OWED JUSTICE:
Thai Women Trafficked into Debt Bondage in Japan

Human Rights Watch/Asia
Human Rights Watch Women's Rights Division

Human Rights Watch
New York · Washington · London · Brussels

ISBN: 1-56432-252-1
Library of Congress Card Number: 00-107963

Cover photo by Kinsey Dinan, © 2000 Human Rights Watch

Cover design by Rafael Jiménez

Addresses for Human Rights Watch
350 Fifth Avenue, 34th Floor, New York, NY 10118-3299
Tel: (212) 290-4700, Fax: (212) 736-1300, E-mail: hrwnyc@hrw.org

1630 Connecticut Avenue, N.W., Suite 500, Washington, DC 20009
Tel: (202) 612-4321, Fax: (202) 612-4333, E-mail: hrwdc@hrw.org

33 Islington High Street, N1 9LH London, UK
Tel: (171) 713-1995, Fax: (171) 713-1800, E-mail: hrwatchuk@gn.apc.org

15 Rue Van Campenhout, 1000 Brussels, Belgium
Tel: (2) 732-2009, Fax: (2) 732-0471, E-mail:hrwatcheu@skynet.be

Web Site Address: http://www.hrw.org

Listserv address: To subscribe to the list, send an e-mail message to
majordomo@igc.apc.org with "subscribe hrw-news" in the body of the message
(leave the subject line blank).

Human Rights Watch is dedicated to
protecting the human rights of people around the world.

We stand with victims and activists to prevent
discrimination, to uphold political freedom, to protect people from inhumane
conduct in wartime, and to bring offenders to justice.

We investigate and expose
human rights violations and hold abusers accountable.

We challenge governments and those who hold power to end abusive practices
and respect international human rights law.

We enlist the public and the international
community to support the cause of human rights for all.

HUMAN RIGHTS WATCH

Human Rights Watch conducts regular, systematic investigations of human rights abuses in some seventy countries around the world. Our reputation for timely, reliable disclosures has made us an essential source of information for those concerned with human rights. We address the human rights practices of governments of all political stripes, of all geopolitical alignments, and of all ethnic and religious persuasions. Human Rights Watch defends freedom of thought and expression, due process and equal protection of the law, and a vigorous civil society; we document and denounce murders, disappearances, torture, arbitrary imprisonment, discrimination, and other abuses of internationally recognized human rights. Our goal is to hold governments accountable if they transgress the rights of their people.

Human Rights Watch began in 1978 with the founding of its Europe and Central Asia division (then known as Helsinki Watch). Today, it also includes divisions covering Africa, the Americas, Asia, and the Middle East. In addition, it includes three thematic divisions on arms, children's rights, and women's rights. It maintains offices in New York, Washington, Los Angeles, London, Brussels, Moscow, Dushanbe, and Bangkok. Human Rights Watch is an independent, nongovernmental organization, supported by contributions from private individuals and foundations worldwide. It accepts no government funds, directly or indirectly.

The staff includes Kenneth Roth, executive director; Michele Alexander, development director; Reed Brody, advocacy director; Carroll Bogert, communications director; Barbara Guglielmo, finance director; Jeri Laber special advisor; Lotte Leicht, Brussels office director; Patrick Minges, publications director; Maria Pignataro Nielsen, human resources director; Dinah PoKempner, general counsel; Jemera Rone, counsel; Malcolm Smart, program director; Wilder Tayler, legal and policy director; and Joanna Weschler, United Nations representative. Jonathan Fanton is the chair of the board. Robert L. Bernstein is the founding chair.

The regional directors of Human Rights Watch are Peter Takirambudde, Africa; José Miguel Vivanco, Americas; Sidney Jones, Asia; Holly Cartner, Europe and Central Asia; and Hanny Megally, Middle East and North Africa. The thematic division directors are Joost R. Hiltermann, arms; Lois Whitman, children's; and Regan Ralph, women's.

The members of the board of directors are Jonathan Fanton, chair; Lisa Anderson, Robert L. Bernstein, David M. Brown, William Carmichael, Dorothy Cullman, Gina Despres, Irene Diamond, Adrian W. DeWind, Fiona Druckenmiller, Edith Everett, Michael E. Gellert, Vartan Gregorian, Alice H. Henkin, James F. Hoge, Stephen L. Kass, Marina Pinto Kaufman, Bruce Klatsky, Joanne Leedom-Ackerman, Josh Mailman, Yolanda T. Moses, Samuel K. Murumba, Andrew Nathan, Jane Olson, Peter Osnos, Kathleen Peratis, Bruce Rabb, Sigrid Rausing, Orville Schell, Sid Sheinberg, Gary G. Sick, Malcolm Smith, Domna Stanton, John J. Studzinski, and Maya Wiley. Robert L. Bernstein is the founding chair of Human Rights Watch.

ACKNOWLEDGMENTS

This report was written by Kinsey Dinan, researcher with the Women's Rights and Asia Divisions of Human Rights Watch, based on research conducted by Therese Caouette, Kinsey Dinan, Yuriko Saito, Piyana Sophanasiri, and Naiyana Supapong. It was edited by Regan E. Ralph, executive director of the Women's Rights Division; Joseph Saunders, deputy director of the Asia Division; and Malcolm Smart, program director of Human Rights Watch. Additional research and editorial input provided by Sidney Jones, Sarah Lai, and Dorothy Q. Thomas. Wilder Taylor, legal and policy director for Human Rights Watch, provided legal review. Production assistance was provided by Tejal Jesrani and Laura Rusu, associates with the Women's Rights Division.

This report would not have been possible without the assistance of a number of individuals and organizations in Japan and Thailand who provided us with essential information and support. In particular, we would like to thank the staff of Mizura, Karabow, HELP Asian Women's Shelter, the Immigration Review Task Force, the Japan Civil Liberties Union, the Kyoto YWCA, and the Minatomachi Medical Clinic in Japan; and the staff of FACE: Coalition to Fight Against Child Exploitation, and the Global Alliance Against Trafficking in Women in Thailand. We would also like to thank the many individuals including several Japanese and Thai government officials whose cooperation was critical to our research.

Finally, we would like to express our deep gratitude to the many other women and men who made invaluable contributions to this report, but whose names have been withheld because of concerns about security and/or confidentiality. These include the many courageous Thai women who shared with us their experiences in Japan and back home. It is hoped that through their testimonies, other women, governments and the international community will have more information securing opportunities for safe interventions and redress in the future.

The Women's Rights Division of Human Rights Watch gratefully acknowledges the generous support of the Ford Foundation, the John D. and Catherine T. MacArthur Foundation, the Sandler Family Supporting Fund, the Moriah Fund, and the Shaler Adams Foundation.

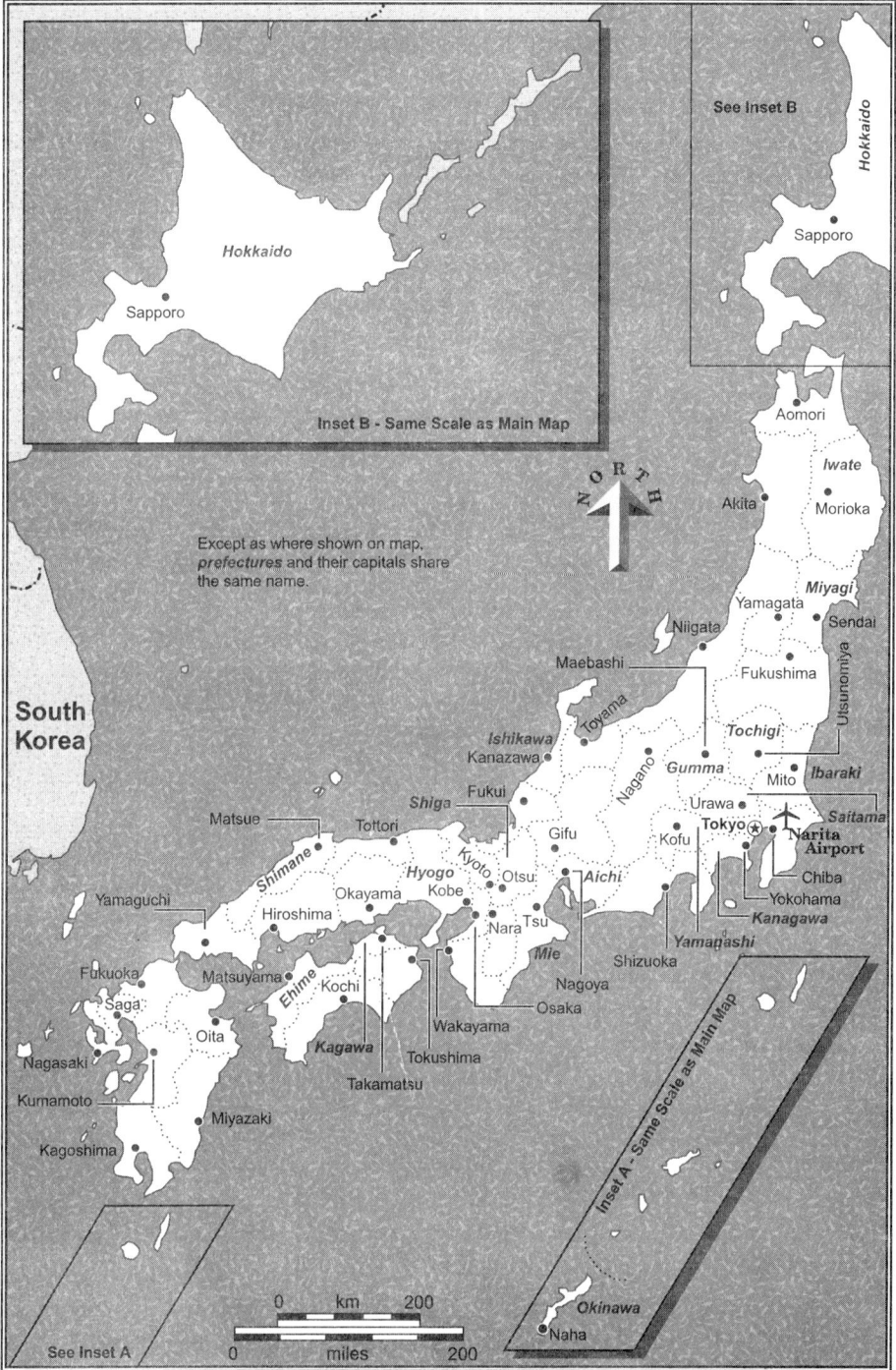

See Inset B

Hokkaido

Sapporo

Inset B - Same Scale as Main Map

Hokkaido

Sapporo

Aomori

Iwate

Akita · Morioka

NORTH

Except as where shown on map, *prefectures* and their capitals share the same name.

Miyagi

Yamagata · Sendai

Niigata

South Korea

Maebashi

Fukushima

Utsunomiya

Toyama

Ishikawa
Kanazawa

Nagano

Tochigi

Shiga Fukui

Gumma

Mito

Ibaraki

Matsue

Tottori

Kyoto Otsu

Gifu

Kofu

Urawa

Tokyo ⊛

Narita Airport ✈

Saitama

Shimane

Hyogo

Okayama Kobe

Aichi

Chiba

Yokohama

Kanagawa

Yamaguchi

Hiroshima

Nara Tsu

Mie

Yamanashi

Shizuoka

Fukuoka

Matsuyama Kochi

Ehime

Nagoya

Osaka

Saga

Oita

Kagawa

Wakayama

Tokushima

Nagasaki

Takamatsu

Kumamoto

Miyazaki

Kagoshima

Inset A - Same Scale as Main Map

0 km 200

0 miles 200

Okinawa

Naha

See Inset A

Prefectures of Japan

Burma

Laos

Vietnam

NORTH

Chiang Rai

Mae Hong Son

Phayao

Nan

Chiang Mai

Lamphun

Lampang

Phrae

Uttaradit

Vientiane

Nong Khai

Loei

Sakon Nakhon

Nakhon Phanom

Rangoon

Tak

Sukhothai

Phitsanulok

Nong Bua Lamphu

Udon Thani

Khon Kaen

Kalasin

Mukdahan

Kamphaeng Phet

Phichit

Phetchabun

Maha Sarakham

Roi Et

Amnat Charoen

Nakhon Sawan

Chaiyaphum

Yasothon

Ubon Ratchathani

Uthai Thani

Nakhon Ratchasima

Chai Nat

12

Lop Buri

Buriram

Surin

Sisaket

Suphan Buri

1

Sara Buri

Kanchanaburi

8

4

Prachin Buri

5

6

7

Sa Kaeo

Ratchaburi

Bangkok (3)

Don Muang Airport

11 10 9

2

Chon Buri

Phetchaburi

Rayong

Cambodia

Chanthaburi

Trat

Phnom Penh

Prachuap Khiri Khan

Chumphon

Ho Chi Minh City

Ranong

1	Ang Thong
2	Chachoengsao
3	Krung Thep Mahanakhon (Bangkok)
4	Nakhon Nayok
5	Nakhon Pathom
6	Nonthaburi
7	Pathum Thani
8	Phra Nakhon Si Ayutthaya
9	Samut Prakan
10	Samut Sakhon
11	Samut Songkhram
12	Sing Buri

Surat Thani

Nakhon Si Thammarat

Phangnga

Krabi

Phatthalung

Phuket

Trang

Songkhla

Pattani

Satun

Hat Yai Airport

Narathiwat

Yala

Provinces and their capitals share the same name.

0   km   150

0   miles   150

Malaysia

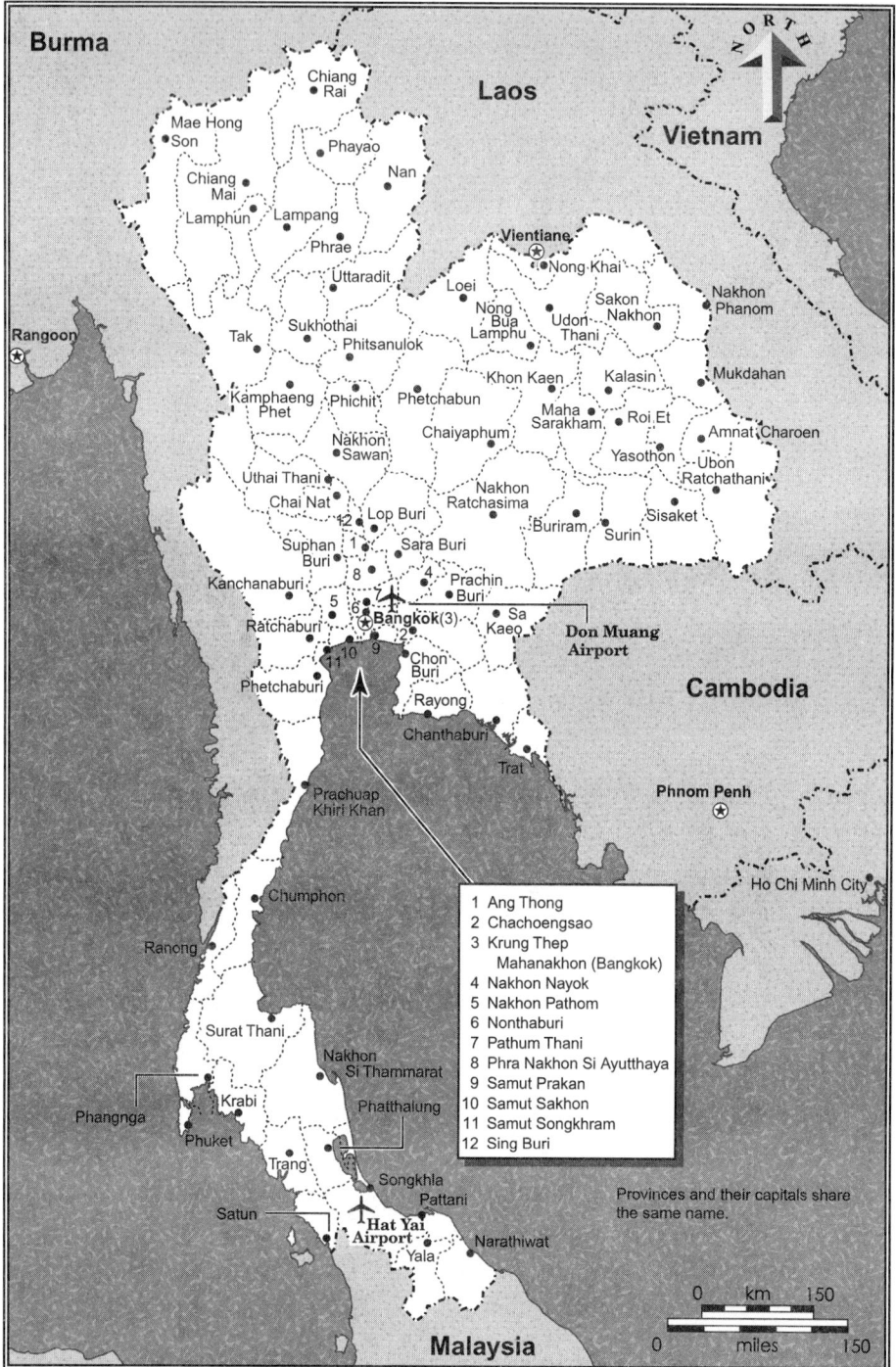

Provinces of Thailand

CONTENTS

I. SUMMARY

In April 1999, the residents at a private women's shelter in Tokyo included two Thai women who had recently escaped from debt bondage in the Japanese sex industry:

> Miew[1] had spent more than two months working as a "hostess" in a "dating" snack bar, serving drinks at the bar and accompanying clients to nearby hotels to provide sexual services. She had been recruited from Thailand with the promise of a generous monthly salary, but when she arrived, she was told that she would have to work without any compensation until she paid off a debt of 5 million yen (approximately US$43,000). Her manager confiscated her passport and warned her that if she tried to escape, she would be followed and caught by Japanese gang members or police. She was housed under constant surveillance in an apartment next door to the bar, where a motion sensitive light outside the door ensured that she could not go outside unnoticed. After working for two months, Miew's debt had risen to 6 million yen (approximately US$51,000), as the cost of room, board, and "protection" fees—as well as a hefty fine for giving the snack bar's telephone number to her parents—well exceeded the amount she had been able to repay.

> Thip came to Japan in March 1999, having been promised a job as a waitress in a restaurant where she could save money. But when she arrived she was told that she owed 4.5 million yen (approximately US$38,500) for the cost of her travel and job placement, and she was put to work in a brothel, where she was kept in a small room and forced to provide sexual services to customers. Thip escaped after working fifteen to sixteen-hour days, every day, for two weeks. The customers paid 12,000 yen (approximately US$100) for eight-minute sessions, but Thip's share was only 2,000 yen. From this amount, Thip was expected

---

[1] To protect the identities of the women victims of trafficking and compulsory labor, each has been assigned a randomly selected name which is used consistently throughout the report. While Human Rights Watch generally refers to interviewees by their first and last names, in this case we have chosen to follow the Thai custom of using nicknames.

to pay 34,000 yen a day for rent and protection money. This meant that she had to serve eighteen clients each day before any earnings were applied toward her debt.

Miew and Thip are among the thousands of women in Thailand who accept offers to work in Japan each year in the hope of providing a better livelihood for themselves and their families. Some are promised jobs as waitresses or factory workers; others are assured high wages as entertainers or sex workers. But nearly all find themselves saddled with exorbitant debts and forced to work under brutal conditions without compensation until they are released.

Trafficking in persons, the illegal but highly profitable transport and sale of human beings for the purpose of exploiting their labor, is a global human rights phenomenon involving hundreds of thousands of victims each year, including thousands of women trafficked from Thailand into debt bondage in Japan. The intermediaries who arrange these women's travel and job placement use deception, fraud, and coercion to place them into highly abusive conditions of employment, where they must repay outrageously high "debts" before they can earn wages or gain their freedom. While in debt, women are kept under constant surveillance and forced to satisfy all customers and all customer demands. Disobedience can lead to fines, physical violence, and even "resale" into higher levels of debt. Escape from these conditions is difficult and dangerous, and may lead to violent retaliation. Governments have an obligation to combat such abuses. To fail to take all possible action is to be complicit. They must clearly identify and punish rights abuses perpetrated by traffickers, aggressively investigating and prosecuting these crimes. They must also address the precarious legal and social position of trafficked persons, with concrete measures to protect victims' rights and provide them with the incentive and resources to cooperate with law enforcement officials. Such measures include exempting trafficked persons from prosecution for offenses directly resulting from their being trafficked; giving them real opportunities to seek justice and compensation for abuses they have suffered; ensuring their access to shelter, medical care, and other services as needed; guaranteeing their personal safety; and facilitating their safe and humane repatriation.

Human Rights Watch, in cooperation with local organizations and researchers, has conducted extensive research regarding the trafficking of women from Thailand to Japan. This report is based on interviews conducted in Thailand and Japan over the six year period from 1994 to 1999, during which we documented serious abuses in the course of women's recruitment, travel, job placement, and subsequent employment. Our interviews in 1999 reveal a clear continuation of the abuses we first documented in 1994, indicating that, despite the increased awareness demonstrated by Japanese and Thai officials regarding the abuses trafficked women suffer, these governments have failed as yet to take adequate steps to respond effectively to the problem.

Findings

Trafficking

The trafficking of women from Thailand to Japan occurs within the context of large-scale regional migration in Asia, which has grown dramatically over the last two decades. Since the late 1980s, this has included large flows of both male and female workers from Thailand to Japan.[2] The vast majority of this migration is illegal, as Japan accepts only a very limited number of legal migrants each year. In practice, the high demand for foreign workers in Japan has fostered the growth of large transnational networks able to bypass legal barriers and facilitate illegal migration into Japan. There is strong evidence that these networks are controlled by powerful organized crime groups, including the Yakuza in Japan and other mafia-like organizations elsewhere. It is these networks that women from Thailand often rely on when they migrate to Japan.

Human Rights Watch interviewed numerous women who had migrated from Thailand to Japan over the past decade, most of whom had worked in "dating" snack bars upon their arrival in the country. They narrated their experiences at length; in some cases, over the course of several meetings. We also interviewed a number of advocates in Japan who are working on behalf of women from Thailand, including lawyers, shelter staff, hotline volunteers, medical professionals, migrants' rights activists, and others. In addition, we interviewed Japanese government officials as well as officials from the Thai Embassy and Thai Labor Office in Japan. Finally, we met with governmental and nongovernmental representatives in Thailand who are involved in efforts to prevent trafficking in persons and provide assistance to victims.

We found that while Thai women's initial decisions to migrate for work were almost always voluntary, women typically were deceived from the time they made their decisions until their arrival in Japan, and most of the women experienced slavery-like abuses, prohibited under international law, during the course of their travel and job placement. Agents in Thailand assisted women in obtaining passports and other travel documentation, took care of all travel arrangements, hired escorts to accompany the women during their travel, and contacted brokers to

---

[2] Migration from Thailand to Japan peaked in 1993. Since then it has slowed somewhat due to Japan's economic difficulties and its related crackdown on illegal migration, but estimates indicate that there are still many tens of thousands of Thai migrants working in Japan each year.

receive the women in Japan. These agents routinely deceived women about the terms and conditions of the work they were going to do; none of the women we interviewed understood the amount and calculation of their debt and the conditions under which they would have to repay it when they arrived in Japan. Many of the women were also deceived about the nature of the work: promised jobs as waitresses or factory workers, they were later coerced into engaging in sex work. Upon arrival in Japan, women were delivered to brokers, who contacted employers and arranged the women's job placement. Most of the women were employed as snack bar "hostesses" with duties included entertaining customers at the bar and accompanying customers to nearby hotels to provide sexual services. Women were given no choice over their occupation, employers, or working conditions, and they received no compensation until they repaid extraordinarily large debts assessed against them, far exceeding the cost of their travel to Japan.

Debt Bondage and Forced Labor

Human Rights Watch found that working arrangements for most of the women from Thailand in Japanese snack bars constituted debt bondage or forced labor, practices prohibited under international law. During their recruitment, women were regularly deceived regarding the amount of debt they would incur, the amount of time it would take to repay this debt, the type of work they would have to perform while in debt, and/or the conditions under which they would be compelled to work. This deception was compounded by the wide discretion employers exercised over debt repayment calculations. Employers used arbitrary and non-transparent methods of account-keeping and routinely increased women's debts with a variety of fines and other expenses. Employers also reserved the power to "resell" indebted women into renewed levels of debt, and the threat of "resale" was often used to exact compliance.

While in "debt," women trafficked from Thailand worked under highly abusive labor conditions. They did not receive any compensation for their labor and had to accept all customers and all customers' requests. They also faced significant risks to their health with only limited access to health care. Severe punishments for refusing or failing to fully satisfy customers meant that women who were in debt had no power to enforce condom use, heightening their risk of exposure to HIV/AIDS and other sexually transmitted diseases. Women were often compelled to submit to even physically abusive clients, and some were subjected to violence by their employers for alleged infringements or acts of disobedience. Women were also forced to work excessively long hours, in some cases even when ill, and their access to medical care was controlled by their boss or manager. Though medical care might be available if a woman succeeded in maintaining a good relationship with her manager, such care also lengthened the period of debt repayment as the cost of any treatment was added to her debt.

Several of the women we interviewed escaped from this situation, but most repaid their debts—over a period of anywhere from several months to two years—and then continued to work in Japan in order to earn money for themselves and their families back in Thailand. There are a number of reasons why escape is unusual. The nature of debt bondage provides women with strong incentives to acquiesce to their managers' demands, as the debt period is typically temporary, but all repayment calculations are at their employers' discretion. Furthermore, escape is difficult and dangerous. Women are kept under near constant surveillance, their passports and other documentation are confiscated, they have little cash, and they are isolated by barriers of language and culture. They are threatened with violent retaliation or "resale" into greater debt if they are caught, and sometimes with retaliation against their family members if they are not. In addition, while Japanese authorities, if contacted, may be willing to facilitate escape attempts, they will also begin deportation procedures, without offering women any opportunity to seek compensation for back wages or damages. Similarly, Thai Embassy officials assist women in returning home to Thailand, but they do not provide women with any assistance in obtaining legal recourse for the abuses they have suffered. Some women find their working conditions so unbearable that they would like to return home, even empty-handed, but most put up with the abuse in hopes of obtaining the money they need to support themselves and their families back home.

Government Responses

The Thai and Japanese governments are well-aware of the abuses described above. Officials from both governments have publicly acknowledged that transnational crime syndicates are involved in trafficking women from Thailand into Japan, that there are currently tens of thousands of undocumented Thai women working in Japan, and that many of these women face extremely exploitative conditions.[3] In fact, the Thai Embassy organized a conference in Tokyo in September 1999 to discuss the abuses faced by Thai women in the Japanese sex industry, and less than four months later, Japan's Ministry of Foreign Affairs sponsored a symposium to discuss the trafficking in persons into Japan, with a focus on trafficking in women and girls from Thailand and other Asian countries into the sex industry. Unfortunately, however, this awareness has not been translated as yet

---

[3] See, for example, Sanitsuda Ekachai, "Conference seeks help for Thai victims: These women are not criminals-envoy," *Bangkok Post,* September 28, 1999; "Govt, NGO officials meet on Thai women's problems," *The Daily Yomiuri,* September 28, 1999.

into effective measures to provide women with the means to protect themselves from abuse or to seek redress for violations.

Japan

Japan's restrictive visa policies have created extraordinary opportunities for profit for those who facilitate the illegal migration of women from Thailand and other countries into Japan. Though there is a strong demand for foreign women workers in Japan and a large number of Thai women willing to migrate, opportunities for legal migration are relatively minimal. Crime syndicates in Japan and abroad have seized upon this opportunity, forming transnational trafficking networks that facilitate women's migration and then compel them to work under highly exploitative conditions.

Japanese officials have publicly acknowledged the slavery-like treatment many of these women endure. However, in policy and practice, their response continues to focus on increased efforts to combat illegal migration, targeting both the migrants themselves and those who facilitate such migration, but entirely failing to address the coercion and deception that is often involved. This response has exacerbated trafficked women's vulnerability.   As "illegal aliens" and "prostitutes," undocumented Thai women working in the Japanese sex industry are viewed as criminals by the Japanese authorities. They get little sympathy from police, immigration officials, and labor officials, and their access to health care is impeded by Japanese policies that exclude undocumented migrants from health care benefits available to other residents of Japan. When police or immigration officials raid establishments that employ undocumented migrant women, the women are arrested as illegal aliens, detained in immigration facilities, and deported with a five-year ban on reentering the country. This punitive treatment is applied regardless of the conditions under which the women migrated to, and worked in, Japan. Even when there is clear evidence of trafficking, debt bondage, or forced labor, no effort is made to provide undocumented migrants with an opportunity to seek compensation or justice. If employers or traffickers are prosecuted at all, they are charged with immigration offenses, such as employing or facilitating the employment of illegal aliens; with procuring prostitutes in violation of the Prostitution Prevention Law; or with operating an un-licensed entertainment business. They are almost never prosecuted for the severe human rights abuses they have committed, such as forced labor, illegal confinement, physical violence, and intimidation.

Thailand

Over the last several years, the Thai government has made eradication of the sexual exploitation of women and children a national priority, adopting a variety of measures aimed at preventing and suppressing the trafficking of women into and out of Thailand for sexual purposes. The Ministry of Labor and Social Welfare offers vocational training programs designed specifically for women and girls to expand their educational and employment opportunities in Thailand. Government officials have launched awareness-raising campaigns that warn women of the dangers of sex work and of migration. The Ministry of Foreign Affairs screens the passport applications of girls and women ages fourteen to thirty-six, rejecting the applications of women suspected of being procured into the sex industry. And the National Assembly enacted legislation designed to facilitate the investigation and prosecution of trafficking agents, including the revised Measures in Prevention and Suppression of Trafficking in Women and Children Act, adopted in 1997. In addition to these efforts, the Thai government provides services to women victims of trafficking. In Japan, Thai Embassy officials assist women in obtaining the necessary documentation and funding to return to Thailand, and victims of trafficking are also eligible for rehabilitative services, such as vocational training and shelter care, after they are repatriated.

These government efforts have helped to raise awareness of the abuses migrant women commonly face in Japan and elsewhere, but their effectiveness in reducing women's vulnerability to such abuses has been limited. Laws to crack down on traffickers have proven difficult to enforce in practice, and other preventative efforts have been undermined by preconceptions about proper roles and occupations for women. Vocational training for women emphasizes traditionally female skills, such as sewing and hair dressing, which do not typically lead to well-paying jobs and thus are not seen as likely to lead to a meaningful alternative career. Information campaigns warn women of the dangers of migration, but fail to provide them with any useful information about their rights or the services available to them when abroad, so that women who decide to migrate despite the risks are unable to protect themselves from exploitation. And the services provided to women victims of trafficking and debt bondage do not include any effort to assist women in seeking back wages or other compensation for the abuses they have suffered.

Finally, the Thai government has abdicated its responsibility for women and girls whose homes are in Thailand, but who lack official Thai citizenship. This problem of denial of citizenship is one affecting hundreds of thousands of people in Thailand. Without Thai citizenship, the vulnerability of such women to trafficking agents is enhanced, both because they are denied access to the same education and employment opportunities as Thai nationals and because they cannot obtain the documents necessary for international travel through legal channels. Even more devastating, once these women leave Thailand it is almost impossible for them to return as the Thai government does not recognize their right of reentry. Consequently, such women who have been trafficked into debt bondage in Japan are obliged to remain in that country in a state of legal and social limbo, separated indefinitely, and perhaps forever, from their homes and families.

Obligations under International Law

Trafficking, debt bondage, and forced labor are practices that are strictly prohibited under international human rights law and treaties binding upon governments. The threat and use of physical force, illegal confinement, and abusive working conditions that women routinely endure also constitute serious abuses of their rights to liberty, security of person, freedom of movement, free choice of employment, fair wages, and safe working conditions. The Japanese and Thai governments are obliged under international law to take concrete steps effectively to prevent and address these human rights abuses and to provide victims with access to justice and compensation. Human Rights Watch found that in the case of women who are trafficked from Thailand to Japan, the Japanese and Thai governments have consistently failed to live up to these obligations.

II. KEY RECOMMENDATIONS

The Japanese and Thai governments have an obligation to takes the steps necessary to prevent and punish the trafficking of women from Thailand to Japan and to protect the rights of trafficking victims, ensuring that they have access to redress for the violations they have suffered and preventing further abuses. The two governments should take the specific measures set out below and in doing so should coordinate their responses to ensure that the trafficking of women, and the further human rights abuses which take place in that context, are swiftly and effectively addressed. The international community can also play an important role in setting appropriate standards for states' response to trafficking in women, and in encouraging the Japanese and Thai governments to implement these standards.

The final chapter of this report provides a more detailed discussion of Human Rights Watch's recommendations to the Japanese and Thai governments, coupled with recommendations to other actors in the international community.

To the Japanese Government

Women trafficked from Thailand to Japan face egregious violations of their basic human rights, and urgent, concrete steps are needed both to reduce their vulnerability to such abuses and to encourage them to seek assistance, protection, and an effective remedy from Japanese law enforcement officials when their rights are violated. Trafficked women must be exempted from penalty for any activities resulting from their being trafficked. They must have the opportunity to seek remedies and redress for the human rights violations they have suffered, including compensation for damages, unpaid wages, and restitution. Their repatriation must be carried out in a safe and humane manner that does not interfere with their ability to seek redress. They must be protected from further violations of their rights and be afforded access to medical care, shelter, and other services as needed. Such steps are necessary to remedy the abuses trafficked women have suffered and to protect them from further traumatization. These measures are also crucial for facilitating the investigation and prosecution of traffickers, thus ensuring that perpetrators are brought to justice and punished, and to deter further abuses.

1. Actively investigate, prosecute, and punish perpetrators of trafficking in persons and/or servitude, imposing penalties appropriate for punishing the grave nature of the slavery-like abuses involved and for deterring further such abuses. Take measures to ensure that the undocumented immigration status of trafficking victims does not impede investigation or prosecution of labor law violations and other offenses.

9

2. Amend laws, including the immigration law, to exempt victims of trafficking and/or servitude from being prosecuted or otherwise punished for any crimes or illegal status that have resulted directly from these practices. While repatriation may be appropriate, punitive measures, including detention pending deportation, should be waived.

3. Guarantee victims of trafficking and/or servitude access to redress for abuses they have suffered, facilitating their ability to seek compensation for damages, withheld wages, and restitution.

4. Protect the safety of victims of trafficking and/or servitude with measures that include strong witness protection provisions and opportunities to seek asylum.

5. Ensure that victims of trafficking and/or servitude have access to essential public services, including appropriate shelter and medical care.

6. Amend detention and trial procedures in both the criminal justice system and the immigration control system to ensure that the rights of detainees, as established by international human rights guidelines, are upheld. Facilitate independent monitoring of procedures and conditions, and thoroughly and promptly investigate all allegations of misconduct.

7. Ratify relevant international conventions, including the Slavery Convention; the Supplementary Convention on the Abolition of Slavery, the Slave Trade, and Institutions and Practices Similar to Slavery; ILO Convention concerning the Abolition of Forced Labour, no. 105; and the International Convention on the Protection of the Rights of All Migrant Workers and Members of Their Families.

To the Thai Government

The Thai government also has a responsibility to protect women in Thailand from trafficking and other human rights violations commonly endured during their migration to Japan. To reduce women's vulnerability to such abuses, the Thai government should strive to improve women's educational and employment opportunities in Thailand, and help prepare women for employment abroad by providing useful information about overseas employment opportunities and about services available to women in destination countries. In addition, Thai officials stationed in Japan, including the Thai Labor Attache, must actively defend the labor rights of *all* migrant workers, irrespective of their immigration status, without discrimination based on sex or occupation. Thailand must also address the widespread problem of "statelessness" among hilltribe and refugee populations in the country. Steps should be taken to facilitate such persons' access to citizenship, and to ensure that all victims of trafficking from Thailand are able return to their homes in Thailand, even when they cannot produce proof of Thai nationality. Finally, one human right cannot be traded for another: efforts to combat trafficking must not discriminate against women and must be consistent with the protection of women's right to freedom of movement and travel.

1.   Expand and improve the services available to women trafficked from Thailand to Japan, so as to facilitate their access to compensation and redress in Japan, guarantee their safe repatriation, and ensure that they have access to appropriate social services upon their return to Thailand.

2.   Improve law enforcement efforts to prevent and punish the trafficking of persons out of Thailand, including efforts to crack down on official complicity in such crimes.

3.   Take steps to reduce women and girls' vulnerability to trafficking by expanding their education and employment opportunities in Thailand and empowering them to protect their rights as workers overseas.

4.   Protect women's right to freedom of movement, including international travel.

5.   Take steps to address the particular vulnerability of hilltribe and refugee women to trafficking and to facilitate their safe repatriation when trafficking abuses occur.

6.   Ratify relevant international conventions, including the Slavery Convention; the Supplementary Convention on the Abolition of Slavery, the Slave Trade, and Institutions and Practices Similar to Slavery; the Convention relating to the Status of Refugees; the Protocol relating to the Status of Refugees; the Convention on the Reduction of Statelessness; and the International Convention on the Protection of the Rights of All Migrant Workers and Members of Their Families.   Remove reservations from Article 7 of the Convention on the Rights of the Child, thereby recognizing the right of *all* children to be registered immediately after birth and to acquire a nationality.

To the Japanese and Thai Governments
Bilateral cooperation is vital to prevent trafficking in persons and respond appropriately to the rights and needs of victims. Though representatives of the Thai and Japanese governments have come together to discuss this problem, they have yet to design or implement concrete bilateral measures to address it. We urge them to:

1. Discuss and implement concrete measures to reduce migrant Thai women's vulnerability to labor exploitation in Japan. Such measures could include expanding the opportunities for legal labor migration by women from Thailand to Japan, and conducting awareness-raising activities for migrant Thai women in both Thailand and Japan.

2. Work cooperatively—and in coordination with relevant Japanese and Thai nongovernmental organizations—to ensure the safe and humane repatriation of victims of trafficking, servitude, and other abuses.

3. Establish a monitoring body, with the financial support of both governments, to assess the cross-border trafficking situation; identify loopholes in existing laws; make recommendations for coordinating government policies to enhance access to services for victims of trafficking and improve the effectiveness of law enforcement efforts; and monitor and publicly report on the implementation of such policies. This body should include representatives from nongovernmental organizations (NGOs) and the Japanese and Thai governments, and should seek input from relevant intergovernmental organizations, such as the International Organization for Migration and the International Labour Organization. The monitoring body should prepare a joint operational plan that both governments are committed to implementing within a reasonable, designated period of time.

III. CONTEXT

The trafficking of women from Thailand into debt bondage in the Japanese sex industry occurs within the context of larger economic and social trends. This chapter begins with an overview of the patterns and characteristics of labor migration between Thailand and Japan, and in the region more generally, to provide a better understanding of some of the forces underlying the movement of women from Thailand to Japan. It also offers a brief description of Japan's large and varied sex industry, and of the role of foreign women within this labor sector. The chapter concludes by introducing the problem of trafficking and the relevant policies and practices of the Japanese and Thai governments.

Labor migration

Regional migration in Asia
Tens of millions of people travel across national borders each year in search of employment. Economic forces in the sending country "push" migrants out when they are unable to find employment in adequately paying jobs; other migrants are "pulled" into the receiving country, usually by rapid economic growth which requires an inflow of cheap, unskilled labor. Migration between Asian countries has grown steadily since the early 1980s, when just over one million Asians were working in other countries in the region, to more than 6.5 million by mid-1997.[4] Labor migration in modern Asia first became a vast enterprise in the 1970s when countries in the Middle East, in search of both skilled and unskilled labor, encouraged the migration of workers from across Asia.[5] This massive flow of workers has continued to climb steadily since the 1970s. Some workers migrate permanently, but most go overseas only for limited time periods to earn money. Of these workers, some migrate legally, others illegally.

Skilled workers usually have little difficulty maneuvering within the legal framework of migration—passports, visas, and work permits—and are often welcomed, especially in boom periods like the 1970s and 1980s, by countries in desperate need of their skills. Unskilled workers' experience with migration is often quite different. In part this is because avenues for legal labor migration in unskilled labor sectors are limited, prompting many workers to migrate illegally,

---

[4] "Toward Regional Cooperation on Irregular/Undocumented Migration," International Symposium on Migration, Bangkok, Thailand, April 21-23, 1999.
[5] Philip Guest and Kritaya Archavanitkul, "Managing the Flow of Migration: Regional Approaches," Institute for Population and Social Research, Mahidol University, IPSR Publication No. 233, 1999.

often recruited by employers and job brokers in receiving countries who are willing to violate immigration restrictions. These "undocumented" migrants are typically excluded from labor law protections and other state services, by law and/or practice. Even when visas are available for unskilled work, there are often large recruiting networks that take advantage of migrants' ignorance and urgent desire to migrate by charging them exorbitant job placement fees and otherwise exploiting them. Furthermore, unskilled work visas are often short term, and renewal may be difficult or impossible. Thus, many workers initially migrate on a contract and then stay on illegally after their contract has expired.[6]

Immigration from Thailand to Japan
    Prior to 1980, foreign travel and immigration into Japan was very limited. The number of foreigners entering the country—including both temporary visitors and migrant workers—surpassed one million for the first time in 1980, almost doubling the figure from five years earlier.[7] This figure has continued to grow since then, exceeding 4.5 million by the late 1990s, with the majority of entrants coming from other Asian countries. The number of foreign nationals registered for long-term residence in Japan has also increased dramatically during this period, nearly doubling from 750,000 in the 1970s to more than 1,400,000 by the mid-1990s. And, even more striking, the number of foreign nationals estimated to be residing illegally in Japan has almost tripled in less than a decade, from 106,000 in 1990 to 283,000 in 1997.[8] The vast majority entered the country through legal channels, but traveled on falsified documents or remained in Japan beyond their visa expiration date, and most are believed to be working in violation of immigration regulations.
    This increase in migration was, in part, the result of Japanese investment and overseas business activities that created contacts and solidified migration networks. As Japanese companies expanded throughout Asia with joint ventures, relationships were established on both formal and informal levels which encouraged exchanges between Japan and its neighbors. Increased contacts facilitated the mobilization of natural and human resources.[9] The rise in both legal and illegal migration from the

---

[6] Pasuk Phongpaichit, "The Illegal Economy of Trafficking in Migrants," in *Voices of Thai Women*, October 1997.

[7] Japanese National Police Agency White Paper on Crime, 1995. Note that these numbers include temporary visitors (i.e. tourists) as well as labor migrants.

[8] Immigration Bureau, Ministry of Justice, Japan, "Immigration." Available: http://www.moj.go.jp/ENGLISH/IB/ib-01.htm; /ib-03.htm; /ib-11.htm; /ib-14.htm. February 2000. Note that this is still a very small percentage of Japan's 65 million person workforce.

[9] Kiriro Morita and Saskia Sassen, "The New Illegal Immigration in Japan, 1980-1992," *IMR*, vol.28(1), 1993, p. 162.

mid-1980s through the early 1990s was also related to the surge in Japan's economy, creating increased demand for unskilled or low skilled labor. With Japan suffering from a labor shortage, migrant workers were willing to take jobs that Japanese no longer wanted, primarily in the construction and service sectors, and the strong appreciation of the yen in the 1980s raised the value of the earnings foreigners could send home.

In addition to Japan's economic boom, the dramatic increase in the migration of Asian women into Japan's sex industry in the 1980s is widely understood as a reaction to the sharp public criticism that Japanese "sex tourism" began to receive around that time. In the late 1960s, "sex tours," primarily to Thailand and other southeast Asian countries, began growing in popularity among Japanese men.[10] By the mid-1970s, package sex tours were being advertised to Thailand, the Philippines, Taiwan, and Korea, and many companies included "weekend sex holidays" overseas as part of employees' yearly bonuses.[11] However, by the end of that decade, Japan was facing heavy criticism for such tours, and efforts grew to bring foreign women into the sex industry in Japan instead.[12] The following years saw unprecedented numbers of foreign women entering the Japanese sex industry, primarily from other Asian countries.

The strong demand for foreign labor in Japan has also been accompanied by policies in several less wealthy countries that encourage workers to migrate abroad in the hope of gaining much-needed foreign currency through remittances, while alleviating unemployment problems at home. Labor exporting policies in the Philippines, for example, are well-known, and over the last few decades, the Thai government has similarly encouraged its nationals to seek employment overseas.[13]

Consistent with migration trends in the rest of Asia, Thai migrants in the 1970s and early 1980s were drawn by the pull of thriving economies in the Middle East, where employment opportunities were more lucrative than those available in Thailand. But in the late 1980s, the destination of unskilled Thai migrants largely

---

[10] Anchalee Singhanetra-Renard, "Networks for Female Migration Between Thailand and Japan," International Seminar on *International Female Migration and Japan: Networking, Settlement and Human Rights,* December 12-14, 1995, Tokyo, Japan, p. 6.

[11] Naomi Hosoda, "The International Division of Labour and the Commodification of Female Sexuality: The Case of Filipino Women in the Japanese Entertainment Industry," thesis submitted to the Department of Political Studies, Queen's University, Ontario, Canada, January 1994, p. 13.

[12] Ibid., p. 14.

[13] Aaron Stern, "Thailand's Migration Situation and its Relations with APEC Members and Other Countries in Southeast Asia," Asian Research Center for Migration, Institute of Asian Studies, January 1998, p. 57.

shifted from the Middle East to Japan, Singapore, and Taipei. Japanese economic expansion included large-scale investment in Thailand, often through joint ventures with Thai companies, thus fostering close economic ties between the two countries.[14] In 1993, the Thai Ministry of Labor estimated that there were 370,500 Thai nationals working abroad—counting both documented and undocumented migrants—including 100,000 in Japan and 216,000 in other Asian countries. This was an increase from only 6,000 Thai nationals working in Japan, and 16,000 in the rest of Asia, in 1988.[15] And migrant workers sent significant amounts of money back to their families in Thailand. In 1995, remittances from overseas Thai workers in Asia totaled roughly US$1 billion. This included about US$100 million from Japan alone.[16] Since 1993, migration from Thailand to Japan has slowed somewhat due to Japan's economic difficulties and its related crackdown on illegal migration, but authoritative estimates suggest that there are still tens of thousands of Thai migrants working in Japan each year.[17]

Male and female migration patterns

Since the dramatic increase in migration into Japan in the 1980s, both male and female migration have followed fluctuations in the Japanese economy, increasing steadily from 1986 through 1992, and then gradually decreasing as Japan slid into recession.[18] Profiles of male and female migrants differ markedly, however. Female Asian migrants are typically younger than their male counterparts. Although males comprise a larger share of the migrants in most age groups, in the fifteen to twenty year-old bracket, women and girls outnumber men and boys by five to two.[19] For males, the largest single migrant group is the forty to forty-nine

---

[14] Singhanetra-Renard, "Networks for Female Migration . . .," International Seminar, December 12-14, 1995, Tokyo, Japan, p. 2.

[15] Overseas Employment Administration Office, Thailand's Ministry of Labor, "Estimated Numbers of Thai Workers Abroad, by Country, 1988-1994," *Yearbook of Labor Statistics.*

[16] Singhanetra-Renard, "Networks for Female Migration . . .," International Seminar, December 12-14, 1995, Tokyo, Japan, p. 11.

[17] These include both documented and undocumented migrants. Scalabrini Migration Center, *Asian Migration Atlas 1999.* Available: http://www.scalabrini.asn.au/atlas/amatlas.htm. February 2000.

[18] Noriyuki Suzuki and Phannee Chunjitkaruna, "Thai Migrant Workers in Japan," paper presented at the International Workshop on Research Project on Thai Migrant Workers in Southeast and East Asia, Chulalongkorn University, Bangkok, Thailand, August 5-7, 1998.

[19] Mizuho Matsuda, "Women from Thailand," *AMPO Japan-Asia Quarterly Review,* vol. 23., no. 4, 1992.

year old age group; seventy percent of all female migrants to Japan are between twenty and twenty-four years old.[20]

Another difference in male and female migration is the type of work they seek. Male migrants are typically employed in occupations that the Japanese have labeled "3K" work—*kitsui, kitanai,* and *kiken,* or, in English, "3D" work—difficult, dirty, and dangerous. These include construction work, factory jobs, and other types of manual labor. Japanese Ministry of Justice statistics on the occupations of undocumented male migrants apprehended in 1995 indicated that 37.4 percent were construction workers, 25.2 percent were production workers, and 9.5 percent were manual laborers. The remaining 27.9 percent were employed in the service industry, as cooks, bartenders, or domestic servants.[21] Some migrant women also work in factories, but the vast majority are employed in the service industry, typically providing entertainment—often including sexual services—to Japanese men. According to the Japan Immigration Association's statistics, 46.5 percent of female illegal migrants apprehended in 1993 were working as hostesses or in direct prostitution,[22] with 22.9 percent in other service work. And the Ministry of Justice's 1995 arrest statistics show that 36.9 percent of undocumented female migrants were working as hostesses, 15.3 percent as waitresses, 8.1 percent as domestics, 4.8 percent as cooks, and 3.4 percent as prostitutes. Only 18.3 percent were employed as production workers or manual laborers; 13.2 percent are listed as "other."[24]

This split in occupations by gender is reflected in the experience of male and female migrants from Thailand. An estimated eighty to ninety percent of female migrants work as sex workers in Japan, typically as hostesses or waitresses who also

[20] Japan Immigration Association, *Statistics on Immigration Control 1994* (Tokyo: 1994).

[21] The National Police Agency, "White Paper of the Police," 1996, pp. 308-309, quoted in International Organization for Migration, *Trafficking in Women to Japan for Sexual Exploitation: A Survey on the Case of Filipino Women* (Geneva: IOM, 1997), p. 7.

[22] The duties of a "hostess" in a Japanese bar generally include flirting with customers and serving drinks and snacks; in some establishments, customers can also pay to take "hostesses" to nearby hotels for sexual services.

[23] Japan Immigration Association, *Statistics on Immigration Control 1994* (Tokyo: 1994).

[24] The National Police Agency, "White Paper of the Police," 1996, pp. 308-309, quoted in International Organization for Migration, *Trafficking in Women to Japan for Sexual Exploitation: A Survey on the Case of Filipino Women,* (Geneva: IOM, 1997), p. 7.

perform sexual services for clients.[25] Others work in bars or restaurants but do not engage in sex work, and a few work in factories. Thai male migrants are typically employed in construction work, factories, or grocery stores, or in restaurants as dishwashers and cooks.[26] There are also some Thai men working as "hosts," providing sexual services to female clients in bars that target migrant Thai women.[27]

Visa policies—skilled and unskilled

Japanese immigration policies reveal a strong bias against foreigners, reflecting a deep-seated commitment in Japan to maintaining a homogeneous society. This commitment is perhaps most clear in Japanese nationality policies, which make it virtually impossible for a person born to non-Japanese parents—including second and third generation descendants of Korean nationals drafted to Japan during World War II—to acquire Japanese citizenship. The same bias was reflected in the 1990 revisions to Japan's Immigration Control and Refugee Recognition Act (hereinafter, the Immigration Control Act). These revisions were adopted in the context of a severe national shortage in unskilled labor, but, while categories of skilled labor visas were expanded, the general prohibition on unskilled labor migration was reinforced. As one immigration officer explained to Human Rights Watch, "Japanese public opinion does not accept giving visas for unskilled labor,"[28] and the Immigration Bureau's web site explains that "[n]ot only do foreign nationals working illegally badly influence market for labor in Japan [sic], they cause various problems concerning customs, security, etc."[29] New provisions in 1990 for cracking down on illegal migration included, for the first time, sanctions on those employing and contracting illegal workers, in addition to penalties for the migrants themselves. When Japan's economy began slipping into recession in 1992, foreigners were

---

[25] A Thai Embassy official in Japan provided this estimate in "40,000 Thai women work as prostitutes in Japan," *The Nation,* September 9, 1994. See also "A multi-million baht business," *Bangkok Post,* Sunday, August 18, 1996; Presentation by Yayori Matsui at the Asian Women's Human Rights Conference, Waseda University, 1995.

[26] See Phongpaichit, "The Illegal Economy . . .," *Voices of Thai Women,* vol. 16, October 1997; "Over 40,000 Thais Suffer in Japan," *Bangkok Post,* January 3, 1997 (summary of research conducted by Suriya Samutkupt and Pattana Kitiarsa).

[27] Human Rights Watch interview with Suriya Samutkupt, Professor of Anthropology, Institute of Social Technology, Suranaree University of Technology, Nakhon Ratchasima province, Thailand, April 27, 1999.

[28] Human Rights Watch interview, Tokyo, Japan, April 15, 1999.

[29] Immigration Bureau, Ministry of Justice, Japan, "Immigration." Available: http://www.moj.go.jp/ENGLISH/IB/ib-11.htm. February 2000.

among the first to be targeted.[30] They were identified as a source of the country's economic difficulties, and crackdowns on illegal migrants were carried out by both immigration and police officers, leading to mass raids and dramatically increased arrests for immigration offenses.[31]

At the same time, the 1990 immigration law revisions attempted to address the serious labor shortage by greatly expanding the availability of visas for second and third generation Japanese emigrants, or *Nikkeis*. This led to a dramatic surge in immigration by ethnic Japanese, particularly from Brazil and Peru, and, by 1992, the number of Nikkeis in Japan had risen to more than 150,000.[32] Two other exceptions to the prohibition on unskilled labor migration have also been made. One is the "entertainer visa," mentioned above. This visa allows foreigners to work in the entertainment industry in Japan for a limited period—typically three months, with the possibility of renewing for an additional three months—under contract with a Japanese employer. While such visas are theoretically available to both male and female applicants, they are granted primarily to women, and, as a result of an agreement between the Japanese and Philippine government, they have been issued

---

[30] Japan's real economic growth rate dropped from 3.8% to 1.0% from 1991 to 1992, and then sunk to .3% in 1993. (International Department, Bank of Japan, "Comparative Economic and Financial Statistics: Japan and other Major Countries," August 31, 1998.)

[31] "Cracking Down on Foreign Workers; Government Exploits Recession Fears: an interview with Kobayashi Kengo," *AMPO Japan-Asia Quarterly Review*, vol. 25, no.1, 1994.

[32] Montse Watkins, "'Coming Back' to Japan: The Nikkei Workers," *AMPO Japan-Asia Quarterly Review*, vol. 23, no. 4, 1992, p. 31.

Further evidence of these restrictive policies is seen in Japan's highly restrictive asylum policies. Though Japan is a signatory to the Refugee Convention and purports to follow the provisions of that Convention, it has approved a strikingly small percentage of asylum applications. In the seven years from 1982 to 1988, Japan approved 192 out of 814 applications for refugee status, and in the following eight years, from 1989 to 1996, Japan approved seventeen out of 514, including only one approval per year in 1994, 1995, and 1996. (Japan Civil Liberties Union, "1998 Report Concerning the Present Status of Human Rights in Japan (Third Counter Report)," October 1998.) In 1998, the number of persons granted refugee status reached a high of sixteen, but this figure fell to eleven in 1999. ("Takuya Asakura, "Asylum said in short supply here," *Japan Times*, December 24, 1999.)

disproportionately to women from the Philippines.[33] Officially classified as "guests," rather than as workers, "entertainers" are excluded from labor law protections, and, although immigration regulations provide detailed instructions regarding wages and job responsibilities for migrants in this category, the regulations are violated with virtual impunity.[34]

Another option available to unskilled migrants seeking work in Japan is the "trainee" visa.[35] According to Immigration Bureau statistics, the number of foreign trainees admitted to Japan quadrupled in the decade following the introduction of these visas in 1982.[36] In 1992, 43,627 foreigners were accepted into Japan on trainee visas, including more than 38,000 from other Asian countries.[37] The trainee visa program operates under the auspices of the Japan International Training Cooperation Organization (JITCO), which was set up under the joint auspices of the Ministries of Foreign Affairs, Justice, International Trade and Industry, and Labor. Trainees enter the country under contract with an employer who is required to provide opportunities for skills development, both through classroom activities and on-the-job training. Again, these laborers are not officially categorized as "workers," but many employers have taken advantage of the policy by using it to bring over unskilled foreign workers, while providing little or no actual training.[38]

---

[33] Pipat Lertkittisusk, "Japan rights groups reach out to Thai counterparts," *Bangkok Post*, July 9, 1990. In 1996, Japan issued a total of 53, 952 entertainer visas. More than a third of these visas were issued to migrants from the Philippines, who accounted for more than 78 percent of total number of "entertainers" admitted from Asia. Only 176 entertainer visas were issued to Thai nationals; the vast majority of Thai entrants entered Japan on temporary visitor visas. (Japan Immigration Association statistics, "The Number of New Entrants Classified by Nationality/Area of Origin and Status of Residence (Purpose of Entry), 1996." Available: http://www.netlaputa.ne.jp/~nakaiofc/Status2.html. December 1999.)

[34] Ma. Rosario P. Ballescas, *Filipino Entertainers in Japan: An Introduction,* (Quezon City: The Foundation for Nationalist Studies, 1992).

[35] Skilled laborers may also enter Japan on trainee visas, but the great majority are issued to unskilled migrants (Morita and Sassen, "The New Illegal Immigration . . ." IMR, vol. 28 (1), p. 153).

[36] Kenichi Furuya, "Labor Migration and Skill Development: Japan's Trainee Program," *Asian Migrant,* vol. viii, no. 1, January-March 1995, p. 8.

[37] Immigration Control Association, "Summarized Statistics on Immigration Control," quoted in Kenichi Furuya, "Labor Migration and Skill Development: Japan's Trainee Program," *Asian Migrant,* vol. viii, no. 1, January-March 1995, p. 9.

[38] See Morita and Sassen, "The New Illegal Immigration . . .," IMR, vol. 28 (1); Furuya, "Labor Migration and Skill Development . . .," *Asian Migrant,* vol. viii, no. 1.

The demand for unskilled migrant labor in Japan has continued to outstrip legal limits on the supply, and the majority of unskilled migrant workers in the country are undocumented.[39] Typically these workers enter Japan through legal channels, though often with falsified documentation, on a tourist or transit visa, and then overstay their visa expiration date and engage in activities outside their visa status. Others sneak into Japan, bypassing immigration controls entirely, and thus enter the country without any documentation at all.

Only a very small number of work visas have been made available to Thai nationals, so the great majority of migrant Thai workers in Japan are undocumented. The Japanese government estimates their numbers based on the number of persons with Thai passports who have entered Japan on temporary visitor visas and then overstayed their visa expiration dates. From 1991 to 1994, Japanese government statistics indicate that Thai nationals constituted the largest group of overstayers, with a total of more than 32,000 Thai overstayers in 1991 and almost 47,000 by the end of 1994.[40] In 1997, Japanese government statistics showed that at nearly 40,000, Thai overstayers continued to represent a significant percentage of the undocumented migrants in Japan (fourteen percent), though their numbers had been surpassed by Korean (eighteen percent) and Filipino (fifteen percent) nationals.[41] Moreover, many believe that the actual number of undocumented Thai migrants in Japan is much higher than the Japanese Immigration Bureau statistics indicate. The Counsellor at the Thai Embassy in Tokyo, for example, told Human Rights Watch that there were approximately eighty thousand Thai "overstayers" in Japan in 1995, including about thirty thousand who either entered with Malaysian or Singaporean passports, or entered Japan illegally by boat.[42]

---

[39] In November 1999, the Mission for the Revitalization of the Asian Economy, which was set up by the Japanese Prime Minister Keizo Obuchi in response to the Japanese economic recession, observed that Japan needed to accept a much wider range of foreign workers in the country (BBC World Service, "Japan 'must open up to foreigners,'" November 17, 1999).

[40] Immigration Bureau, Japan's Ministry of Justice,"Foreigners staying without legal documents by country of origin," March 1996. Note that the number of Thai overstayers peaked in mid-1993 at 55,383, and then began to gradually decline.

[41] Immigration Bureau, Japan's Ministry of Justice, "Change in Number of Illegal Overstayers by Nationality (Place of Origin)," January 1, 1997.

[42] Human Rights Watch interview with Udom Sapito, Counsellor, Royal Thai Embassy, Tokyo, Japan, May 19, 1995.

Criminal networks

The wide gap between the demand for unskilled foreign labor and the legal opportunities for migration under Japanese immigration policy has encouraged the development of a large underground business in procuring illegal foreign labor.[43] Typically, women in Thailand are recruited by relatives, friends, or other acquaintances, who promise them high-paying jobs in Japan and introduce them to trafficking agents. The agents then make arrangements for the women's travel and job placement, obtaining the necessary documentation, contacting job brokers in Japan, and hiring escorts to accompany the women on their trip. When the women arrive in Japan, job brokers receive them and deliver them to employers.

The agents, brokers, and employers in these operations often have ties to powerful organized crime syndicates. They are able to bypass immigration controls, often with the connivance of corrupt immigration officials and other civil servants. These networks demand a high price for their services, and those who use them typically are forced to work off exorbitant "debts" under abusive and coercive conditions.[44] Many migrants are unable to distinguish in advance between legal and illegal work opportunities, and thus may not realize that they are dealing with underground agents and brokers—or mafias—until after they have been cheated, incurred heavy debts, and arrived illegally in Japan.[45] In other cases, operators of Japanese entertainment businesses—often Thai nationals who have lived in Japan for extended periods of time—recruit women themselves, either directly or through

---

[43] See International Organization for Migration, "Trafficking in Migrants: IOM Policy and Activity" (Geneva, May 1997) for a general discussion of how the "unabated demand for migration, coupled with stricter entry controls or requirements, has provided entrepreneurs with a potential for profit."

[44] See Pasuk Phongpaichit, Sungsidh Piriyarangsan, and Nualnoi Treerat, *Guns, Girls, Gambling, Ganja: Thailand's Illegal Economy and Public Policy* (Chiang Mai: Silkworm Books, 1998), p. 166; Yayori Matsui, "Trafficking in Asian Women and Prostitution in Japan," *Asia-Japan Women's Resource Center Newsletter*, no. 1, August 1995, pp. 29-31; Pisan Manawapat, "From sex, exploitation to finally crime in Japan," *The Nation*, January 16, 1993.

[45] "Villagers cheated through offers of work in Japan," *Bangkok Post*, October 2, 1995. Human Rights Watch similarly found that women migrating from Thailand typically did not understand the legal implications of their migration decisions until after they had arrived in Japan or had committed themselves to going.

Thai contacts. But in these cases too, women often arrive in Japan saddled with enormous debts and vulnerable to serious human rights abuses.[46]

The extensive involvement of the Japanese Yakuza[47] in facilitating illegal immigration, including the procurement of women from Thailand and other countries into the Japanese sex industry, is well-known and documented.[48] Japanese and Thai police exchange information on Yakuza activities in an effort to stem the flow of Thai women into Japan, and Japanese police officers are consistently quoted in the press blaming the Yakuza for both the surge in illegal migration into Japan generally, and, more specifically, the flow of Thai women into the sex industry.[49] The Yakuza's ties to criminal groups in migrants' countries of origin, including Thailand, China, Hong Kong, Korea, Taiwan, the Philippines, Russia, Colombia, and Mexico, have also been well-documented.[50] Arrests of Thai agents accused of sending women to Japan to engage in sex work have revealed links to Yakuza members in Japan, and there have been credible reports of ties between ethnic

---

[46] See "Prostitution ring broken in Shinjuku," *Asahi Shimbun* (English version), August 12, 1999; "Three Thai arrested for arranging prostitution in Japan," Kyodo New International Inc., August 16, 1999; "Over 40,000 Thais Suffer in Japan," *Bangkok Post,* January 3, 1997; Chitraporn Vanaspong, "A multi-million baht business," *Bangkok Post,* August 18, 1997, p. 4.

[47] "Yakuza" refers to long-standing organized crime groups in Japan that are now officially known as "Boryokudan."

[48] See Phongpaichit, Piriyarangsan, and Treerat, *Guns, Girls, Gambling, Ganja: Thailand's Illegal Economy and Public Policy*, p. 166; Donald Wilson, "The Sinking Sun," *The Sunday Nation,* September 4, 1994, pp. C1, C3; Matsui, "Trafficking in Asian Women and Prostitution in Japan," *Asia-Japan Women's Resource Center Newsletter,* no. 1, pp. 29-31; David E. Kaplan and Alec Dubro, *Yakuza: The Explosive Account of Japan's Criminal Underworld* (Reading, Massachusetts: Addison-Wesley Publishing Company, Inc., 1986).

[49] See Sonni Efron, "In Japan, a Thriving Business in Illegal Immigrants," *International Herald Tribune,* February 4, 1997, pp. 1, 10; "Japanese, Thai police to discuss crime crackdown," *Bangkok Post,* March 6, 1995; "Crackdown helping to cut down prostitution in Japan," *Bangkok Post,* December 14, 1994;

[50] See Michael Vatikiotis, Sachiko Sakamaki, and Gary Silverman, "On the Margin: Organized crime profits from the flesh trade," *Far East Economic Review,* December 14, 1995; "Hokuriku Special: Illegal immigrants find new gateway," *Japan Times,* April 19,1999; Gregory Gross, "Mexican women forced to be sex slaves: Taken to Japan, they were victimized by organized crime," *San Diego Union-Tribune,* May 3, 1996, p. A-1; "Crackdown helping to cut down prostitution in Japan," *Bangkok Post,* December 15, 1994; "Japan: the Illusion of Immigration Control," in Wayne, Cornelius, Philip Martin and James Hollifield [eds.], *Controlling Immigration a Global Perspective,* 1994; Human Rights Watch interview with Rutsuko Shoji, Director, HELP Asian Women's Shelter, Tokyo, Japan, April 8, 1999.

Chinese crime syndicates operating in Thailand and the Yakuza.[51] Criminal syndicates in Thailand are involved in sending women to other parts of the world as well, including the United Kingdom, France, the United States, Australia, and South Africa.[52]

The Sex Industry in Japan

Government policies

Foreign women employed in the Japanese sex industry are part of an enormous undertaking, with estimated gross annual earnings of between four and ten trillion yen (US$33.6 billion - 84 billion), approximately one to three percent of Japan's GNP.[53] The wide range in estimates may in part reflect different decisions about what types of enterprises to include, as Japan has a large and varied sex entertainment industry, with both legal and illegal components. "Prostitution," narrowly defined as the sale of sexual intercourse on a repeated basis, was

---

[51] See Chitraporn Vanaspong, "A multi-million baht business," *Bangkok Post,* August 18, 1996, p. 4; "Girls pack up and quit Japan," *Bangkok Post,* August 9, 1996; "Yakuza links may have led to flesh trade gang leader's killing," *The Nation* (Bangkok, Thailand), March 8, 1995, p. A5; "Three men arrested for supplying prostitutes," *Bangkok Post,* February 9, 1994, p. 6; Hiroshi Komai (translated by Jens Wilkinson), *Migrant Workers in Japan,* (London: Kegan Paul International, Ltd., 1995), p. 78; Vatikiotis, Sakamaki, and Silverman, "On the Margin . . .," *Far East Economic Review*; Phongpaichit, Piriyarangsan, and Treerat, *Guns, Girls, Gambling, Ganja: Thailand's Illegal Economy and Public Policy,* p. 166; Wilson, "The Sinking Sun," *The Sunday Nation*; Matsui, "Trafficking in Asian Women and Prostitution in Japan," *Asia-Japan Women's Resource Center Newsletter,* no. 1, pp. 29-31; David E. Kaplan and Alec Dubro, *Yakuza: The Explosive Account of Japan's Criminal Underworld* (Reading, Massachusetts: Addison-Wesley Publishing Company, Inc., 1986).

[52] See R. Robin McDonald, "Human Contraband: Asian women expected jobs, not prostitution," *The Atlanta Constitution,* August 31, 1999, p. C8; "U.S. Says Asian Women Held In Prostitution Scheme," *Reuters,* August 20, 1999; Andrew Drummon, "Flesh Market: More and more Thai women are being tricked into prostitution by global traffickers," *Bangkok Post,* May 23, 1999; "France bids adieu to 40 vice girls," *Bangkok Post,* April 7, 1999; "Thai sex slaves working in SA," *Bangkok Post,* September 6, 1994.

[53] See "Weekend Economic Forecast," Asahi Newspaper, April 6, 1991; HELP Asian Women's Shelter, "An Alternative Report (Non-Governmental) To the United Nations," 1993; and "Women From Across the Sea: Migrant Workers in Japan," published by Asian Women's Association, Tokyo Japan 1988, p.45, respectively. The dollar figures have been calculated using the average yen-dollar exchange rate for the nine year period from 1990-1998: 119 yen to the U.S. dollar. Average yearly rates fluctuated between 94 and 145 yen to the U.S. dollar during that period.

prohibited in Japan for the first time in 1958, under the Prostitution Prevention Law. A wide range of sexual acts, however, have remained outside the purview of prohibitions on prostitution, and businesses involving the sale of such services are regulated under the Law on Control and Improvement of Amusement Businesses (hereinafter, the Entertainment Businesses Law).

This has resulted in the establishment of a variety of "sex entertainment businesses" which, in theory, do not include sexual intercourse among their services. These include "image clubs," where role playing and oral sex are the norm; "pink sarons,"[54] which are similar to the image clubs without the role playing; and "SM Clubs," where customers can engage in activities such as cross-dressing and anal sex. These businesses fall under Japan's Entertainment Businesses Law, which regulates the types of services they may provide, specifies detailed reporting requirements, establishes zoning restrictions, and sets minimum age levels for clients and employees. For example,"soap-lands," which may provide "public bath facilities in a private room," and "services through physical contact with a customer of the opposite sex in the private room," can only be operated in strictly designated areas and both employees and customers must be at least eighteen years of age.[55] There are also a number of businesses that routinely include sexual intercourse, but evade legal sanctions by arranging for sexual activities to occur off-premises, making anti-prostitution provisions difficult to enforce. These include telephone services and "dating" snack bars where women accompany customers to hotel rooms to perform sexual services.[56] Finally, a number of brothels continue to operate throughout the country. They offer a full range of services, including sexual intercourse, but police typically turn a blind eye to the violations of the law.[57]

Role of foreign migrants

There are an estimated 150,000 non-Japanese women employed in the Japanese sex industry, primarily from other Asian countries such as Thailand and the Philippines.[58] These women are typically employed in the lower rungs of the

---

[54] This term is taken from the English expression, "pink saloon."

[55] Entertainment Businesses Law, Article 4, 4-1. See the "Japanese Government Response" chapter for a more detailed description of this law.

[56] SWEETLY (Sex Workers! Encourage, Empower, Trust and Love Yourselves!) publication.

[57] Human Rights Watch interview with Momocca Momocco, founder of SWEETLY (Sex Workers! Encourage, Empower, Trust and Love Yourselves!), Kyoto, Japan, April 12, 1999.

[58] "Prostitution in Asia Increasingly Involves Trafficking," *Trafficking in Migrants,* no. 15, June 1997.

industry. Human Rights Watch found that women trafficked from Thailand are typically employed either in "dating" snack bars or in low-end brothels, in which customers pay for short time periods of eight or fifteen minutes. Abuses are common as job brokers and employers take advantage of foreign women's vulnerability as undocumented migrants: they cannot seek recourse from the police or other law enforcement authorities without risking deportation and potential prosecution, and they are isolated by language barriers, a lack of community, and a lack of familiarity with their surroundings. Compounding the difficulty and danger of escape, women in "debt" are kept under constant surveillance, their wages are withheld, and their passports and other documentation are confiscated, depriving them of proof of identity. In addition, the Yakuza is heavily involved in the operation of many of these establishments; bar and brothel owners are often Yakuza members themselves, or else pay protection money to the Yakuza in exchange for assistance both in "disciplining" women who disobey orders or attempt to escape and in evading police and immigration raids.[59] As one Japanese sex worker—and sex workers' rights activist—explained to Human Rights Watch, "Foreign sex workers are kept isolated, without information about Japan, and their passports are confiscated. Japanese women are too knowledgeable about their rights, so owners use foreigners. Other Asian woman, in particular, are viewed as controllable by Japanese men."[60]

The brokers and employers involved in recruiting foreign women into Japan derive enormous profits from their earnings. Even at the lower end of the sex

---

[59] The Yakuza's involvement in the procurement and employment of foreign women in the Japanese sex industry is well-documented. See Vatikiotis, Sakamaki, and Silverman, "On the Margin . . .," *Far East Economic Review*; Matsui, "Trafficking in Asian Women and Prostitution in Japan," *Asia-Japan Women's Resource Center Newsletter*, no. 1, pp. 29-31; Alexandra Black, "Japan: Foreign Women Workers Forced into Flesh Trade," an Inter Press Service Feature, September 16, 1994; Wilson, "The Sinking Sun," *The Sunday Nation*; "Japanese ordeal ends for girl in tearful reunion," *The Nation*, April 8, 1994; Pisan Manawapat, "From sex, exploitation to finally crime in Japan," *The Nation*, January 16, 1993; "MPD: Thai Women Help Businessmen Close Deals," *The Daily Yomiuri*, October 10, 1992, p. 3.

Human Rights Watch interviews with women from Thailand who worked in the Japanese sex industry—including one woman who was the manager of a snack bar—as well as with women's shelter staff and other advocates in the field consistently confirmed that Yakuza members operate some sex establishments directly, while providing protection and disciplinary services to others.

[60] Human Rights Watch interview with Momocca Momocco, founder of SWEETLY (Sex Workers! Encourage, Empower, Trust and Love Yourselves!), Kyoto, Japan, April 12, 1999.

industry, fees are significant, and brokers and employers take a large cut by entirely withholding wages from women in debt and taking up to fifty percent of the fees from non-indebted women. Women from Thailand who work in "dating" snack bars reported that clients were charged fees of 20,000 to 30,000 yen (US$170-250[61]) for two hours and 30,000 to 50,000 yen (US$250-340) for a full night. While in debt, the women typically worked seven nights a week, servicing between one and three clients a night, and all of their earnings went to their employer. Using conservative figures, a noted Thai economist estimated the gross annual income generated by Thai sex workers in Japan as 310,500 million yen (US$3.3 billion).[62]

Trafficking

A Global Problem

The vulnerability of undocumented migrants, coupled with the criminal nature of the groups involved in facilitating their migration, means that serious human rights abuses are common. This is particularly true in the case of women's migration into sex work. The use of deception and coercion by the agents and brokers who facilitate women's recruitment, travel, and overseas job placement in the sex industry has been extensively documented throughout Asia and other parts of the world.[63] This problem of trafficking in women has been on the international agenda for the last one hundred years, but efforts to clearly define the scope of the problem and to adopt concrete measures to remedy it have met with little success.[64]

---

[61] These dollar amounts were calculated using the average yen-dollar exchange rate over the nine year period from 1990-1998.

[62] Phongpaichit, Piriyarangsan, and Treerat, *Guns, Girls, Gambling, Ganja: Thailand's Illegal Economy and Public Policy*, p. 171. This amount was calculated for 1995 using an estimated 23,000 Thai sex workers, an average fee per client of thirty thousand yen, and an average rate of 1.5 clients per day, 300 days per year. The dollar figure was calculated using the average exchange rate for 1995. (Note that due to a miscalculation, the book cites a total of 3,105,000 million yen (one decimal point too many), but the figures used to make this calculation are those noted in this footnote.)

[63] See "Prostitution in Asia Increasingly Involves Trafficking," *Trafficking in Migrants*, no. 15, June 1997.

[64] Human Rights Watch understands that a definition of trafficking should include all acts related to the recruitment, transport, transfer, sale, or purchase of human beings by force, fraud, deceit, or other coercive tactic, for the purpose of placing them into conditions of forced labor or practices similar to slavery, in which labor is extracted through physical and/or non-physical means of coercion, including blackmail, fraud, deceit, isolation, threat or use of physical force, or psychological pressure. For a more detailed discussion of the definition of the term, see the "International Legal Standards on Trafficking" chapter.

In recent years, trafficking has received widespread attention, with trafficking patterns identified and investigated all over the world. The *Asia Migrant Bulletin,* for example, has documented the trafficking of migrants from the Philippines, Thailand, China, Indonesia, Burma, Sri Lanka, Bangladesh, India, Nepal, and, more recently, from other Asian countries such as Vietnam, Laos, Cambodia, and Fiji. Migrants from these countries have been trafficked to Japan, Taiwan, Hong Kong, Macau, Malaysia, Singapore, Thailand, India, and further to Australia, the Middle East, Europe, and the United States.[65] The International Organization for Migration (IOM) publishes a quarterly newsletter entitled "Trafficking in Migrants" that has included accounts of trafficking from all over the world, including Southeast Asia, East Asia, South Asia, the Middle East, Western Europe, Eastern Europe, South America, Central America, and North America.[66] The global scale of the trafficking problem was also highlighted at the Beijing Women's NGO Forum in September 1995.

Despite the increased attention, the actual extent of trafficking, both in terms of the number of persons trafficked and in terms of the profits made by traffickers, is still not known. In part this is because international attention has focused largely on the problem of trafficking of women for prostitution, often with the assumption that all migration into sex work is by definition coercive. However, other definitions acknowledge that men, women, and children are trafficked into a wide variety of labor sectors, including domestic labor, factories, construction, and criminal activity, including smuggling.[67] And some have stressed the fact that many women voluntarily decide to migrate for sex work and not all fall victim to trafficking abuses in the process.[68] Estimating the magnitude of trafficking operations is also difficult because of the illegal nature of the activity, and documenting the number of women trafficked can be particularly difficult because the victims often end up in informal—or illegal—labor sectors. One IOM study estimated that up to four million persons are trafficked internationally each year—with those involved in the trade making a profit of up to $7 billion—but this

---

[65] *Asia Migrant Bulletin,* July-December, 1995, Volume III, No. 3&4.

[66] See *Trafficking in Migrants,* no. 10 (March 1996) - no. 19 (July 1999).

[67] 1998 Regional Conference on Trafficking in Women Report, Nov. 3rd - 4th, Bangkok, Thailand.

[68] Jo Doezema, "Loose Women or Lost Women? The re-emergence of the myth of "white slavery" in contemporary discourses of 'trafficking in women,'" presented at the ISA Convention, Washington, D.C., February 17-21, 1999.

study defined trafficking to include all facilitation of illegal migration for a profit, whether or not elements of coercion or deception are involved.[69]

Into the Japanese sex industry

The trafficking of women into the sex industry in Japan has been a significant problem for many years. It first received attention in the late 1970s and early 1980s, when women from the Philippines began migrating to Japan in large numbers, often falling victim to gross abuses in the process. In 1981, the governments of Japan and the Philippines officially acknowledged the demand for Filipina "entertainers" in Japan, and agreed to facilitate the process of issuing "entertainer visas" to women from the Philippines. Over the course of the next decade, the number of entertainer visas issued to applicants from the Philippines increased from about nine thousand to more than forty thousand per year.[70] The evidence suggests that these visas have improved women's position vis-a-vis agents, brokers, and employers, making them less vulnerable to abuse and exploitation in the workplace than migrant women who enter Japan on tourist or transit visas.[71]

There are limits, however, to the advantages Filipina women possess. Many continue to enter Japan on tourist visas, unable to obtain one of the still limited number of entertainer visas. This problem has been exacerbated by the heightened application requirements imposed by the Philippines government in the 1990s,[72] which were adopted in response to reports of serious abuses of Filipina women

---

[69] International Organization for Migration, "Trafficking in Migrants: IOM Policy and Activities" (Geneva, May 1997).

[70] Hosoda, "The International Division of Labour . . .," thesis submitted to the Department of Political Studies, Queen's University, Ontario, Canada, p. 14.

[71] Human Rights Watch interview with Rutsuko Shoji, Director, HELP Asian Women's Shelter, Tokyo, Japan, April 8, 1999. In *Filipino Entertainers in Japan: An Introduction*, Ballescas also finds that Filipina women working in Japan on entertainer visas enjoy somewhat better conditions than those with tourist visas.

[72] There is some evidence that policies of the Japanese and Philippine governments to discourage women from coming to Japan as entertainers—including stricter visa requirements by the Japanese Immigration Office and stiffer conditions imposed on women leaving to work as entertainers by the Philippines' labor department—have pushed an increasing number of Filipina women into abusive marriages with Japanese nationals. (Luz Rimban, "Rights: Marriage is Ticket to Living in Japan," *Inter Press Service,* January 1998. Available: http://www.oneworld.org/ips2/jan98/japan.html. October 1999.)

working in Japan on entertainer visas.[73] Moreover, peculiarities in the regulations governing entertainer visas significantly reduce their effectiveness in protecting the women's rights. The most obvious problem is that while Filipinas who enter Japan on entertainer visas have the right to work, they are officially classified as "non-workers" and are not covered by Japanese labor laws.[74] Consequently, any appeals for violation of their contracts, which are frequent, must be directed to immigration authorities rather than labor officials, and enforcing labor standards is not an Immigration Bureau priority.[75] One study of Filipina workers in the Japanese entertainment industry found that even those women with entertainer visas, or "contract workers," are commonly subjected to labor violations and other abuses by their employers. Nonetheless, the study concluded that the contract workers generally suffered less abuse, both in terms of financial exploitation and other rights violations, than their non-contract worker counterparts from the Philippines.[76]

Trafficking of women from Thailand into Japan's sex industry reached large-scale proportions in the late 1980s, and remains an egregious problem more than a decade later. No effort has been made by the Japanese and Thai governments to regularize the migration of Thai women, as in the case of Filipina migrants discussed above, even though the evidence suggests that such measures could reduce their vulnerability to abuse. Japanese economic recessions in the 1990s, coupled with an increase in the enforcement of immigration law, have had a dampening effect on migration flows, and, according to Japanese government statistics, the number of female Thai "overstayers" has been gradually declining

---

[73] The exploitation of Filipina entertainers in Japan received widespread attention after Maricris Sioson, a twenty-two-year-old Filipina entertainer, died in Japan on September 14, 1991. Her death certificate indicated that she died of hepatitis, but when an autopsy was performed in the Philippines, at her family's request, Dr. Arizala of the Philippine National Bureau of Investigation found that she had suffered severe blows to the head and two stab wounds, one in the thigh and one in the genital area. Dr. Arizala determined that though she was suffering from the early stages of hepatitis, her death was due to traumatic head injuries. Appeals were made to the Japanese government to investigate her death, but the Japanese police continued to insist that she died of natural causes. (Equality Now, "Japan: The Death of Maricris Sioson," *Women's Action 4.1,* December 1993.)

[74] Ballescas, *Filipino Entertainers in Japan: An Introduction*, p. 9.

[75]Human Rights Watch interview with Rutsuko Shoji, Director, Asian Women's Shelter HELP, Tokyo, April 8, 1999.

[76] Ballescas, *Filipino Entertainers in Japan: An Introduction*.

from a high of almost 30,000 in 1993.[77]   However, even by official Japanese government estimates, the number of female overstayers from Thailand continues to exceed 20,000,[78] and as pointed out above, this excludes the numerous women from Thailand who have entered the country on non-Thai passports. Moreover, our research indicates that the abuses new entrants commonly suffer at the hands of their traffickers and initial employers in Japan remain largely unchanged.

---

[77] This fits the general pattern of undocumented migration in Japan. According to Japanese government estimates, the number of foreign nationals illegally residing in Japan peaked at 297,000 in 1993, and had fallen to 283,000 by 1997, the last year for which such statistics were available at the time of this publication. (Ministry of Justice, Japan, "Estimated number of illegal stays by foreign nationals."   Available: http://www.moj.go.jp/ENGLISH/IB/ib-11.htm. February 2000.)

[78] The most recent statistics available from the Japanese government at the time of this publication were for January 1997, at which time there were an estimated 22, 574 Thai women overstaying their visas in Japan. (Immigration Bureau, Ministry of Justice, Japan, "Change in illegal stays by country of origin," March 1997.)

IV. PROFILES

In this chapter, Human Rights Watch profiles four women who were trafficked from Thailand into servitude in Japan. Human Rights Watch interviewed numerous women who recounted similar experiences, and in the chapters that follow, we describe and analyze the common patterns and abuses that emerged through our research. Yet, to fully relay the gravity of this issue, and its impact on the women affected, we can do no better than to begin by repeating here the stories of individual women, as told to Human Rights Watch. In these testimonies, women describe their experiences from the time of their recruitment in Thailand through their release—or escape—from debt bondage in Japan. While each woman's story is unique, their testimonies are typical of many others gathered by Human Rights Watch. They also reflect some of the key variations we noted in women's accounts.

Pot[79]

Pot was recruited to work in Japan in 1990 when she was twenty-seven years old.

> A friend I knew from the market in Nakhon Sawan told me about
> the opportunity to work in factories in Japan. I had divorced my
> Thai husband when I was four months pregnant and now my son
> was three years old and I had to raise him by myself and was
> finding it difficult to make enough money. My parents asked me
> not to go, but I thought if I went for just one year I could make
> money for my family and son. I didn't realize what kind of work
> I was going to do until I was on my way to Japan, and I didn't
> realize I was in debt for 380 bai [3.8 million yen; US$26,000][80]

---

[79] Human Rights Watch and FOWIA interview, Ibaraki prefecture, Japan, June 1, 1995.

To protect the identities of the women victims of trafficking, each has been assigned a randomly selected name which is used consistently throughout the report. While Human Rights Watch generally refers to interviewees by their first and last names, in this case we have chosen to follow the Thai custom of using nicknames.

[80] Here and below, to convert Japanese yen into U.S. dollars, we use the average exchange rate for the relevant year and then round off. Where the year cannot be easily determined from the context, a footnote will specify which year's average rate was used.

until I arrived at the snack.[81] I was told by the recruiters in
Thailand that I would work in a factory and would get fifty
percent of my salary until my debt was paid off. I was angry and
freaked out about my situation.

After describing the good job opportunities in Japan, Pot's friend introduced her to
an agent in Bangkok who made the arrangements for her travel. First, he helped her
obtain her travel documents. She applied for and received her own passport, but the
agent took care of all of the paperwork and negotiations with the officials. Then he
took Pot to get her Japanese visa. "The agent told me to go to a certain window at
the visa section at the Japanese Embassy. I got my visa without anyone asking me
any questions or having to talk at all because the agent filled out all the forms for
me." The agent also gave Pot money for clothing, but Pot sent most of it to her
family instead. The day Pot's visa arrived, the agent put her in a hotel room at the
Central Hotel in the Ladprao area of Bangkok and would not let her go out. Pot
recalled:

> It was a big room and four or five other women going to work in
> Japan were also kept there. I was surprised to be locked up
> because I was not allowed any chance to say goodbye to my
> family, even over the phone. I heard the agents talking about the
> price for each woman being between 150-160 bai [1.5-1.6
> million yen; US$10,000-11,000], but I couldn't really understand
> what they were talking about and did not realize that we were
> being sold into prostitution. I was feeling suspicious but still
> wasn't clear about what was going on. I stayed at the hotel for
> several days. During that time, I saw that if a woman did not get
> approved for a Japanese visa, then the agent exchanged her real
> passport for a false one.

Two weeks after her initial decision to go to Japan, Pot was put on a flight to
South Korea with four other women from the hotel room and a Thai man nicknamed
Dee. Dee told them which immigration officer to go to at the airport. "In hindsight
I believe that the immigration officer at Don Muang airport in Bangkok knew what

---

[81] Snack bars, often referred to simply as "snacks," will be described in greater
detail in the next chapter. In brief, they are common venues where Japanese go for
relaxation and conversation. Many do not involve sexual exchanges, but in the
establishments women referred to as "dating" snack bars, clients are allowed take the
hostesses out of the bar for sexual services.

I was going to do in Japan better than I did at the time, as the officer was buddy-buddy with my escort and just kept smiling at me and the other Thai women as he stamped our passports." When Pot got to South Korea she was put in a room with fifty other Thai women and seven or eight men. "Most of the women were under twenty years old and from the north of Thailand. All fifty women were guarded, controlled, and watched by the men at all times. I knew that there was something wrong and began talking to the other Thai women there. This is where I learned that all of the women were going to work in prostitution, because some of the women had worked in prostitution before and knew that they were going to do so in Japan. I didn't know what to do. I just thought that once I got to Japan I would change my job immediately."

All fifty Thai women were put on the same flight to Narita airport, just outside Tokyo. The men who were accompanying them went through immigration control first, and then waited near the immigration officers to give explanations when needed. A few of the women were not allowed into Japan, but most were. From the airport, Dee put Pot and several of the other Thai women into a van with a Khmer woman named Chan, who was from one of the refugee camps close to the Thai border with Cambodia. Chan brought the women to Tokyo, and spent the next five days taking them to different places around the city. "Chan was trying to sell me and the others like cattle. Then, on the fifth day, a Thai woman bought me and took me to another woman named Chan in Ibaraki prefecture who paid 380 bai [3.8 million yen; US$26,000] for me. I had known since Korea that I was being sold as a prostitute, but I didn't realize until I got to the snack that this 380 bai that I was bought for was to be my debt."

There were ten to twenty women working at the snack at any given time. Pot worked there for nearly three months and then was sent—still in debt—to another city in Ibaraki to work as a telephone service girl.[82] After two months there, she was sent back to the snack bar where she worked for another three months.

> In all, I worked for eight months to pay back my debt and I had calculated that I must have paid it back long ago, but the mama[83] kept lying to me and said she didn't have the same records as I did. During these eight months, I had to take every client that wanted me and had to work everyday, even during my menstruation. The mama also made me and the other women

---

[82] Working for a telephone service is similar to working in a 'dating' snack bar, except that customers arrange 'dates' by telephone, rather than at a bar.

[83] Managers at the snack bars are typically women referred to as "mama" or "mama-san" by the hostesses.

work for her during the day and wouldn't allow us to eat much saying we would get too fat. I was like a skeleton during that time. While I was in "tact" [under contract, or in debt], the mama paid for everything except for my health care and birth control pills. This was all added to my debt. I tried to keep track of my own records quietly, but I didn't know all the additional expenses that the mama was adding to my debt. And I did not want the mama to know I was keeping track for fear that she would get angry.

While she was in debt, Pot worried about her family back in Thailand. "I did not have any money to send home unless a client gave me a good tip. I just wanted to pay off my debt and get enough money to go home. But the mama was always swearing at me for saving money. The mama threatened me, saying that if I made any trouble she'd sell me again and double my debt. During the first three months I was never allowed out of the apartment except with the mama or a client. Even after three months I was allowed out only along with others and was warned not to make any friends." Some of the clients were abusive too. "Once a Yakuza member took me out for the night. He brought me to a hotel room and first injected himself with heroin and then tried to force me to inject. I refused and struggled. He beat me until I was almost dead. Then he took a rubber band out and strapped it around my arm and was just about to inject me when he passed out. I tried to move and after some time was able to get out of the hotel and fled back to my apartment. I didn't dare tell anybody what happened or seek medical help for my injuries."

Despite the terrible conditions, Pot did not try to escape. "When the Japanese police came around I knew that I had overstayed my visa and that the mama had my passport. I never dared to run away or even considered running to the police without my documents. Without my documents I was sure I would be arrested and jailed. . . . I tried to be cooperative with the mama and not make any troubles for myself." After paying off her debt, Pot continued to work at the snack bar for another year, trying to save enough money to return home. While she was working there, she met a man who asked her to marry him, and she agreed. When they went to register the marriage, the official resisted. "The provincial official asked me how I could register as an 'overstayer.' I had already found out how it was done so I explained it to him. Then the official claimed my documents were fake. I explained that if they were fake, I would not have tried to come here to register legally." Eventually, she and her husband were successful.

Kaew[84]

Kaew lives in a village in Chiang Rai province in northern Thailand. She has three sons and was married to an abusive husband, who drank too much and was either unable or unwilling to work. In May 1992, Kaew went to Japan on a ninety day tourist visa, hoping to earn enough money to care for her children. "I had three kids, my husband drank, and we had no money," Kaew explained, "so I had to do something." Several years earlier, Kaew had traveled to southern Thailand, to the city of Hat Yai in Songkhla province, to work as a sex worker. "I went back and forth several times trying to make money, leaving my children with my mother." Next she tried working in Singapore. She met a man there who asked her to move in with him, but he did not give her enough money to send home to her children, so she left and returned to her village. Again, she tried to reconcile with her husband, but he was still violent and drinking heavily. Finally, she left him, and moved into her parents' house with her children. A few months later, someone in the village asked her if she wanted to go to Japan, and she agreed. That person told her about an agent in Bangkok.

When she arrived in Bangkok, she was taken to an apartment with about thirty other women from northern and northeastern Thailand. They were all told to undress, and a woman examined their busts, stomachs, hips, and vaginas. Kaew was thirty-one years old, well above the average age of new recruits for the Japanese sex industry. But she looked young, and "the agent in Bangkok decided I was beautiful enough to go to Japan, though I had to get a nose job first and they kept messing it up; they had to do it four times to get it right. The agent wanted me to get my eyes done too, but I refused. Other women got plastic surgery for their breasts, eyes, or other body parts. Women who were not beautiful enough were given a bus ticket home to their village."

Kaew was given 100 baht (US$4) a day while she waited in Bangkok with other women who were going to Japan. She waited in Bangkok for seven months because the agent used her to get passports and visas for the other girls.

> They used me because I was older, so it was easier for me. I got five passports for other women—each time getting married to change my surname. If I think about it now, [the agents] were very, very clever. They could even make birth certificates; they could do everything. They were so clever, and in Japan [the brokers] are even more clever.

---

[84] Human Rights Watch and FOWIA interviews, Chiang Rai province, Thailand, September 13, 1997, October 4, 1997, and April 25, 1999.

After seven months, I threatened to go home because I wasn't making any money, so they sent me to Japan. My escort was a Western man named Gary. He took the women to Japan one-by-one. He had many passports and worked with the airline. He had a visa that allowed him to go back and forth between Japan and Thailand through his banana business. He was handsome and dressed up and spoke Thai. I told the immigration officials that I was going to visit a banana factory in Japan to see how it worked and I had a letter from the company in Thailand. Gary had 150 bai [1.5 million yen; US$12,000] with him. Gary and I were separated by the immigration officers at the airport and asked questions about the company, but we had prepared before. I had practiced for two or three nights before I left, and learned to write my new name in English.

At Narita airport, someone was waiting for me and took the clothes and jewelry that they had given me to wear. The person took me to the mama's house in Tokyo. There were lots of women there and people came to choose women and buy them. I was bought on the third day, and told that my price was 380 bai [3.8 million yen; US$30,000]. After three or four days of working at the snack bar, I realized how much 380 bai was.

Kaew explained that she had understood there would be some debt for the airplane ticket and other expenses, but she had never been told how high her debt would be, and she was shocked at the amount. "The other girls said to me, 'that's a lot of debt and you're old; you'll never pay it off.' Then I prayed that it would only take six or seven months to pay it off, and I went with all of the clients I could. ... The mama said to me, 'don't let your period come, or you'll never finish paying your debt.'" So Kaew also took contraceptive pills daily, though she had been sterilized at age twenty-one, so that she would not menstruate and could work every day.[85] She got her mother to send the pills from Thailand, so that she would not have to buy them from her mama and increase the level of her debt.

---

[85] The pills were designed to be taken in twenty-eight day cycles, with twenty-one days of pills followed by seven days off (or seven days of placebos) to allow for menstruation. Contraceptive pills, or oral contraceptives, are designed to prevent pregnancy and/or regulate menstruation. They are not designed to prevent menstruation.

The boss would tell me to go with a man, and I couldn't refuse. Girls were beaten if they didn't agree, and the owner was close to the Yakuza so he knew how to fight. Women were also fined for coming back late, fighting with each other, or not agreeing to sit with a client, so I did what I was told. Other women were beaten so badly they had to take days off; I wasn't beaten or given fines because I obeyed.

Some clients were good, and some were abusive. . . . I had up to three clients a night because I needed to pay off my debt, and after six months the mama said I had paid off 250 bai [2.5 million yen; US$20,000]. I kept track in a notebook and this sounded about right—I was paying back about 40 or 50 bai [400,000-500,000 yen; US$3000-4000] per month, and I could have paid off the rest of the debt soon. But while I was working, I met a man who was a friend of the owner. He came to the snack bar often, but he never took women out, he just talked to them. I had to talk to him, and at first I was upset because I knew he wasn't going to pay to take me out, but then he gave me tips just to sit and talk. He told the owner that he liked me and asked to buy out my contract, and the owner agreed since it was his friend. Usually, they didn't allow men to buy women out.

So he paid the 130 bai [1.3 million yen; US$10,000] that I owed and set me up in an apartment. He gave me money, and I also continued to work at the same snack bar, but I wasn't in debt so I earned money. Women working without debt still had to go with a customer if he picked her out, but I didn't have to try flirting and all anymore because I wasn't so worried about money. On Tuesdays, I spent the day with my boyfriend, and the other days I worked. I continued to work there for almost two years after my debt was paid, and then I was arrested.

Kaew's snack bar was in Nagano prefecture, about three hours west of Tokyo by train.

All of the local police came to the snack bar, just like in Thailand, and they were very nice—there were no problems. But then police came from Tokyo. They were cleaning up in preparation for the Olympics in Nagano, and an undercover

police officer from Tokyo came to the snack bar. She said she
was a tour operator from Tokyo—there were a lot of tours from
Tokyo—and that she wanted to see the women. When the
women lined up, the officer took out her ID and arrested us all.
I always kept 10 bai [100,000 yen; US$980[86]] in my pocket to
pay for my ticket to Thailand in case I was arrested and deported,
so I had that with me. I also had my passport—the mama had
kept it while I was in debt, but after my contract was paid I
carried it at all times. I gave my money and passport to the
officer, and she let me get my stuff, and then I was taken to jail
[an immigration detention facility in Tokyo]. Five days later I
returned to Thailand. I didn't have to stay long because I had my
passport and enough money for the trip home. . . . When I left,
I just got onto the plane like other passengers. There were
twenty-four of us arrested together at the snack bar, and we were
sent back to Thailand in groups of three or four.

Now Kaew is back in her village in Thailand. She worries that her sons are
embarrassed about the work she did while they were growing up.

Whenever I think too much, I get sad. But then I remember
when I could only feed my children rice and soup. My husband
didn't help, so my kids had to stay with my mother while I went
to earn money. That guy was physically abusive too. He would
come home drunk and beat me. I tried to work it out with him.
But things never changed. The oldest son knows everything I
did. He remembers before, knows the choices I've made. I
worry that my children will be embarrassed by me, by the fact
that I was a prostitute. But I tell my kids: "I had many men on
my chest and I cried, but I closed my eyes and thought of my
kids." I don't know if they really listen or if it's in one ear and
out the other.

Asked what she would say to other women who wanted to go to Japan, Kaew
replied,

---

[86] This U.S. dollar amount was calculated using the average yen-dollar exchange
rate in 1994.

It's all good luck or not. It was good luck that I had a good
snack bar, and bad luck that I got arrested, and good luck that I
found a good boyfriend. If you talk to different women, you will
get very different stories. Some women start to gamble, spend
their money on hosts, and drink. It gets difficult to remember
why you're there, for the young especially. Some are less
obedient than me, so they have problems. The snack bar next
door to me was run by the Yakuza so it was worse. Some women
are killed or followed if they escape, or even if they are arrested.
Some are followed to Thailand, so many don't go back to their
families right away, but wait. Now I want to go back to Japan to
visit, but only legally. When I was in Japan, I had no rights
because the job was illegal. I'd like to go back to see,
independently. I'm trying to go legally, with a passport, so that
I'm allowed to be there.

Chan[87]

Chan grew up in the province of Korat (now called Nakhon Ratchasima), in
northeast Thailand. She went to school through the eighth grade, but was unable
to find a job with a decent salary, so she eventually decided to go to Japan. Chan
was twenty-three years old at the time. She had known the recruiters for a long time
through her aunt, and, with their help, Chan applied for her passport and a Japanese
visa. She told the Japanese Embassy that she was a nurse and was going to stay
with a family in Japan who had lived previously in Thailand. Then the recruiter
introduced Chan to the agent, who paid the recruiter 30,000 baht (US$1,200). The
agent told Chan that her debt would be about 800,000 baht (US$32,000), but that
she would be able to pay it back in about three months.

Chan left for Japan in December 1993. The week before she left, she stayed
with the agent in the Ladprao area of Bangkok, where she met other Thai women
who were also going to Japan. Chan was escorted to Japan by a Thai woman, and
after they passed through immigration at Narita airport, this woman introduced her
to a broker. The broker took Chan to a snack bar in Chiba prefecture; the mama
was a Thai woman and her husband was a Japanese man with Yakuza connections.
Chan said that the mama was very strict. "Although I knew about the debt before
I left," she explained, "I was lied to about the conditions and the fact that I would
have to pay extra for everything and have it added to my debt."

[87] Human Rights Watch and FOWIA interview, Bangkok, Thailand, March 2, 1995.

Chan was housed in an apartment with three other Thai women. The mama, who lived in the same building, confiscated Chan's passport and return plane ticket to Thailand. Every night the women had to be ready for the van that came to pick them up at 7 p.m., and then they worked until 2 a.m. They were expected to help with the running of the snack bar, entertaining guests and serving clients, and they were not given any days off. "We weren't exactly forced to take clients, but we were pressured and if we didn't cooperate our life could be made very difficult. So, everyone learned to do as they were instructed. I had to take clients from the first day. I had never done this type of work before and had to serve about three or four clients every night. The mama told us we had to work hard to pay off our debts within five months or she would sell us again. We were forced to take birth control pills with no days off, so I never had my period." Each month, 100,000 yen (US$980[88]) was added to Chan's debt for her expenses. She knew this included 30,000 yen (US$290) per month for housing, but she did not know how the rest of the money was divided. Chan was also penalized if her weight exceeded fifty-four kilograms (119 pounds), and once a month, the women were tested for AIDS and charged 10,000 yen (US$100) for the test. Once, while Chan was working, immigration officers raided the snack bar. But a telephone call received just before the raid warned those there so that most of the women, including Chan, were able to run out; the others, however, were arrested.

After Chan had been at the snack bar for two months a client showed her where the Thai Embassy was and explained how she could escape. Chan went into the embassy to begin the process of preparing her documents to return home, but she did not dare escape then, because she did not want to get the client in trouble. About a month later, another client left Chan to take a taxi back to her apartment. Instead, she took the taxi to Tokyo and surrendered herself to the Japanese immigration authorities. The next day, Chan went to the Thai Embassy, where officials called her snack bar, demanding Chan's passport and money for her return trip home.

Chan was deported in February 1994. After she got back to Thailand, an agent followed her to her home in Korat, asking for the rest of the debt. "I was afraid so I left my family's home and came to Bangkok. I am still afraid that they are following me even though one year has passed. I am afraid that if they catch up with me they will kill me. I heard in Japan that that is what they do to those who don't repay their debt. I know that is why very few women dare to escape.

---

[88] This U.S. dollar amount was calculated using the average yen-dollar exchange rate in 1994.

Everyone I knew stayed and finished their debt. But I couldn't stay in Japan because I don't like to be bossed around."

Nuch[89]

Nuch is the youngest of four children. She went to school until she was twelve years old, finishing the fourth grade, and then went to work as a farmhand for about 30 baht (US$1.20) per day. When she was fifteen years old she went to Bangkok to work as a maid, earning 400 baht (US$16) per month. She returned to her village after only a month because she was homesick, but over the next twelve years she went back and forth to Bangkok several times looking for work. She spent two weeks there selling Thai sweets, several months working as a nanny, three years working in a shop, and three months sharpening knives. During her last trip to Bangkok, she spent a month working as a maid, and then got a job at a diamond shop. After two years there, her salary had reached 3,500 baht (US$140) per month, with four days off each month.

While she was working at the diamond shop in 1992, an acquaintance told her that she should go to work in Japan and introduced her to a dress-maker, who then brought Nuch to an agent. "The agent told me she could find a job for me in a Thai restaurant in Japan and that I could make several tens of thousands a month. The agent agreed to pay for all of my expenses, saying that I could pay her back once in Japan." Then Nuch met another agent, an older Thai man named Lek. He explained that she would have to pay back 380 bai (3.8 million yen; US$30,000), and she agreed. "I didn't know anything about exchange rates or different currencies so I didn't know how much [380 bai] was, but it didn't sound like a lot. I asked him how long it would take me to pay it back, and the agent said five months." Nuch and her roommate decided to go to Japan together. Nuch's roommate was only eighteen years old, and she didn't want to ask her parents for permission to go to Japan so she had to use a false passport.[90] Nuch was twenty-seven years old at the time, so the agent took her to get her real passport. Then Lek and his wife took Nuch to get her Japanese visa. She told the embassy officials that she was going on holiday, and a week later she received her visa.

Nuch left for Japan on March 26, 1992. Lek's wife went with her. "I didn't carry my own passport to go through Thai immigration. The wife gave both of our passports to immigration and talked to them. I arrived in Japan at night. At Narita airport immigration, the wife told me to go to a specific line and she went in another

---

[89] Human Rights Watch and FOWIA interview, Bangkok, Thailand, March 3, 1995 and March 26, 1995.

[90] Persons under twenty years old must have their parents' permission to get a passport in Thailand.

one. She went through first and then came to help me. The wife spoke Japanese and got me through. Then we took a taxi to a hotel in Tokyo. The wife told me I would work at a Thai restaurant that belonged to a Thai woman." The next morning, a Japanese man came to the hotel to get Nuch and took her to an apartment in Tokyo. There were three or four other Thai women at the apartment, and many Thai men as well. Everyone slept in the same room, and Nuch was told that a Thai woman named Ice was the 'boss.' "Ice told me I was to stay here and that I shouldn't speak Thai outside the apartment. Ice told me I couldn't escape and not to even try."

Nuch stayed in the apartment for two days without going out and did not talk to anyone. She thought it was strange that the women worked all night, but she did not ask any questions. After two nights, Nuch was told to pack up her things and get dressed. Two other Thai women were told to do the same. "Another woman took the three of us. We traveled all day by train. Once off the train, I was separated from the others and brought straight to a snack bar. I was very cold because I had no winter clothes. The snack bar was very small and had only four other Thai women there. They worked and slept at the snack shop. The mama was a Taiwanese woman." Nuch stayed there for two nights, and nobody came to the restaurant. She still did not understand that she was to work as a prostitute.

After two days, the Japanese man who had picked her up at the hotel in Tokyo the morning after she arrived in Japan came to the snack bar to get her. During the next two weeks, this man took Nuch to different apartments and restaurants. Nuch said she was not forced to stay with him, but she had no passport or money, nor any idea where else to go. Finally, Nuch was taken to a snack bar that was owned by a Thai woman and her Japanese husband, a member of the Yakuza. The other Thai women at the snack bar told Nuch that she would have to prostitute herself. "They told me there was no way out and I would just have to accept my fate. The snack bar had many customers who I saw drinking alcohol and singing. I was told I had to go to sit with them. I knew then what had happened to me. That first night I had to take several men, and after that I had to have at least one client every night." Nuch said that the mama didn't actually "force" her to take clients, but she found clients for her, and Nuch always accepted them because she did not think she could refuse. During her time at the snack bar, Nuch never saw a doctor, nor received any health check-ups.

Nuch did not keep track of her debt. The mama bought her clothing, birth control pills, and medicine when she was sick, and added these expenses to her debt, but did not tell Nuch how much was added. After two months, the mama told Nuch she had paid off 20 bai (200,000 yen; US$1600). Around that time, Nuch went out one day with a male Thai acquaintance. When she returned, the mama told her to get her bags packed. The same Japanese man that had picked Nuch up at the hotel in Tokyo and then eventually taken her to this snack bar, came to get her and brought her to Tokyo to see Ice.

> When I first got to the apartment a Thai man slapped my face and said 'they told you not to meet other Thai.' Then Ice took me into another room. There Ice beat me, mostly by kicking me everywhere, while I sat in a chair. Ice beat me for over an hour saying 'I told you not to speak to any Thai.' I couldn't fight back because there were many men outside the room. When Ice finished she took a visa photo of me and forced me to write a contract. I said I couldn't write, but Ice forced me to write the contract by telling me each letter in Thai. I was forced to write that 'if I try to escape again, I agree to be killed,' and then Ice forced me to sign it. Then Ice photocopied it and said she would give a copy to the next mama I was sent to work for. Ice then asked me, 'do you want to go into a brothel where you'll never come out or pay back a debt of 700 bai [7 million yen; US$55,000]. I didn't know what a brothel was, but it didn't sound good so I agreed to having my original debt doubled.

Ice sent Nuch to work at another snack bar, where she worked for the next seven months. This time she kept better track of how much she earned. "I had to take all the clients that were introduced to me and was never given a day off. I was given birth control and charged 1,000 yen [US$8] per month. The only money I ever had was the tip money I saved. With the tip money, I had to buy my own food, except for rice, with the other women." While Nuch worked at this snack bar, the mama took her and the other women to a hospital for blood tests on two occasions. The first time, the mama talked to the doctor and told Nuch that there was no problem. The second time, one of the other Thai woman from Nuch's snack bar, who had been working their long and could speak a lot of Japanese, heard the doctor tell the mama that Nuch was blood positive. "The Thai woman told me that blood positive just means that you have to get some injections. The mama told me 'never mind, it's a minor problem.' The mama never took me to see the doctor again."

A few weeks later, Nuch was taken to a house in Nagano to have her blood checked again, and then she was taken to see Ice. Ice threw away Nuch's house registration, letters from her mother, and any other papers or documents she found. Then she gave Nuch her passport with a new visa saying she had just arrived in Japan. Two days later, Nuch was taken to a snack bar in Niigata prefecture. The mama there was Taiwanese and had a Japanese husband and two teen-age daughters. Ice reminded Nuch not to tell anyone that she had ever been to Japan before and told her to not to tell anyone, especially the clients, that she was Thai. The other Thai women working at this snack bar explained to Nuch that Japanese men do not like Thai women because they think they have AIDS. Nuch was told that her debt was 380 bai (3.8 million yen; US$30,000).

Nuch described this snack bar as "very strict." "Once I slipped and said I was from Thailand. The client asked the mama if it was true that I was from Thailand. It was a big problem. The mama's daughter slapped me, and the Japanese husband of the mama told me, 'if you tell another person you are Thai again you will have a name, but no body.' This meant he would kill me and only my name would be left. The mama's daughter slapped me again another time, when I was told to serve a very rude, drunk and dirty client whom I had been forced to have sex with several times before and couldn't stand it. She slapped me because I wasn't eager enough to take this particular client."

Nuch lived above the snack bar with the seven other Thai women who worked at the snack bar. "We were watched at all times. When we had to go out with clients, the mama hired taxis to wait for us at the hotel and bring the women back. There was never any chance to escape." They also worked extremely long hours, without any days off. "We worked at the snack bar from 6 p.m. to 3 a.m., and at 9 a.m. we were woken up to clean the house and the snack bar before lunch. After lunch we worked in the field out behind the snack bar until dinner. We were given birth control pills and told not to take the white pills (for the week to have a period). So we never had our periods while working there. We worked and took clients everyday."

A few weeks after Nuch began working there, the mama found out that Nuch had been in Japan before. "I asked another Thai woman to help me write a letter to send to my mother. It had been a long time since I had written to my mother. I had never told my mother what I was forced to deal with or the details of my life. I just wanted to tell my mother that I was well and everything was okay. But, while I was telling the other Thai woman what to write, I slipped and said 'sorry I haven't written to you for a long time. I have moved to another restaurant.' The Thai woman who was transcribing the letter asked me for more details. I told her then that I got sick and my blood was positive. Then this Thai woman went and told the mama—to get some extra points by telling on me." The mama and her daughter told Nuch to take off her clothes and checked her for sores. Then they told her she would have to work extra hard in order to pay off her debt quickly, and the mama told the cashier to give Nuch a lot of clients.

So Nuch continued to work and after three months had paid off about 100 bai (1 million yen; US$8000[91]). Two of the Thai women at the snack bar had been there nearly two years and had not yet finished paying back their debts. Another Thai woman had been there one and a half years and was also still paying back her debt. Nuch was never taken to see a doctor, and while the snack bar provided condoms and told the clients to use them, they seldom did. "In all my time in Japan only about ten clients ever used condoms and even then they broke a couple of times. I did not know about AIDS then or what 'blood positive' meant."

After about three months, a group of five Japanese men came into the snack bar. They appeared much neater than the usual clients. These men asked Nuch where she was from in Japanese, and she told them she was from Malaysia. Then they asked her something in Malaysian, but she could not answer. The five men came to the snack bar on three different occasions, and then one morning, the police came to arrest the women. "They asked me and the others in Thai if we wanted to go home, and if so to get our clothes. Only myself and one other woman got our clothes. Everyone was arrested, the mama, her husband, the two Taiwanese friends, and the seven Thai women. One Thai woman had just finished off her debt after two years and was about to be paid for the first time for twenty clients. She was especially upset."

Nuch was taken to a police station and questioned. The police told her they would help her to get home, but instead she was detained for the next several months in solitary confinement, though she never understood why. While she was in jail, a doctor tested her blood three times, but did not tell her anything. Eventually, Nuch was transferred to an immigration detention center, where she was held until the Thai Embassy issued her travel documents. In March 1993, Nuch went to the airport with the Japanese immigration officers and ten other Thai nationals. Upon arrival at Don Muang airport in Bangkok, the ten Thais were taken to the immigration office in the airport. Nuch was taken to a shelter where she has been living ever since. She understands now that she has HIV/AIDS.

---

[91] This U.S. dollar amount was calculated using the average yen-dollar exchange rate in 1992.

V. INTERNATIONAL LEGAL STANDARDS ON TRAFFICKING IN WOMEN

Trafficking, debt bondage, forced labor, and other abuses commonly suffered by women during their migration from Thailand to Japan, and their subsequent employment in Japan, constitute violations of these women's human rights. These rights are enumerated in international conventions that Japan and Thailand have acceded to or ratified, thereby committing their governments to take the steps necessary to uphold these rights and to provide redress when violations occur.[92] By allowing perpetrators to exploit migrant women with virtual impunity —and by failing to check corruption among government officials who facilitate these crimes—the Japanese and Thai governments fail to live up to their international obligations and exacerbate women's vulnerability to abuse.

To the extent that the failure to protect the human rights of migrant women from Thailand reflects discrimination on the basis of gender, race, nationality and/or immigration status, it also amounts to a violation of the prohibition of discrimination in the protection of human rights, as established under the International Covenant on Civil and Political Rights (ICCPR).[93] The Human Rights Committee, the international treaty body responsible for monitoring states' compliance with the ICCPR, has made it clear that human rights apply regardless of nationality or statelessness, and that states have a responsibility to guarantee basic human rights equally for both citizens and aliens.[94] Women's right to equal

---

[92] Under Article 2 of the International Covenant on Civil and Political Rights (ICCPR), states have the obligation to protect the rights of all individuals in their territory and to ensure that any person whose rights have been violated has access to an "effective remedy." Japan ratified on June 21, 1979. Thailand acceded on October 29, 1996.

[93] ICCPR, Article 2(1): "Each State Party to the present Covenant undertakes to respect and to ensure to all individuals within its territory and subject to its jurisdiction the rights recognized in the present Covenant, without distinction of any kind, such as race, color, sex, language, religion, political or other opinion, national or social origin, property, birth or other status."

[94] Human Rights Committee, General Comment 15, "The position of aliens under the Covenant" (Twenty-seventh session, 1986), in which the Committee explained: "In general, the rights set forth in the Covenant apply to everyone, irrespective of reciprocity, and irrespective of his or her nationality or statelessness. Thus, the general rule is that each one of the rights of the Covenant must be guaranteed without discrimination between citizens and aliens. Aliens receive the benefit of the general requirement of non-discrimination in respect of the rights guaranteed in the Covenant, as provided for in article 2 thereof. This guarantee applies to aliens and citizens alike. Exceptionally, some of the rights recognized in the Covenant are expressly applicable only to citizens (art. 25),

enjoyment of human rights has been reaffirmed by the Convention on the Elimination of All Forms of Discrimination Against Women (Women's Convention).[95] When governments fail to effectively prevent or respond to abuses —as is true in the case of trafficking in women from Thailand to Japan—it constitutes a violation of specific obligations that the states have undertaken under the terms of that convention. Finally, many of the abuses documented in this report are prohibited under Japanese and Thai domestic legislation,[96] and governments have an obligation to exercise due diligence in enforcing their laws, providing all persons with equal protection under the law and equal access to legal remedies for violations.[97]

---

while article 13 applies only to aliens. However, the Committee's experience in examining reports shows that in a number of countries other rights that aliens should enjoy under the Covenant are denied to them or are subject to limitations that cannot always be justified under the Covenant."

[95] Women's Convention, Article 3: "States Parties shall take in all fields, in particular in the political, social, economic and cultural fields, all appropriate measures, including legislation, to ensure the full development and advancement of women , for the purpose of guaranteeing them the exercise and enjoyment of human rights and fundamental freedoms on a basis of equality with men." Ratified by Japan on June 25, 1985. Acceded to by Thailand on August 9, 1985.

[96] See the "Japanese Government Response" and "Thai Government Response" chapters for a discussion of relevant domestic legislation.

[97] ICCPR, Article 26: "All persons are equal before the law and are entitled without any discrimination to the equal protection of the law. In this respect, the law shall prohibit any discrimination and guarantee to all persons equal and effective protection against discrimination on any ground such as race, color, sex, language, religion, political or other opinion, national or social origin, property, birth or other status."

General Assembly resolution 48/104 of 20 December 1993, the Declaration on the Elimination of Violence against Women, notes States' responsibility to "[e]xercise due diligence to prevent, investigate and, in accordance with national legislation, punish acts of violence against women, whether those acts are perpetrated by the State or by private persons."

See also: Committee on the Elimination of All Forms of Violence Against Women, "Violence Against Women," General Recommendation No. 19 (eleventh session, 1992), U.N. Document CEDAW/C/1992/L.1/Add.15, in which the Committee observed, "Under general international law and specific human rights covenants, States may also be responsible for private acts if they fail to act with due diligence to prevent violations of rights or to investigate and punish acts of violence, and for providing compensation."

Trafficking in women—a human rights violation

Trafficking in persons is condemned under international human rights law with provisions that place an explicit obligation upon states to take steps to stop this practice. The Women's Convention directs states to "suppress all forms of traffic in women and exploitation of prostitution of women."[98] Trafficking in children is further condemned in the Convention on the Rights of the Child[99] (Children's Convention), which requires States Parties to "take all appropriate national, bilateral and multilateral measures to prevent the abduction of, the sale of or traffic in children for any purpose or in any form."[100] Finally, the 1949 Convention on the Suppression of Trafficking in Persons and the Exploitation of the Prostitution of Others, denounces "the traffic in persons for the purpose of prostitution."[101]

"Trafficking" has been used in international legal instruments to refer to the movement of, and trade in, human beings, usually in connection with slavery, prostitution, and/or sexual exploitation. However, none of these documents articulates a clear definition of the term, so a precise legal meaning has yet to be established. In recent years, increased attention to the global problem of trafficking in persons has led to a widespread push to develop a working definition of trafficking that encompasses the full nature and scope of the abuse. Further impetus for such efforts was provided by the United Nations' decision to draft a convention against transnational organized crime, supplemented by an optional protocol on trafficking in persons. To this end, the Ad Hoc Committee on the Elaboration of a Convention against Transnational Organized Crime (Ad Hoc Committee) was established by General Assembly resolution in December 1998, with a mandate to draft the convention and the trafficking protocol by the end of 2000. In February 2000, the Office of the United Nations High Commissioner for Human Rights (UNHCHR), the Office of the United Nations High Commissioner for Refugees (UNHCR), the United Nations Children's Fund (UNICEF), and the International Organization for Migration (IOM) submitted a joint statement to the Ad Hoc Committee recommending the following definition of trafficking: "the recruitment,

---

[98] Article 6.

[99] Ratified by Japan on April 22, 1994. Acceded to by Thailand on March 27, 1992.

[100] Articles 34 and 35, respectively.

[101] Note that the primary focus of this convention is not trafficking, but prostitution. The term "trafficking" is not defined in the document, nor is any distinction made between coercive and non-coercive practices on the part of persons involved in the prostitution of others. Human Rights Watch believes that a key defining element of the human rights abuse of "trafficking in persons" is the coercive and slavery-like nature of the practice.

transportation, transfer or harboring or receipt of any person for any purpose or in any form, including the recruitment, transportation, transfer or harboring or receipt of any person by the threat or use of force or by abduction, fraud, deception, coercion or abuse of power for the purposes of slavery, forced labor (including bonded labor or debt bondage) and servitude." They noted that "servitude" should be understood in this context to include "practices that have been defined elsewhere as 'contemporary forms of slavery,' such as forced prostitution."[102] The United Nations High Commissioner for Human Rights, Mary Robinson, also submitted an "Informal Note" to the Ad Hoc Committee explaining that, in describing the purposes for which persons are trafficked, the committee should drop the "imprecise and emotive" term "sexual exploitation," and refer instead to trafficking for "forced labor and/or bonded labor and/or servitude," terms that explicitly include coercion and can be applied to any type of labor or service.[103] Human Rights Watch understands that a definition of trafficking should include all acts related to the recruitment, transport, transfer, sale, or purchase of human beings by force, fraud, deceit, or other coercive tactic, for the purpose of placing them into conditions of forced labor or practices similar to slavery, in which labor is extracted through physical and/or non-physical means of coercion. Such coercion may include blackmail, fraud, deceit, isolation, threat or use of physical force, or psychological pressure. We support the evolving international consensus that trafficking must be understood to apply to all labor sectors, including, but not limited to, the sex industry, while being limited to those instances in which some form of coercion is present. This consensus reflects the recognition that persons "trafficked" for various types of employment endure similar violations, as well as the conviction that distinguishing between voluntary and coercive acts is crucial to maintaining respect for the ability of women to purposefully and voluntarily migrate

---

[102] Ad Hoc Committee on the Elaboration of a Convention against Transnational Organized Crime, "Note by the Office of the United Nations High Commissioner for Human Rights, the Office of the United Nations High Commissioner for Refugees, the United Nations Children's Fund and the International Organization for Migration on the draft protocols concerning migrant smuggling and trafficking in persons," February 22, 2000. A/AC.254/27/Corr.1 (A/AC.254/27 was originally submitted on February 8, 2000 but UNHCR was omitted from the title).

[103] Ad Hoc Committee on the Elaboration of a Convention against Transnational Organized Crime, "Informal note by the United Nations High Commissioner for Human Rights," June 1, 1999. A/AC.254/16.

for work.[104] The United Nations Special Rapporteur on Violence Against Women, Radhika Coomaraswamy, adopted a definition of trafficking that incorporates both of these elements in a report released in February 2000. The report dealt with human rights violations suffered by women during both voluntary migration and trafficking, with trafficking in persons defined as "the recruitment, transportation, purchase, sale, transfer, harbouring or receipt of persons: (i) by threat or use of violence, abduction, force, fraud, deception or coercion (including abuse of authority), or debt bondage, for the purpose of: (ii) placing or holding such person, whether for pay or not, in forced labor or slavery-like practices, in a community other than the one in which such person lived at the time of the original act described in (i)."[105]

Other relevant standards for combating trafficking in women

The United Nations High Commissioner for Human Rights has pointed out that trafficking in persons is not a single event, but a series of actions involving a variety of actors and abuses.[106] Combating trafficking in women requires policies and practices designed to prevent and provide redress for all of the human rights violations involved, thus deterring further abuses and encouraging victims to turn to law enforcement officials when violations occur.

Forced labor, servitude, and practices similar to slavery

Women trafficked from Thailand are subjected to a range of slavery-like practices during their travel, job placement, and employment in Japan, practices clearly condemned under international law. The women we interviewed described being "bought" and "sold" by agents, brokers, and employers. They spoke of their purchase "price," and explained that the person who "bought" them demanded strict obedience, using a variety of coercive tactics to ensure their acquiescence. The slavery-like nature of these practices was illustrated perhaps most clearly by the

---

[104] The Global Alliance Against Trafficking in Women (GAATW), a Bangkok-based NGO, has been one of the leading organizations worldwide in documenting the global phenomenon of trafficking in women and articulating a working definition of the term. Its definition fulfills all of these criteria.

[105] Commission on Human Rights, "Report of the Special Rapporteur on violence against women, its causes and consequences, Ms. Radhika Coomaraswamy, on trafficking in women, women's migration and violence against women, submitted in accordance with Commission on Human Rights resolution 1997/44," E/CN.4/2000/68, 29 February 2000, paragraph 13.

[106] "Message from the High Commissioner, Mary Robinson, to the Asia-Pacific Symposium on Trafficking in Persons," Tokyo, Japan, January 20, 2000.

fact that employers and brokers maintained the power—and believed it was their right—to "resell" women at their discretion.

Under the ICCPR, Japan and Thailand have an obligation to take the steps necessary to prevent all forms of slavery, the slave-trade, servitude, and forced or compulsory labor, and they must provide remedies for the victims when violations occur.[107] Slavery and the slave-trade are defined under the Slavery Convention as, respectively, "the status or condition of a person over whom any or all of the powers attaching to the right of ownership are exercised" and "all acts involved in the capture, acquisition or disposal of a person with intent to reduce him to slavery; all acts involved in the acquisition of a slave with a view to selling or exchanging him; all acts of disposal by sale or exchange of a slave acquired with a view to being sold or exchanged, and, in general, every act of trade or transport in slaves." Several practices similar to slavery are elaborated under the Supplementary Convention on the Abolition of Slavery, the Slave Trade, and Institutions and Practices Similar to Slavery. This convention condemns debt bondage, serfdom, compulsory marriage, and the pledge of a child's labor to another person by the child's guardian as institutions and practices similar to slavery. According the convention, "A person of servile status" means a person in the condition or status resulting from any of the following practices:

> (a) Debt bondage, that is to say, the status or condition arising from a pledge by a debtor of his personal services or of those of a person under his control as security for a debt, if the value of those services as reasonably assessed is not applied towards the liquidation of the debt or the length and nature of those services are not respectively limited and defined;

> (b) Serfdom, that is to say, the condition or status of a tenant who is by law, custom or agreement bound to live and labor on land belonging to another person and to render some determinate service to such other person, whether for reward or not, and is not free to change his status;

> (c) Any institution or practice whereby:

---

[107] Article 8 provides: "No one shall be held in slavery; slavery and the slave-trade in all their forms shall be prohibited," "No one shall be held in servitude," "No one shall be required to perform forced or compulsory labor." Ratified by Japan on June 21, 1979. Acceded to by Thailand on October 29, 1996.

(i) A woman, without the right to refuse, is promised or given in marriage on payment of a consideration in money or in kind to her parents, guardian, family or any other person or group; or
(ii) The husband of a woman, his family, or his clan, has the right to transfer her to another person for value received or otherwise; or
(iii) A woman on the death of her husband is liable to be inherited by another person;

(d) Any institution or practice whereby a child or young person under the age of 18 years, is delivered by either or both of his natural parents or by his guardian to another person, whether for reward or not, with a view to the exploitation of the child or young person or of his labour.[108]

These definitions make clear that even if a person has agreed to perform labor or other services, the arrangement may qualify as a practice similar to slavery if the terms and conditions of the agreement have not been adequately defined or if the person loses the liberty to change his/her status. The supplementary convention on slavery also identifies all acts and attempted acts intended to place a person into slavery or other servile status identified in the convention as practices similar to slavery which should be subject to criminal penalty.[109]

As parties to the International Labor Organization (ILO) Convention 29 concerning Forced or Compulsory Labor, Japan and Thailand have made an additional commitment to "suppress the use of forced or compulsory labor in all its forms within the shortest possible period."[110] This convention defines forced or compulsory labor as "all work or service which is exacted from any person under the menace of any penalty and for which the said person has not offered himself

---

[108] Articles 1, 7(b).
[109] Article 6.
[110] Article 1.

voluntarily," and specifically prohibits "forced or compulsory labor for the benefit of private individuals, companies or associations."[111]

The most common abuse that Human Rights Watch documented in the trafficking of women from Thailand to Japan was debt bondage. Women were forced to work without wages until they repaid extraordinarily high "debts," amounts exponentially exceeding any costs incurred through their travel to Japan. Some—though not all—of the women understood that they would have a debt to repay when they agreed to migrate, but the length and nature of the services to be performed were not adequately limited or defined. Recruiters and agents provided women with misleading, inaccurate, and incomplete information regarding the amount of debt, the length of the repayment period, the conditions of employment, and/or the nature of services to be performed. After the women arrived in Japan, they had no control over the terms or conditions of their employment. A woman's initial debt was typically based on the "price" negotiated by her broker and employer, and her employer then enjoyed full control over her working conditions and debt repayment calculations. In addition, many of the women we interviewed indicated that the value of their labor was not "reasonably assessed" and "applied towards the liquidation of the debt." Rather, employers augmented debts with arbitrary expenses, fines, and dishonest account keeping, and even maintained the power to "resell" women into higher levels of debt before their initial debt was paid off.

Human Rights Watch also documented a number of other coercive tactics that were used to control women during their travel, job placement, and employment. These included the threat and use of physical harm against the women and/or their family members, strictly enforced rules against going outside without permission and an escort, and other forms of intimidation and isolation. When agents, brokers, and employers used such tactics to extract labor or to place women into a state of servitude, they acted in violation of the prohibitions against forced or compulsory labor, practices similar to slavery, and servitude. Many of these tactics threaten to violate other protected rights as well, such as the women's right to life; to freedom

---

[111] Ratified by Japan on November 21, 1932 and by Thailand on February 26, 1969. Note also that in Japan, "in the field of labor law, it is generally accepted that the ratified conventions of the ILO have legal effect at national level. . . . In several cases, including a few Supreme Court decisions, the Courts have declared or implied that a legislative provision which contravenes one of the ILO conventions is null and void." (Dr. R. Blanpain [ed.], *International Encyclopedia for Labor Law and Industrial Relations,* vol. 7, p.52).

from cruel, inhuman or degrading treatment; to liberty and security of person; and to freedom of movement and freedom to choose her residence.[112]

There is also a component of sex discrimination in the acts of violence inflicted on trafficked women. In 1992, the Committee on the Elimination of All Forms of Violence Against Women (CEDAW), established to monitor compliance with the Women's Convention, explained that the general prohibition against gender discrimination "includes gender-based violence—that is, violence which is directed against a woman because she is a woman or which affects women disproportionately. It includes acts which inflict physical, mental, or sexual harm or suffering, threats of such acts, coercion or other deprivations of liberty."[113] The committee also noted: "States may also be responsible for private acts if they fail to act with due diligence to prevent violations of rights or to investigate and punish acts of violence, and to provide compensation."[114]

Labor rights violations

Human Rights Watch also documented violations of women's labor rights in Japan that were the direct result of trafficking. These abuses constitute violations of both Japanese domestic legislation (see the "Japanese Government Response" chapter for a discussion of Japanese labor laws) and international human rights law. To provide adequate redress for trafficked persons and to deter further violations, Japan must take the steps necessary to prevent these abuses, punish offenders, and compensate victims. The Thai government should also adopt measures aimed to protect its nationals from labor rights abuses both at home and abroad and to facilitate Thai women's ability to seek compensation for labor rights violations suffered in Japan.

The International Covenant on Economic, Social and Cultural Rights (ICESCR) recognizes the right to fair wages, reasonably limited working hours, and rest days.[115] In violation of these standards, the women we interviewed were given no compensation at all for months or longer, while they worked excessively long

---

[112] ICCPR, Articles 6(1), 7, 9(1), 12(1).

[113] Committee on the Elimination of All Forms of Violence Against Women, "Violence Against Women," General Recommendation No. 19 (eleventh session, 1992), U.N. Document CEDAW/C/1992/L.1/Add.15.

[114] Ibid.

[115] Article 7(a)(d). Ratified by Japan on June 21, 1979. Acceded to by Thailand on September 5, 1999.
Note that persons under the age of eighteen years old are also entitled to further labor protections under the Convention on the Rights of the Child (see Articles 32 and 34), ratified by Japan on April 22, 1994 and acceded to by Thailand on March 27, 1992.

hours—without days off for rest or, in some cases, even illness—to pay off illegal and arbitrarily inflated "debts." The ICESCR also provides that all workers have a right to safe and healthy working conditions.[116] Despite this guarantee, women reported that their safety and health were jeopardized by employers who limited and, in some cases, denied them access to health services and medication; compelled them to accept physically abusive clients; and coerced them into performing sexual services without condoms, exposing them to the risk of contracting HIV and other sexually transmitted diseases.

Kept under constant surveillance and threatened with retaliation if they tried to escape, women from Thailand working in debt bondage in the Japanese sex industry had little choice but to accept these conditions. Moreover, even when they were released from debt—or detained by Japanese officials—they were not given any opportunity to seek redress. As stated above, the ICCPR requires that states guarantee all persons equal protection under the law. Consequently, trafficked women must have the same access to Japanese labor law protections as all other persons in Japan. Though the women's immigration status did not permit their employment under Japanese immigration laws, this does not affect their labor rights vis-à-vis their employers—according to either international law or Japanese domestic law—and should not have affected their ability to seek compensation in Japan for work they had done.[117] In addition, as parties to the ICESCR, Japan and

---

[116] Article 7(b).

[117] As noted above, the labor rights established under ICESCR apply to all, without discrimination based on nationality or other status. And though few states have ratified the international conventions that deal explicitly with the rights of undocumented migrant workers, these instruments have emphasized the importance of this principle. ILO Convention 143 (the Convention concerning Migrations in Abusive Conditions and the Promotion of Equality of Opportunity and Treatment) states: "Without prejudice to measures designed to control movements of migrants for employment by ensuring that migrant workers enter national territory and are admitted to employment in conformity with the relevant laws and regulations, the migrant worker shall, in cases in which these laws and regulations have not been respected and in which his position cannot be regularized, enjoy equality of treatment for himself and his family in respect of rights arising out of past employment as regards remuneration, social security and other benefits." And, according to the Migrants' Convention, while states should take steps to eliminate the employment of migrants in an irregular situation, "The rights of migrant workers vis-à-vis their employer arising from employment shall not be impaired by these measures." The Japanese government recognizes this standard in principle and does not make legal distinctions regarding workers' labor rights based on their immigration status, but in practice, we found that undocumented women trafficked from Thailand had little access to Japanese labor rights protections.

Thailand have undertaken to uphold the rights provided under this covenant without discrimination based on sex, nationality or other status.[118]   The Japanese government's failure to prosecute labor rights violations endured by trafficked women allowed employers to continue unjustly to enrich themselves and thus encouraged the continued exploitation of the women.   The failure of Thai government officials charged with protecting the labor rights of Thai nationals in Japan to assist female migrants only encouraged this injustice.[119]

---

[118]Article 2(2): The States Parties to the present Covenant undertake to guarantee that the rights enunciated in the present Covenant will be exercised without discrimination of any kind as to race, color, sex, language, religion, political or other opinion, national or social origin, property, birth or other status. Article 2(3) allows developing countries some discretion with regard to the rights of non-nationals: "[d]eveloping countries, with due regard to human rights and their national economy, may determine to what extent they would guarantee the economic rights recognized in the present Covenant to non-nationals." However, this exception does not apply to the highly developed country of Japan.

The nature of states' obligation to guarantee the rights provided under ICESCR was elaborated by the Maastricht Guidelines on Violations of Economic, Social and Cultural Rights, (Maastricht, January 22-26, 1997). This document is not binding, but provides good guidance for the implementation of the covenant. According to the Maastricht Guidelines, "any discrimination on grounds of race, color, sex, language, religion, political or other opinion, national or social origin, property, birth or other status with the purpose or effect of nullifying or impairing the equal enjoyment or exercise of economic, social and cultural rights constitutes a violation of the Covenant" (Article 11).

[119] See discussion in the "Thai Government Response" chapter.

VI. RECRUITED IN THAILAND—SOLD ON JAPAN

The trafficking of women from Thailand to Japan involves a wide range of actors: the initial recruiter who contacts the women; the agent in Thailand who pays the recruiter, arranges travel documents, and holds the women until they are ready to leave; the escorts who accompany the women to Japan, often via other countries such as Singapore, Malaysia or South Korea; the brokers who meet the women upon their arrival and pay the agent for delivering them; and the procurers who run the sex establishments and pay large sums of money to the brokers for the acquisition of the women.[120] In some cases, these networks also rely on the cooperation of government officials who prepare false documents and/or turn a blind eye to violations, apparently in return for bribes.

The strong demand for Thai women's labor in Japan, coupled with restrictive immigration policies, has provided an ideal environment for these networks to flourish. Women who wish to migrate from Thailand to Japan for work are rarely able to make the arrangements themselves and instead rely on intermediaries to obtain the necessary travel papers, negotiate border controls, and arrange their job placement. Research by Human Rights Watch and others indicates that, in most cases, these intermediaries engage in serious human rights abuses, and women who agree to migrate for lucrative employment opportunities find themselves trafficked into compulsory labor.

Trafficking networks use deception, the threat and use of physical force, and other forms of coercion to place women from Thailand into debt bondage employment in Japan. The agents and brokers derive enormous profits by "selling" the women for amounts exponentially greater than the costs they have incurred, and this "price" becomes the basis of a woman's debt, which she must repay through months of grueling unpaid labor. Agents regularly misrepresented the conditions under which women would work upon their arrival in Japan, giving false or misleading information about crucial issues, such as the type of work they would do, the range of choice they would have, the amount of money they would owe, and the amount of money they would earn. Agents failed to explain the legal implications of the women's travel and employment as well as the highly controlled circumstances under which they would be forced to repay their "debt." Furthermore, once a woman agreed to go to Japan, and the agent began to make arrangements, women lost the ability to safely change their decision or negotiate the terms of their agreement.

---

[120] Note that though the terms agent and broker are often used interchangeably, in this report we will refer to the person in the sending country as the agent and to the person in the receiving country as the broker.

Methodology

Human Rights Watch traveled to Japan and Thailand several times over the six year period from 1994 to 1999. In Japan, we conducted interviews in Tokyo and Kyoto, and in Chiba, Kanagawa, Ibaraki, Nagano, Nagoya, and Osaka prefectures; in Thailand, we traveled to Bangkok and to the provinces of Chiang Mai, Chiang Rai, and Phayao. We interviewed women who had recently escaped from debt bondage, as well as women who had paid off their debts and either returned to Thailand or continued working in Japan; we could not interview women while they were in debt bondage, due to the heavily controlled conditions of their employment. Our interviewees included twenty-three women[121] from Thailand who described the circumstances under which they came to Japan. Most of these interviews were conducted together with Friends of Women in Asia (FOWIA), a Thai NGO based in Bangkok. We also received detailed testimonies from thirty-five other women, twenty-eight of whom were interviewed by local researchers[122] and seven by staff members at a women's shelter in Japan. In addition, we have drawn on the results of interviews with 170 Thai women that were conducted by staff at the House for Women "Saalaa"[123] between September 1992 and May 1995, as well as the work of Dr. Suriya Samutkupt, a professor of anthropology at Suranaree University of Technology in Thailand. Dr. Samutkupt met with almost one hundred Thai women working in the sex industry in Ibaraki prefecture while conducting research in Japan in 1995, 1996, and 1997. He explained to Human Rights Watch that he was not able to speak to any of the women who were then working in debt bondage, but the women he talked to had arrived in Japan in "debt" and "described the hell that they went through."[124]

In the great majority of the cases we documented, abuses qualifying as trafficking occurred during women's recruitment, travel, and job placement (see table below). All but one of the women Human Rights Watch interviewed or obtained a detailed interview transcript for explained that agents in Thailand

---

[121] Note that though we spoke to girls under the age of 18, we use the term "woman/women" throughout this report.

[122] In one of these cases, the researchers spoke to the woman's parents, not the woman herself.

[123] This is a nongovernmental organization that was founded as a shelter for foreign women in 1992. The results of its interviews with shelter residents were published in 1995: Nobuyo Tomita, "From Thailand to Japan: The Reality of Trafficking in Women, Voices from a Shelter," in Women's Research and Action Committee [ed.], *NGOs' Report on the Situation of Foreign Migrant Women in Japan and Strategies for Improvement*, 1995, pp. 23-28.

[124] Human Rights Watch interview, Nakhon Ratchasima, Thailand, April 27, 1999.

arranged their travel and job placement in coordination with contacts in Japan.[125] The great majority of these women described elements of deception and coercion that amounted to trafficking for debt bondage or forced labor. In many more cases, there were strong indications of coercion—for example, the women had extraordinarily high "debts" to pay off when they began working—but the women did not provide enough information about the terms and conditions of their employment to reach definitive conclusions about whether the situation constituted debt bondage. The women's initial employment was nearly always in the entertainment industry, typically in a "dating" snack bar, where their work included providing sexual services to male clients.[126] The abuses that the women suffered during the course of their migration and initial employment in Japan are described below and illustrated with examples from the women's testimonies.[127] Due to circumstances, and to their personal decisions, some of the women did not discuss all of the issues dealt with in this report. Human Rights Watch's findings were confirmed by the groups and individuals we spoke to in Thailand and Japan.

---

[125] Only one woman, Gap, arranged her travel documents and plane tickets herself, though she was still in debt to her aunt, who ran a snack bar in Japan, when she arrived. Furthermore, when Gap went to Japan a second time, after being deported for immigration violations, she did go through an agent who prepared false documentation for her and then placed her into indebted sex work at a snack bar. (Interview by M. N., Chiang Rai province, Thailand, October 12 and 17, 1997.)

[126] There are many different types of snack bars in Japan, many of which do not offer sexual services. See the next chapter for a brief discussion of these establishments.

[127] There may be some repetition of women's testimonies as different abuses associated with trafficking and forced labor are discussed. In particular, elements of the cases described in the "Profiles" chapter are referenced in this chapter to illustrate specific human rights violations.

Table: Cases documented by Human Rights Watch
(twenty-three women were interviewed by Human Rights Watch; thirty-five testimonies were provided to Human Rights Watch by local researchers and advocates)

Trafficked?	total	snack bar hostess	other position
Yes	41	37 (all in debt)	1 (lover and domestic servant of a snack bar owner; no debt) 1 (mama and lover of a snack bar owner; no debt) 2 (brothel; in debt)
Not clear	14	11 (all in debt)	1 (factory; in debt) 1 (exotic dancing; in debt) 1 (massage parlor; in debt)
No	3		1 (came with husband— managed a Thai restaurant) 1 (factory; no debt—she paid 200,000 baht (US$8,000) in advance) 1 (dish washing)
TOTAL	58	48 (all in debt)	10 (2 in snack bars)

Recruits

As seen in the case histories described in the "Profiles" chapter, the women we interviewed had different backgrounds and expectations when they left for Japan. But they had similar motivations in going. Most of the women said that they were attracted by the high salaries promised; they wanted to provide a better standard of living for themselves and their families and were often coping with difficult relationships or other family problems. Saalaa, a shelter for foreign women in Kanagawa prefecture in Japan, similarly reported that most of the women there had been persuaded to go to Japan by promises of large wages, though some also wished to separate from husbands or boyfriends.[128] The women trafficked from Thailand were generally recruited while they were in their twenties, but some went to Japan when they were under eighteen or over thirty.[129] Most of the women Human Rights Watch interviewed were Thai nationals, but there is also a problem of women and girls without Thai citizenship being trafficked out of Thailand and into Japan. These include migrants from neighboring countries such as Burma, China, Laos and Cambodia; "hilltribe" people, who may have been born in Thailand but have no records to prove their nationality; and "refugees," who were permitted to live in Thailand only as long as they remained within designated refugee camps. These women find themselves even more vulnerable to exploitation because of the discrimination and economic disadvantages that they face in Thailand, and once they leave the country they are often unable to return.[130]

The following are excerpts from the testimonies provided by several of the women Human Rights Watch interviewed about their decisions to work in Japan. Though all of them made consensual decisions to migrate to Japan for work, and many knew they would be employed as sex workers, each of these women were subsequently trafficked into coercive labor conditions:

- Rei grew up in southern Thailand. She completed the twelfth grade in school and then got a job as a receptionist for five months. For the next four years, she took many different jobs, but didn't keep any of them for more than five months. During much of that time, Rei had no job at all. So, she said, "I heard about many women going to work in Japan, and I knew many agents in my

---

[128] Tomita, "From Thailand to Japan . . .," p. 25.
[129] Saalaa's findings support this. See Tomita, "From Thailand to Japan . . .," p. 27.
[130] See the "Deportation as 'Illegal Aliens'" and "Thai Government Response" chapters for a more detailed discussion of these populations and the problem of "statelessness."

neighborhood who could arrange for me to go. I knew I would have to be a prostitute, but the promise of a good salary was very appealing."[131]

- Phan was born in Burma. She is the second of seven children. In 1985, when Phan was fourteen years old, she and her sister moved to Thailand to join their parents and siblings, who had moved there a year earlier. The next year, when Phan was fifteen and her parents were having difficulty finding enough money to support the family, Phan began working at a brothel in Chiang Rai province. After about four years of working as a sex worker in Thailand and Malaysia, Phan was approached by a Thai man who asked her if she wanted to go work in Japan.[132]

- Soi was born in Chiang Rai province and was a seamstress in Bangkok. She was making 3000 baht (US$120[133]) a month. Soi was twenty-four years old when she was recruited in 1990. A Thai friend whom she had known for two years asked her if she would be interested in going to Japan. As Soi recalled, "[My friend] didn't tell me what kind of work there was, but said I could make a lot of money. I was interested."[134]

- Bua was an only child, and her father died when she was young. She lived with her mother, grandmother, and grandfather. After she finished sixth grade, she stopped going to school. She wanted to continue her studies, but the school was far from her house and her family could not afford to send her. When she was fifteen years old, her friends went to work as sex workers, and she went with them. Over the next four years, she worked variously in Bangkok, southern Thailand, and her village, sending money home to support her family. In 1991, she met someone who asked her to go to Japan.[135]

---

[131] Human Rights Watch and FOWIA interview, Bangkok, Thailand, January 17, 1995.

[132] Human Rights Watch and FOWIA interview, Chiang Rai province, Thailand, October 5, 1995.

[133] Here and below, we use an exchange rate of 25 baht to the U.S. dollar for all dates before July 1997. For converting amounts to and from Japanese yen, we use the average exchange rate for the relevant years and then round off. Where the year cannot be easily determined from the context, a footnote will specify which year's average rate was used.

[134] Human Rights Watch interview, Japan, March 1994.

[135] Interview by M. N., Phayao province, Thailand, October 15, 1997.

Expectations and understanding of the process of recruitment and job placement, and of the work they would be doing in Japan, differed greatly among the women we interviewed:

- At age twenty-three, when Bun was asked to go to Japan, she was heavily in debt and agreed to go in order to pay back her debt and make some additional money. But when she arrived in Japan, she found that she had been misled about the conditions and financial arrangements of her employment. "I left for Japan in August 1994 with the agreement that I could either work in a restaurant or as a prostitute as I wished. . . . [The day after I arrived,] I was ordered to strip dance on a table at a snack bar and play stripping games with the customers." In addition, Bun found herself saddled with an outrageous and unexpected "debt." "I didn't know I was going to be in debt 400 bai (4 million yen; US$39,000). I only knew that I would have to work for free for two or three months."[136]

- Faa, who worked at a sewing shop in Udon Thani province before going to Japan, explained to Human Rights Watch that she knew she was going to work as a sex worker, but not that she would have to work off a debt. At nineteen, she arrived in Japan to find that she had to work every day for the next five months without compensation as she struggled to pay the money she "owed."[137]

- The Thai man who recruited Phan to work in Japan told her that she would have to pay off a debt of 100,000 baht (US$4,000) and that it would take her about two or three months to do so. "I said I wanted to go, but I didn't have any documents. They said, 'no problem,' they could arrange all the documents. I saw so many other girls going to Japan, so I agreed." Later, when Phan arrived in Japan, she found that her debt was more than seven times the amount to which she had agreed.[138]

In the interviews Human Rights Watch conducted, the majority of the women indicated that they knew they would be working as sex workers in Japan, and some had already worked in this industry in Thailand. Others were promised jobs as

---

[136] Human Rights Watch and FOWIA interview, conducted during a number of meetings, Tokyo, Japan, early 1995.

[137] Human Rights Watch and FOWIA interview, Chiang Mai province, Thailand, October 3-4, 1995.

[138] Human Rights Watch and FOWIA interview, Chiang Rai province, Thailand, October 5, 1995.

waitresses or factory workers, though in almost all cases they were placed into the sex industry when they arrived. Saalaa found that of the 170 Thai women who stayed at the shelter from 1992 to 1995, 158 had worked as indebted sex workers in Japanese snack bars. And while a majority of these women knew that they would be working in restaurants or bars with at least the option to perform sex work, only a quarter of the women understood that they would have to sell sexual services, and a third expected work outside of the entertainment industry altogether.[139] Siriporn Skrobanek, Executive Secretary of the Foundation for Women (FFW) in Thailand,[140] told Human Rights Watch that according to FFW's research, when women from Thailand first began migrating to Japan in the late 1980s, only about ten percent of the women knew they were going into sex work. A decade later, it has become more difficult to deceive women about the type of the work they will do in Japan, but Siriporn Skrobanek explained that recruiters are increasingly targeting women in northern villages who do not have previous experience of working in the Thai sex industry, because they consider such women easier to deceive about the financial arrangements and other aspects of the work.[141]

None of the women whom Human Rights Watch interviewed had fully understood the economics of the situation they were entering, nor had any clear idea of the kind of conditions they would face. While some women were told that they would be in debt, the amount of the debt and/or the amount of time it would take to repay the debt was misrepresented. Furthermore, women were not told how debt repayment calculations would be determined. This was left to the discretion of their employers in Japan, who routinely used the woman's "debt" to extract labor under abusive and coercive conditions. And the methods of coercion that employers regularly applied to ensure that women fully repaid their "debts" were, of course, not described by recruiters or agents.[142]

Finally, women did not have a clear understanding of the legal implications of their migration. Agents handled women's travel and job placement arrangements, often obtaining falsified documentation for them and always providing escorts to accompany them on their trip. Women were given only as much information as they needed to get through immigration procedures. In many cases, women traveled to Japan legally, on their own passports with Japanese tourist or transit visas, and

---

[139] Tomita, "From Thailand to Japan . . .," p.28.

[140] Siriporn Skrobanek is also the Coordinator of the Global Alliance Against Trafficking in Women (GAATW), which was formed at the International Workshop on Migration and Traffic in Women organized by the Foundation for Women in Chiang Mai, Thailand, in October 1994 and has over 150 individual and organizational members.

[141] Human Rights Watch interview, Bangkok, Thailand, April 23, 1999.

[142] The same pattern was confirmed in the findings published by Saalaa.

they did not understand that their visa status prohibited them from working. Other women traveled to Japan on falsified passports, in which their name and/or travel history had been changed, but they did not necessarily know that false documentation had been prepared for them until after they arrived at the airport in Thailand, or even later. In other cases, women were told to memorize fake names and stories before they left Thailand, so they realized that they would be deceiving the airport authorities. But in these cases too, the arrangements were made by the agents, and women were required to follow the agents' instructions. Once a woman had agreed to go to Japan and an agent had begun to make preparations on her behalf, the woman was in the agent's debt; she was not allowed to change her mind. Moreover, the women traveled under conditions of deception; the promises of their recruiters and agents had not yet been proven false.

Many women Human Rights Watch interviewed spoke of their surprise and confusion regarding their legal status and Japanese laws in general:

- Jaem, who entered Japan at age sixteen, stated, "I didn't know the law and I didn't know that coming to Japan and doing this kind of work was illegal. Before I went to Japan, nobody told me that it was illegal. I don't know Japanese law at all. Now I understand that whatever Thai people do in Japan is illegal."[143]

- "I didn't know anything before I went to Japan. The agents never told me that I would be legal or that I would be illegal. They just took me to make a passport and told me that I would work at a restaurant as a waitress with a good income. . . . I didn't know Japanese law. But after I arrived in Japan I knew that I was illegal, so I just hid and escaped when police came," explained Aye, who went to Japan in 1992 at age twenty-seven, after having been a sex worker since the age of fourteen or fifteen in Thailand.[144]

- Jo, who traveled to Japan in 1990 at age twenty-three after seven years of sex work in Thailand, confided, "I never knew the law in Japan or even in Thailand. When I arrived in Japan I knew that I had come illegally, so I was afraid of being arrested. They [her bosses at the snack bar] said that if you meet police or immigration officers you have to run away from them. Everybody said that we stayed illegally, but nobody explained what was legal or illegal."[145]

---

[143] Interview by M. N., Phayao province, Thailand, September 1997.

[144] Interview by M. N., Phayao province, Thailand, September 28, 1997.

[145] Interview by M. N., Phayao province, Thailand, October 8, 1997.

Our interviews with women who have worked in Japan, as well as with nongovernmental organization (NGO) representatives in Japan and Thailand, suggest that many of them understood that they were taking a risk in migrating to Japan for work. Some women had heard firsthand stories about abusive conditions in Japan, or knew women who had returned to their villages in Thailand sick and empty-handed. Awareness of the dangers of migration has increased as a result of information campaigns launched by the Thai government and local NGOs as well.[146] But women also knew there was the possibility of making large amounts of money in Japan and thereby improving the standard of living of their parents, children, and other family members. In some cases, they lived near large houses built with remittances sent by women working in Japan, and they saw women who had returned to their villages after achieving financial success in Japan. As Yui explained to Human Rights Watch, "when I was nineteen years old, a villager invited me to go work in Japan. I knew three or four women from the village had already died in Japan, but other women got a lot of money, so I decided to go."[147]

Naiyana Supapong, who served as the Director of Friends of Women in Asia (FOWIA) from 1992 to 1998, helping women who had decided work overseas in Japan, Hong Kong, and other countries, explained:

> Women only get positive information from agents and returning women, but they don't know about the negative things. So I gave them both—the positive and the negative information. I said to them, "some women are successful, but do you know about the suffering behind their success?" . . . Most of the women said: we've heard about the bad situations, but some women have good luck, and we hope we'll be one of them. So most went anyway—they had already made the decision to go when I met them—but this way they were better prepared.[148]

And, according to another Thai NGO worker,

---

[146] Human Rights Watch interview with Chitraporn Vanaspong, Information Officer at ECPAT International (End Child Prostitution, Pornography and Trafficking in Children for Sexual Purposes), Bangkok, Thailand, April 22, 1999.

[147] Interview by M. N., Phayao province, Thailand, October 1997 and December 1997.

[148] Human Rights Watch interview, Naiyana Supapong, Bangkok, Thailand, April 28, 1999.

In the case of Japan, lots of women know what they'll do and know they'll have hardships, but they still want to go because they are so poor. The Social Welfare Department tries to prevent them from going with information campaigns in the villages saying how hard it will be in Japan, that they'll be beaten, etc. A police officer who is also a song writer (Police Colonel Surasak Sutharom) even wrote a song about exporting women, saying that it is not a heaven but a hell. There were also ex-sex workers on talk shows on television saying don't go to Japan. But still women want to go.[149]

Recruiters

Most of the women explained that they were first approached by a relative, neighbor, or other acquaintance, who told them about opportunities to work in Japan:

- Rei's recruiter was a Thai man who lived in her neighborhood. He was known as the "boss lek" and was known to have arranged jobs for many women in Japan.[150]

- Khai was recruited in 1991, at age sixteen, by a client while she was working as a masseuse and sex worker in a massage parlor in southern Thailand. As she explained to Human Rights Watch, "a client invited me to work in Tokyo. I explained that I had no identification, but he said he could get me a passport because he was a member of parliament. So I agreed, and the client took me to a place to have my body checked. There I saw many other Thai girls trying to go to Japan. I was told I would work as a server."[151]

- Faa had left her village in Thailand to work in a sewing shop in Bangkok. When she was nineteen years old, her relatives in Bangkok convinced her to go to work in Japan.[152]

---

[149] Human Rights Watch interview with Chitraporn Vanaspong, Information Officer at ECPAT International, Bangkok, Thailand, April 22, 1999.

[150] Human Rights Watch and FOWIA interview, Bangkok, Thailand, January 17, 1995.

[151] Human Rights Watch and FOWIA interview, Osaka prefecture, Japan, May 27, 1995.

[152] Human Rights Watch and FOWIA interview, Chiang Mai province, Thailand, October 3-4, 1995.

- Nam had been working at a restaurant in Chiang Rai Province when she was invited to go to Japan by a friend in 1991. As she recalled, "I could not find a job in Thailand and I saw that many women in the village had gone to Japan, so I decided to go." She was twenty-eight years old at the time.[153]

If a woman expressed interest in going to Japan, the recruiter typically offered to introduce her to an agent who could make all the arrangements. Once a woman agreed to see an agent, the recruiter hurried to make the introduction. After that, the woman generally did not see her recruiter again. Chan was recruited to go to Japan in 1993, by friends of her aunt's whom she had known for a long time. She told Human Rights Watch that one of these friends "introduced me to an agent, and the agent gave her [the recruiter] 30,000 baht [US$1200[154]]."[155]

Agents

The women interviewed by Human Rights Watch and Saalaa typically identified their agent as a Thai man, whom they referred to as "boss." When there was more than one agent, the women called them *boss yai* (big boss) and *boss lek* (little boss). Of the Thai women in contact with Saalaa shelter from 1992-1995, almost eighty percent of the 158 women who had worked as indebted snack bar hostesses when they arrived in Japan reported that their agents were Thai, while an additional thirteen percent dealt with agents from Japan.[156] This corroborates the experiences of our interviewees, most of whom were first introduced to Thai agents, though others said their agents were from Japan, Singapore, or Malaysia. The agent paid the recruiter for the introduction, and then made arrangements with a broker in Japan to receive the woman. Some agents have contacts with brokers in many different countries so they are able to move women according to the demand. For example, according to a report in a major Thai newspaper in 1994, the arrest of three agents in Bangkok revealed a book noting the expenses for sending women to Japan, the United States, Australia, Sweden, South Africa and Italy. These agents were arrested following leads given to the Acting Thai Police Chief by seven

---

[153] Interview by M. N., Chiang Rai province, Thailand, August 4, 1997.
[154] This dollar amount was calculated using the average yen-dollar exchange rate for 1993.
[155] Human Rights Watch and FOWIA interview, Bangkok, Thailand, March 2, 1995.
[156] Tomita, "From Thailand to Japan . . .," p. 27.

Thai women who had been arrested in South Africa and claimed to have been trafficked by them.[157]

In some cases, agents inspected women's bodies first to ensure that they were suitable for the work overseas:

• Khai explained that the first thing her recruiter did when she agreed to go to Japan in 1991 was take her to "a place where I had my body checked."[158]

• As mentioned in the "Profiles" chapter, Kaew recounted that when she was introduced to an agent, "the agent in Bangkok decided that I was beautiful enough to go to Japan, though I had to get a nose job first, and they kept messing it up—they had to do it four times to get it right. The agent wanted me to get my eyes done too, but I refused. Other women got plastic surgery for their breasts, eyes, or other body parts. Women who were not beautiful enough were given a bus ticket home to their village."[159]

Agents also handled women's travel arrangements, including booking their flights and assisting them in obtaining the necessary travel documentation. Thai and Japanese government policies have made it difficult for women to obtain passports and Japanese visas legally, but agents are able to overcome these legal barriers through a variety of tactics, including obtaining authentic passports and then switching the photographs; arranging "marriages" to facilitate passport and visa applications; booking flights to the United States or other destinations with a layover in Japan, as transit visas are easier to obtain than tourist visas; and using passports from third countries such as Singapore where visas are not needed to enter Japan. While most of the women we interviewed traveled on Thai passports, others used passports from Malaysia, Singapore, and even Japan. Over half of the women we interviewed said agents used false passports to secure their Japanese visas and entrance into Japan:[160]

---

[157] "Three men arrested for supplying sex workers," *Bangkok Post*, February 9, 1994.

[158] Human Rights Watch and FOWIA interview, Osaka prefecture, Japan, May 27, 1995.

[159] Human Rights Watch interview, Chiang Rai province, Thailand, April 25, 1999.

[160] The same breakdown was found among women from Thailand at the Saalaa shelter for foreign women. Out of 158 women, seventy-seven had entered Japan using false passports, and seventy-four had entered using authentic ones with their own names (the remaining seven cases are unknown). Tomita,"From Thailand to Japan . . .," p.28.

- As described above, Khai had no identification or citizenship papers when she was recruited to work in Japan, but the recruiter promised to take care of that for her. "I was told to say I was another person and given all the woman's documents—her house registration and identification card—and sent to make a passport under this person's name. Getting the passport was no problem, even though I couldn't sign my own name, let alone the name they gave me. I went to apply for the passport with the agent, and then the agent went to collect it on another day. When I went to apply for a Japanese visa, I was never asked any questions and got the visa without difficulty."[161]

- The agent who made arrangements for Korn was equally adept at fixing documents. When she first decided to go to Japan in 1993, she applied and received her own passport with the help of the agent. However, when she was unable to pass the interviews with the Japanese embassy for a visa, the agent produced a new passport for her, complete with visa, within a week. She did not know whether the new passport was in her name, because she was never allowed to hold it.[162]

- In Rei's case, her agent, whom she referred to as "boss lek," helped her obtain her passport and a Japanese tourist visa. "The boss lek gave me 1,000 baht (US$40) to apply for my passport. Then he gave me another 500 baht (US$20) to collect it and 50 baht (US$2) to deliver it to him. The boss lek accompanied me to the passport office the first time, but I went to collect my passport by myself. Then, boss lek took me to the Japanese Embassy and told me what to do. However, I actually went into the Embassy alone and did it myself. The boss lek told me to tell the Embassy that I was going to Japan to look at a plastic factory, since I am the boss of a plastic factory in Thailand. Boss lek gave me a letter which stated that I was the boss of a factory. I also gave the Embassy a phone number for the factory. When the Embassy called the 'factory'—it was actually the boss lek's number—the boss lek answered and said I was gone to a meeting for the day. The embassy never called again. I got my Japanese visa a couple days later."[163]

---

[161] Human Rights Watch and FOWIA interview, Osaka prefecture, Japan, May 27, 1995.

[162] Human Rights Watch and FOWIA telephone interviews, Kanagawa prefecture, Japan, May 1995.

[163] Human Rights Watch and FOWIA interview, Bangkok, Thailand, January 17, 1995.

- Miew explained that she agreed to go to Japan because, "I was told I could work in Japan as a waitress at a restaurant or snack bar and serve alcohol or food and sit down and talk with customers. I was also told I would get a monthly salary and extra tips, and I wanted to go because my family's business in Thailand had collapsed and I wanted to help support them. The 'boss' in Thailand arranged everything for the trip. In late January 1999, I left Thailand from the southern border and went to Singapore. Then I left Singapore on a ticket for Los Angeles via Japan. I traveled with a passport that the boss gave me. ʼThe first page of the passport had been changed with my name, photo, age, and sex, but the other pages were from someone else who had lived in the United States for ten years and had even been to Japan before."[164]

- Kay was twenty-seven years old when she went to Japan from Thailand's Lop Buri province. Kay entered Japan in 1988 on her own passport, but her agent had arranged a marriage for her to facilitate the visa application process. According to Kay the agent told her that, "a 'Mrs.' on my passport would make it easier for me to get a Japanese visa. I met the man who was to be my husband at the district government office when we registered our marriage, and I have never seen or heard of him since."[165]

The women's testimonies suggest that in some cases agents relied on the cooperation of government officials to procure travel documents. Several women, for example, reported that they had obtained Japanese visas without having to answer a single question, despite an official Japanese policy heightening scrutiny of Thai visa applicants. A Thai government official stationed in Tokyo in 1995 affirmed these suspicions, explaining to Human Rights Watch that agents in Thailand could then procure Japanese visas from Embassy staff for approximately 40,000 baht (US$1600) each.[166] The Thai press has also published reports of Thai

---

[164] Human Rights Watch interview, Tokyo, Japan, April 16, 1999.

[165] Human Rights Watch and FOWIA interview, Chiba prefecture, Japan, May 20, 1995.

[166] Human Rights Watch and FOWIA interview, Tokyo, Japan, May 19, 1995.

officials preparing false documentation to facilitate applications for Japanese visas in return for bribes.[167]

Once an agent began to make the travel arrangements and obtain the necessary documentation, the women were obliged to follow the agent's instructions. Agents used a combination of persuasion, deception, and coercion to ensure that the women stood by their decisions to go to Japan. Invariably, they misled women regarding the financial arrangements and other conditions under which they would work. In some cases agents spoke to the recruits about their costs and the debt the women would incur, and women often understood that they would have to repay agents for their travel costs. But agents frequently lied about the amount of debt, or the amount of time it would take women to repay it. And those who did not lie outright used vague and misleading jargon that made it virtually impossible for the women to understand the nature of their financial arrangements prior to arriving in Japan.

---

[167] In 1994, newspaper reports revealed that officials from Thailand's Commerce Ministry and Foreign Ministry had been investigated for providing false documents to Thailand's Passport Division and the Japanese Embassy. The scam was discovered by a Japanese Embassy official who became suspicious when he received visa applications from about ten young Thai women under a document issued by the Commerce Ministry's Export Promotion Department stating that the women would be going on an "educational tour" in Japan. The official called the Commerce Ministry to verify the authenticity of the document, speaking first to a junior officer who verified the document, and then to a senior official who said that he had never approved such a trip. A police investigation was subsequently launched by the Police Department's Crime Suppression Division (CSD), and after a three-month investigation warrants were issued for the arrest of seven junior officials from the Commerce Ministry as well as three Foreign Ministry officials. Investigators found that each of the ten officials was paid at least 5,000 baht (US$200) for his assistance in delivering a woman to Japan, for a total of 50,000 baht (US$2,000) paid per women. The investigation also uncovered a second scam used by traffickers to obtain Japanese visas: a Thai police captain responsible for overseeing the security of the Japanese Embassy was accused of using his ties with embassy staff to get visas for Thai women. He married the women one at a time, applied for their visas, and then filed for divorce, and he was paid about 50,000 baht (US$2,000) for each women who successfully obtained a visa. And investigators further alleged that agents paid immigration police at Don Muang airport to stamp women's passports without checking the validity of the passport or visa, and they concluded that agents trafficking women from Thailand to Japan pay a total of at least 70,000 baht (US$2800) per woman: 10,000 baht (US$400) to the initial recruiter, 50,000 baht (US$2000) for the visa, and 10,000 baht (US$400) to the airport immigration police. (Preecha Sa-ardsorn, "Flesh Trade export gang falls victim to its own greed," *The Nation* (Bangkok, Thailand), September 7, 1994.)

For example, traffickers referred to 10,000 yen (about US$84[168]) as one *bai* (a Thai word for paper note) and then discussed prices, expenses, and debts in terms of bai:

- When Khai agreed to go to Japan in 1991, she was told that she would owe 120 bai [1.2 million yen; US$9,000] when she arrived. As she explained, "I didn't know how much that was, but I thought it was about 30,000 baht [US$1,200] because I asked what the price was of the round-trip ticket from Bangkok to Tokyo. When I arrived in Japan I was taken to Shinjuku [an area in Tokyo] and sold to a mama for 120 bai. Later she told me that I owed 280 bai, and then she added 70 bai more to cover additional expenses. In total I had to pay off a debt of 350 bai [3.5 million yen; US$26,000]."[169]

- Wanna said that the agent in Thailand told her that she would be doing sex work and that she would have a debt to repay, but she told us that after she arrived in Japan, "I was surprised when I heard my debt was 700,000 baht [3.3 million yen (330 bai); US$28,000]."[170]

- Keak went to Japan in 1988 at the age of twenty-three after eight years as a sex worker in Thailand. She went through a Malaysian escort in Bangkok, and was told that her debt would be 300,000 baht (1.5 million yen; US$12,000). But after arriving in Japan, "I was shocked to hear that my debt was 2.8 million yen [550,000 baht; US$22,000]. I cried without eating for two days."[171]

- Aye explained, "I didn't know anything before I went to Japan. [The agents] said I could earn 20,000 to 30,000 baht [US$800 - 1200] per month. But when I went to Japan [in 1992], they told me that I owed a debt of 300 bai [3 million yen; 600,000 baht; US$24,000]."[172]

---

[168] This dollar amount was calculated using the average yen-dollar exchange rate over the nine year period from 1990-1998: 119 yen to the U.S. dollar.

[169] Human Rights Watch and FOWIA interview, Osaka prefecture, Japan, May 27, 1995.

[170] Interview by M. N., Chiang Rai province, Thailand, August 5, 1997. Since it is unclear what year Wanna went to Japan from her testimony, this dollar amount was calculated using the average yen-dollar exchange rate over the nine year period from 1990-1998: 119 yen to the U.S. dollar.

[171] Interview by M. N., Chiang Rai province, Thailand, August 6, 1997.

[172] Interview by M. N., Phayao province, Thailand, September 28, 1997.

While explicit threats were generally unnecessary to elicit women's compliance while their travel arrangements were being made, several of the women Human Rights Watch interviewed spoke of being confined to a hotel room during that time. And a few women were expressly forbidden from going out unescorted or from making any contact with friends or family during this period, which usually lasted about a week though sometimes was as short as two or three days. Thus, women who had voluntarily agreed to go to Japan found themselves confined against their will, deprived of their basic right to freedom of movement, and unable to change safely their decision to go to Japan.

- As Bun recalled, "Once I agreed to go, I was put in a room by the agent and not allowed to go around. The agent gave me a passport, and I went to Japan a week after Du did with a *farang* [Westerner] escort. We told immigration that we were on our honeymoon."[173]

- Pong decided to go to Japan in 1986. She was eighteen years old and had been working at a bar in southern Thailand for two years. "On the day I agreed to go, my friend introduced me to an agent. I let him take a photo of myself and went home. Two or three days later I was called to go to a hotel. I stayed there for twenty-four hours—I wouldn't have dared to go out—and left the next day. At the airport, I was given a passport with a false name."[174]

- Phan was working in a brothel in Hat Yai near the Malaysian border in January 1991 when she was invited to go to work in Japan. She agreed because it sounded as though she could make more money, but she had no documents. The agents assured her they could take care of everything. Two days later, they helped her escape from the brothel and then held her in a hotel for five days until she left for Japan. During that period, she was guarded and not allowed out of the room.[175]

- Sri is from a village in the province of Phra Nakhon Si Ayutthaya. In 1985, Sri was a twenty-one-year-old sex worker in a massage parlor in Bangkok, when a client invited her to go to work at a massage parlor in Macau. Sri agreed, and the client introduced her to an agent. The agent said he liked Sri and would

---

[173] Human Rights Watch and FOWIA interview, conducted during a number of meetings, Tokyo, Japan, early 1995.

[174] Human Rights Watch interview, Chiang Rai province, Thailand, April 24, 1999.

[175] Human Rights Watch and FOWIA interview, Chiang Rai province, Thailand, October 5, 1995.

send her to Japan where she could make more money. After Sri agreed, the agent brought her to an apartment in Bangkok. "The agent wouldn't let me out of the apartment at all. I was kept there with five other girls." The women were held for three days before beginning their trip to Japan.[176]

Escorts

Women were accompanied on their flights to Japan by escorts who were responsible for delivering the women to brokers, or the brokers' associates, in Japan. Most of the interviewees reported that their escorts were Thai men, though others were escorted by women and/or non-Thais, and in some cases the escorts changed as the women traveled through other countries on their way to Japan. Most of the women we talked to met the escort for the first time in the airport or as they were boarding the airplane; none of the women we interviewed saw their escorts again after they were delivered to brokers in Japan. The escorts facilitated the women's departures from Thailand and entry into Japan, often via third countries, such as Malaysia, Singapore, or South Korea. In some instances, escorts contacted agents in transiting countries to change passports or to collect or deliver other women. The escorts held the women's travel documents, tickets, and money during the trip. None of the women interviewed by Human Rights Watch were allowed to carry their own passports except briefly when passing through immigration, after which they were immediately taken from them again by the escort. And those women who stopped in other countries along the way reported that they were strictly guarded at all times.

- Janya was twenty years old in August 1991 when she was sent by an agent in Bangkok to Kuala Lumpur to meet a Malaysian woman who escorted her to Japan. "I entered Japan through Narita airport. I was carrying a Singaporean passport with a Malaysian-Chinese name on it and my photograph. I came with the Malaysian woman and her five year old daughter. I was a little worried because the passport was fake, but the Malaysian woman told me I didn't have to say anything. She told me to just practice writing my new name and said that she would take care of everything at customs. Nothing happened at customs; I got through easily."[177]

---

[176] Human Rights Watch and FOWIA interview, Osaka prefecture, Japan, May 26, 1995.

[177] Human Rights Watch interview, Tokyo, Japan, March 14, 1994.

- Nat did not even realize she would end up in Japan when she left Thailand at age twenty and traveled with a friend and two escorts to Malaysia. When she and her friend arrived in Malaysia, they were taken to Kuala Lumpur and placed in a large apartment with about one or two hundred other Thai women. Nat was confined to that apartment for a month while agents prepared a Malaysian passport for her. As she recalled, "They gave us meals, but the only things to do were watch television and sleep. We were not allowed to go out." When the passport was ready, she flew to Narita airport in Japan.[178]

- Thip flew to Japan via Singapore in 1999. "I began the trip to Japan on my own passport. I didn't have a visa for Japan—I didn't know that I needed one. I flew from Bangkok to Singapore on my passport, but on the flight from Singapore to Japan, about thirty minutes before arrival, the Japanese man who was escorting me gave me a Japanese passport and told me to use it with the immigration officers in Japan. I was very surprised, and I asked why. He answered, 'a Japanese passport will make it easier for you to enter Japan,' and I didn't know what else to do, so I did as he said."[179]

Several women explained that they were able to pass through customs despite patently false stories and/or documentation, and, based on the suspicious behavior they observed, at least two of the women concluded that airport immigration officials had collaborated with their traffickers:

- Khai entered Japan in December 1991 with five other people who were posing as her "family": three other girls who were to be her "sisters," another woman who was the "mother," and a man who was the "father." But, she explained, "none of us were related, or looked like it for that matter. All the women were actually going to work, and the man was the agent." Khai was also traveling on a false passport with a description that did not match her physical characteristics. "I knew in my fake passport the woman was 162 centimeters and I was not even 150 centimeters. But I memorized all the details and passed [through airport immigration] with no problems."[180]

- Sri traveled to Japan from Hat Yai airport in 1985 with five other Thai women. "At the Thai immigration in Hat Yai, they asked me what I was going to do in

---

[178] Interview by M. N., Chiang Rai province, Thailand, September 3, 1997.
[179] Human Rights Watch interview, Tokyo, Japan, April 16, 1999.
[180] Human Rights Watch and FOWIA interview, Osaka prefecture, Japan, May 27, 1995.

Japan. The officer was laughing and I believe he knew exactly what we were going to do. Then the [escort] arranged all of our passports with the immigration officer and we passed through without any other questions asked."[181]

• Pot flew to Japan via South Korea in 1992. She was put on a flight to South Korea with four other Thai women and one Thai man nicknamed Dee. "Dee told me and the other four women the specific Thai immigration officer to go to . . . In hindsight I believe that the immigration officer at Don Muang airport in Bangkok knew what I was going to do in Japan better than I did at the time of my departure. Because the officer was buddy-buddy with Dee and just kept smiling at us [the Thai women] as he stamped our passports."[182]

• Nuch said that when she arrived in Japan in 1993, her escort "told me to go in a specific line and she went in another line at Narita immigration. She went through first and then came to help me. She spoke Japanese and got me through."[183]

We found that those traveling on false passports often traveled through Hat Yai, a Thai city in Songkhla province near the Malaysian border.[184] Nid , who went to Japan in 1991, explained to Human Rights Watch that "most women who use false passports go through Hat Yai [airport] because it is easier to pass immigration."[185] Sean confirmed that, when she went to Japan in 1992, she had to fly through Hat Yai because "I had a fake passport and Hat Yai could arrange my departure without any problems."[186] There are also agents in Hat Yai who can arrange for women to travel to Malaysia by boat. Nat, whose experiences in Malaysia are described above, traveled from Hat Yai to the Thai coast, where, she explained, "Two men were waiting and they took me and my friend on a small boat. Both were policemen. On the boat, my friend and I were told not to tell anyone that the two men were police. . . . After about two hours, the boat arrived at a pier with fishing

---

[181] Human Rights Watch and FOWIA interview, Osaka prefecture, Japan, May 26, 1995.

[182] Human Rights Watch and FOWIA interview, Ibaraki prefecture, Japan, June 1, 1995.

[183] Human Rights Watch and FOWIA interview, Bangkok, Thailand, March 1995.

[184] See interviews with Nat, Nid, Sean, Phan, Faa, and Sri.

[185] Human Rights Watch and FOWIA interview, Tokyo, Japan, May 20, 1995.

[186] Human Rights Watch and FOWIA interview, Nagano prefecture, Japan, May 24, 1995.

nets everywhere. The border police seemed to have been informed about our arrival and immediately opened the lock for the wire fence." Nat and her friend had arrived in Malaysia; a month later, Nat flew to Japan on a Malaysian passport.[187]

Allegations that corrupt officials are involved in facilitating trafficking operations have been supported by a number of sources, including Thai officials. A Thai Labor Affairs Officer stationed in Tokyo told Human Rights Watch about a case in which a twenty-year-old Thai woman entered Japan with the passport of a fifty-year-old woman; only the photo had been replaced. The Thai woman had explained to the officer that she used a password, as she had been instructed, and passed through immigration at Narita airport without any questions asked.[188] There have also been reports in the Thai press of collaboration by both Thai and Japanese officials in such scams. During the investigation of the murder of two Thai agents in March 1995, the Northern Bangkok Metropolitan Division Deputy Commander, Kongdej Chusri, told reporters that he believed that for there to be trafficking in women, both Thai and Japanese officials had to be involved in the trafficking of women. He explained, "It is difficult to leave Thailand and enter Japan with a fake passport. Without assistance from the immigration authorities, it would be almost impossible for them to slip through the tight control [of immigration]."[189] And a study published by Chulalongkorn University of Thailand in 1998 noted that agents who exploit Thai labor migrants, facilitating their travel arrangements and then subjecting them to indentured labor, are "aided by corrupt police and other

---

[187] Interview by M. N., Chiang Rai province, Thailand, September 3, 1997.

[188] Human Rights Watch and FOWIA interview, Tokyo, Japan, May 19, 1995.

[189] Chaiyakorn Bai-ngern, "Yakuza links may have led to flesh trade gang leader's killing," *The Nation* (Bangkok, Thailand), March 8, 1995, p. A5.

In another case, *The Nation* reported that in an interview with a Special Branch policeman in the Thai border city of Hat Yai, "The policeman said flesh trade gangs cannot work alone. Some legal travel couriers, tourist police and immigration police are also involved in the business, providing cooperation to the gangs. An immigration policeman at Hat Yai Airport who is involved in the flesh trade would receive Bt3,000-5,000 [US$140-200] from the gangs for each woman sent out of Thailand, the policeman said. If the woman was sent to Singapore, the immigration official would get Bt3,000. But, if she was sent to Taiwan or Japan, he would get Bt5,000. The policeman said tourism police involved in the business would receive monthly financial support from the gangs, as would some local policemen. According to the police officer, some of the gangs have connections with senior government officials, especially officials in the Foreign Ministry." ("Thai border a haven for illegal immigrant trade," *The Nation* (Bangkok, Thailand), September 7, 1994.)

government officials in the immigration office, the airport authority, and other offices."[190]

Brokers

After the women passed through immigration and customs in Japan, they were typically handed over to a broker, who either went to the airport to meet the women, or sent someone to pick them up. According to our interviews, most of the brokers were either Japanese men or Thai women, but some women also reported that certain Thai and Taiwanese men had acted as brokers. The brokers provided the connection between the agents in Thailand and the employers in Japan, and they held the women while making arrangements for their "procurement." In a few cases, the escorts served as brokers, delivering the women directly to procurers. While a woman's placement was being arranged, she was confined and denied access to the outside world. Women were also deprived of their passports, which were held by the brokers and then given directly to the procurers.

Descriptions of the brokers' "job placement" activities indicated that the women were treated as property, rather than as job applicants. The women consistently referred to being "sold," and they had no opportunity to negotiate their "contract" nor any ability to select or refuse their placement. In the majority of the cases documented by Human Rights Watch, women were placed into work in the sex industry, usually as "hostesses" in "dating" snack bars.[191] This was true regardless of the type of job promised by recruiters and agents in Thailand. Interviews with NGO staff, Thai Embassy officials, and others in Japan who work with women from Thailand, as well as with women returning from Japan to Thailand, confirmed this. The women's shelter Saalaa reported that out of the 170 Thai women who stayed in the shelter from 1992 to 1995, 158 (eighty-five percent) were "sold to small bars called snacks."[192]

The following cases provide examples of recruits' first few days in Japan. Here and below we focus on women who were placed into employment in snack bars:

---

[190] Pasuk Phongpaichit, Sungsidh Piriyarangsan, and Nualnoi Treerat, *Guns, Girls, Gambling, Ganja: Thailand's Illegal Economy and Public Policy* (Chiang Mai: Silkworm Books, 1998), p. 157.
[191] We also interviewed a woman who was forced to work in a low-end "brothel." These establishments are at the bottom rung of the sex industry. Customers at these establishments pay for very brief periods of time—as little as eight minutes — and women must serve numerous men each night.
[192] Tomita, "From Thailand to Japan . . .," p. 23.

- Phan arrived at Narita airport in Japan in early 1991. She and three other Thai women were then taken by their escort to an apartment where they were handed over to a Taiwanese broker. All of the women were told to shower, after which they drove through the night to Kofu city in Yamanashi prefecture. There they were given some winter clothes and told to shower again and change. According to Phan, the women "were sold by the Taiwanese broker for 150 bai [1.5 million yen; US$11,000] each. The broker explained that our debt would actually be 380 bai [3.8 million yen; US$28,000] to cover all our travel and other expenses. Then we were taken to different snacks. I was taken to a snack bar run by a Taiwanese mama. I was given another 20 bai [200,000 yen; US$1,500] to pay for clothes and told my total debt was 400 bai [4 million yen; US$30,000]."[193]

- Pong told us that when she and her sister arrived in Japan, "we were handed over to a Thai man who lived in Japan. He took us to a Thai woman, the broker, where I stayed for two nights. Then this woman sold me and my sister. I saw the money changing hands and didn't know at first what it was about, but then realized I was being sold. . . . We were told at the time of purchase that we were six months in debt. This was the first I had heard about the debt."[194]

- Rei was escorted to Japan by a wealthy woman whom she knew from her village in Thailand. When they arrived at Narita airport, the escort handed Rei a passport and money to show to the immigration officials. After Rei passed smoothly through immigration control, the escort took back the passport and money and brought Rei to a hotel in Tokyo by train. Rei recalled, "I stayed at the hotel with my escort for two nights. On the third day, I was bought by a Taiwanese mama and taken to Ibaraki prefecture by car. I didn't find out where I was until about a week later when I asked a woman I was working with."[195]

- When Pot arrived at Narita airport in 1990, she was handed over to a Thai woman named Chan and put into a van with several other women. Chan spent the next five days taking the women around to different locations in Tokyo. "She was trying to sell us like cattle. Then on the fifth day a Thai woman

---

[193] Human Rights Watch and FOWIA interview, Chiang Rai province, Thailand, October 5, 1995.
[194] Human Rights Watch interview, Chiang Rai province, Thailand, April 24, 1999.
[195] Human Rights Watch and FOWIA interview, Bangkok, Thailand, January 17, 1995.

bought me and took me to another woman named 'Chan' in Ibaraki prefecture, who paid 380 bai [3.8 million yen; US$26,000] for me. When I got to the snack I learned that the 380 bai that I was bought for was to be my debt."[196]

Procurers/Employers

Once the women were "sold" to snack bar owners or managers, their procurers demanded that they work to repay their purchase price—plus other fees and expenses. As one women recalled, "When I refused [to work as a snack bar hostess], I was told, 'we bought you so we want you to give us back that amount of money.'"[197] According to interviewees, the bar owners were typically Japanese men with close ties to the Yakuza, often referred to as "boss," while managers, referred to as "mama" or "mama-san," were almost always foreign women, typically the wife or girlfriend of the owner. Most of the women interviewed by Human Rights Watch worked under Thai or Taiwanese mamas, and a few interviewees pointed out that the mama herself was often living and working in Japan in violation of immigration law, like the women who work for her. For example, one woman we interviewed explained that she became a "mama" when a client paid off her debt in one snack bar and then forced her to repay another debt by working as the mama in a snack bar he owned.[198] The mama operated the bar for the owner and managed both the working and living arrangements of the women who worked there. She was also the one who kept track of women's "debts," and she exercised strict control over those whose debt had not yet been paid off, as is discussed further below. In some cases, women were procured by mamas who were not directly employed by one snack, but instead had connections to several different snacks, where they brought the women to work each day. This arrangement was particularly common in the Kabuki-cho district of the Shinjuku ward in Tokyo, an entertainment district with numerous small snack bars and other sex venues.

---

[196] Human Rights Watch and FOWIA interview, Ibaraki prefecture, Japan, June 1, 1995.

[197] Human Rights Watch and FOWIA interview, conducted during a number of meetings, Tokyo, Japan, early 1995.

[198] Human Rights Watch and FOWIA interview with Sri, Osaka prefecture, Japan, May 26, 1995.

VII. SERVITUDE IN THE "SNACK BARS"

While I was in Japan, I worked like a slave to pay off my debt. It took almost one year.[199]

Women recruited and transported into Japan for sex work typically were subjected to a period of servitude in the sex industry when they arrived, and forced to work without pay until they repaid exorbitant "debts," equivalent to around US$25,000 to US$40,000.[200] In most cases, the conditions under which such "debts" were imposed, calculated, and repaid clearly constituted debt bondage, a slavery-like practice outlawed by international law.[201] The women involved also reported a range of other coercive tactics which were used to ensure their obedience while they were "in debt," such as the imposition of "fines" for misbehavior, the confiscation of their passports and other identification documentation, threats of "resale" into renewed debts and/or worse conditions, strict controls on the women's freedom of movement and communication, and threats and use of physical force. In some cases, the conditions women described amounted to forced labor. Furthermore, "indebted" women were compelled to work under highly abusive labor conditions, subjected to excessive work hours, abuse by clients, and significant risks to their physical and mental health.

This chapter describes women's experiences after they were trafficked from Thailand and "sold" in Japan. It begins with a brief description of the type of snack bar in which most of the women who were interviewed by Human Rights Watch had worked, and then describes the methods which were used to coerce women to work in these establishments for months—or longer—effectively without pay or recompense, and often at serious risk to their physical and mental health. Escape from these conditions was difficult and dangerous, and most of the women we interviewed stayed in debt bondage until their employers determined that their debts

---

[199] Interview by M. N., Phayao province, Thailand, September 1997.

[200] Note that given fluctuations the exchange rate during the 1990's, U.S. dollar equivalents for amounts calculated in terms of Japanese yen may vary substantially. Throughout this report, when converting Japanese yen into U.S. dollars, we use the average exchange rate for the relevant year(s) and then round off. Where the year cannot be easily determined from the context, a footnote will specify which year's average rate was used.

[201] Whether or not someone has entered into debt "voluntarily," when the amount of debt, the conditions of work, and/or the terms of debt repayment are defined—or can be changed—at the employers' discretion, it is debt bondage labor, a practice strictly proscribed by international law. See the chapter on "International Legal Standards" for more details.

were "finished." Other women, however, did manage to escape, and their compelling stories are also recounted below.

Snack bars

Though debt bondage and other slavery-like practices occur in a variety of work places, the discussion below focuses on the conditions in Japanese snack bars where the vast majority of our interviewees worked. Snack bars, often referred to simply as "snacks," are a common venue where many Japanese go for relaxation and conversation. The many different types of snack bars are not necessarily distinguishable to outsiders but are well known to the locals in the area. A *baishun*—or prostitution—snack bar is one which involves sexual exchanges and is almost exclusively patronized by men. The women interviewed by Human Rights Watch distinguished between different types of baishun snacks by the arrangements of sexual exchanges. As noted in the previous chapter, most of the women we interviewed were placed in "dating" snack bars, in which clients may take women out of the bar for sexual services. Of the forty-eight interviewees who were placed in snack bars when they arrived in Japan, all but one of the women described going out with customers to provide sexual services as their primary responsibility.[202] All discussion of snack bars below refers to "dating" snacks.

"Dating" snack bars typically employ anywhere from five to twenty women as "hostesses"[203] and a female manager, who is called "mama" or "mama-san." Both the hostesses and the mamas are most commonly from Thailand, the Philippines, or Korea, although there are also women from other countries, including Japan. When a man enters the bar, he is immediately greeted by the mama, who comes to his table and asks what he wants to drink and what kind of woman he would like. If the customer is a regular, the mama will know without having to ask. Clients can choose a hostess for either two hours or a whole night, and they may take her out of the snack if they wish. Typically, a hostess is taken by her client to a nearby hotel, and the client is then responsible for paying for the hotel room and for returning the woman to the snack or the apartment where she lives, depending on the time. According to the women we interviewed, average fees were 20,000 to

---

[202] The only exception is Bun who said she had to dance on a table at the snack bar and play strip games with the customers, but does not mention going out of the bar with clients. (Human Rights Watch and FOWIA interview, conducted during a number of meetings, Tokyo, Japan, early 1995).

[203] "Hostess" is the term commonly used to refer to the women who work as prostitutes in the snack bars.

30,000 yen (US$170-250[204]) for two hours and 30,000 to 40,000 yen (US$250-340) for the night, and the money was given directly to the mama. The women explained that once paid for, a woman was expected to satisfy all of the client's demands.

The operation of baishun snack bars is closely tied to the Yakuza.[205] The owners are often Yakuza members (or former members) themselves, or else are linked to Yakuza gangs to which they pay regular protection money. The Yakuza are powerful and dangerous groups with connections to police and other government officials. According to our interviews with women who worked as hostesses, as well as with advocates and researchers in this field, the Yakuza's involvement in snack bar operations has important implications for women's ability to challenge the terms or conditions of their employment and to seek redress for violations. Women spoke of their fear of Yakuza retaliation for disobedience or escape attempts, and several advocates pointed to Yakuza involvement in the snack bar industry as a key reason behind the lack of adequate police response to abuses.[206] Sri, who worked as a mama in Kofu from 1985 to 1992, told Human Rights Watch that she paid the Yakuza 8 bai (80,000 yen; US$630[207]) per month to protect her snack bar, follow clients who did not pay, and follow girls who tried to run away.[208]

Many women also alleged that corrupt police officers—together with Yakuza—helped to protect snack bar operations. Several women explained to Human Rights Watch that police or immigration officials either exempted their snack bars from raids, or else gave their owners advance warning, in return for bribes:

- Pot explained that the owners of her snack bar and others paid a "tax" to the police so that their hostesses would not be arrested in raids. "When there are raids on snack bars everyone agrees it is because the owner didn't pay the necessary tax."[209]

---

[204] These dollar amounts were calculated using the average yen-dollar exchange rate over the nine year period from 1990-1998.

[205] "Yakuza" refers to organized crime groups that are now officially known as the "Boryokudan."

[206] In particular, see Human Rights Watch interviews with Rutsuko Shoji, Director, HELP Asian Women's Shelter, at shelter office, Tokyo, Japan, April 8, 1999, and with Kinhide Mushakoji, Director, IMADR, at restaurant, Tokyo, Japan, April 9, 1999.

[207] This dollar amount was calculated using the average exchange rate from 1992.

[208] Human Rights Watch and FOWIA interview, Osaka prefecture, Japan, May 26, 1995.

[209] Human Rights Watch and FOWIA interview, Ibaraki prefecture, Japan, June 1, 1995.

- According to Chan, "immigration came once, but there was a telephone call which notified the snack just before and so almost all of the women ran out. Those who didn't get out were arrested."[210]

- Janya said that "the bar owners were not afraid of the police because the police warn them in advance of inspections by immigration officials. I never saw this, but I heard about it often."[211]

- Nung recalled that while she was afraid of immigration and police officers, the "boss" at the snack bar was not. "Boss easily got information about immigration crackdowns. So during immigration crackdowns, the Thai people stayed at the apartment and the snack was closed."[212]

Debt Bondage

All of the women whose cases Human Rights Watch documented—either through directly conducting in-depth interviews or drawing upon detailed interview transcripts from other researchers—and who were placed into employment as snack bar hostesses upon their arrival in Japan, reported having to repay a substantial debt to their employers.[213] The amount of the women's debts varied, but most of the women were told they owed between 3 million and 5 million yen (US$25,000 - 42,000[214]) when their work began. Our findings have been corroborated by researchers, advocates, and government officials in Japan and Thailand.[215] The

---

[210] Human Rights Watch and FOWIA interview, Bangkok, Thailand, March 2, 1995.

[211] Human Rights Watch interview, Tokyo, Japan, March 14, 1994.

[212] Interview by M. N., Chiang Rai province, Thailand, August 6, 1997.

[213] Of the fifty-eight women who described their initial job placement in Japan, fifty-four reported having to repay a debt after they arrived in Japan, including the two women who were placed in brothels, one who worked in a massage parlor, one who did exotic dancing, and one woman who worked in a factory (the other factory worker paid 200,000 baht in advance and was not in debt when she arrived in Japan).

[214] These dollar amounts were calculated using the average yen-dollar exchange rate over the nine year period from 1990-1998.

[215] See, for example, Human Rights Watch interview with Rutsuko Shoji, Director of HELP Asian Women's Shelter, Tokyo, Japan, April 8, 1999; Human Rights Watch interview with Rieko Aoki, Secretary of Kyoto YWCA, Kyoto, Japan, April 11-13, 1999; Human Rights Watch interview with Nopporn Ratchawej, First Secretary of the Royal Thai Embassy, Tokyo, Japan, April 15, 1999. See also Human Rights Watch interview with Suriya Samutkupt, Professor of Anthropology at Suranaree University of Technology, Nakhon Ratchasima, Thailand, April 27, 1999.

women's shelter Saalaa, for example, found that of the Thai women who worked in Japanese snack bars, more than ninety-five percent arrived in debt. Moreover, in ninety-five percent of those cases, the women "owed" more than 3 million yen (US$24,000[216]), which they were forced to reimburse through sex work under highly coercive conditions. Saalaa published a report on these findings which points out that although this amount is called a "debt," this is a misnomer, as the women have not actually borrowed the money.[217]

Human Rights Watch found that while the crime of debt bondage was closely linked to the crime of trafficking—as women were placed into debt bondage by the same networks that arranged their travel to Japan—women also could be "sold" into debt bondage in snack bars by persons unconnected to their travel into the country. Human Rights Watch interviewed two women who accepted job offers while they were already in Japan in 1995 and then found themselves in debt bondage, with debts of 300 bai (3 million yen; US$32,000):

• Korn came to Japan in 1993. Her first debt was 380 bai (3.8 million yen; US$34,000), which she paid off in three months, working as a sex worker at a snack bar. Then Korn and her friend Gaew, another sex worker from Thailand, met a Thai woman who told them they could earn a lot of money at another snack bar in Chiba prefecture. So, as Korn explained, "we both came to work the snack on March 23, 1995. But, upon arrival at the snack, we realized we had been sold for 300 bai [3 million yen; US$32,000] each and were in debt again for this amount. As soon as we realized we had been tricked we tried to escape."[218]

The actual time it took women to repay their debt, and the work they had to perform while in debt, often differed greatly from the promises made at the time of recruitment. Mamas used arbitrary and non-transparent methods of account-keeping, and women had no control over the initial level or on-going calculation of their debt. Not surprisingly, abuses were rampant. In virtually every case Human Rights Watch documented, debts were increased at employers' discretion as fees

---

[216] This dollar amount was calculated using the average yen-dollar exchange rate over the five year period from 1990-1994.

[217] Nobuyo Tomita, "From Thailand to Japan: The Reality of Trafficking in Women, Voices from a Shelter," in Women's Research and Action Committee [ed.], *NGOs' Report on the Situation of Foreign Migrant Women in Japan and Strategies for Improvement,* 1995, pp. 23, 25, 28.

[218] Human Rights Watch and FOWIA telephone interviews, Kanagawa prefecture, Japan, May 1995.

were levied for housing, food, clothing, medication, fines, and other expenses. Some women were never told how much their debt was to begin with, and in any case, the details of the debt repayment calculations were never fully explained:

- Unable to find a job that paid a good salary, Chan left Thailand for Japan in 1993, when she was twenty-three years old. Chan told Human Rights Watch, "I was charged 100,000 yen [US$900] a month for all my expenses, and this amount was added to my debt. All I knew was that this included 30,000 yen [US$270] per month for housing. I didn't know how the rest of the money was divided."[219]

- Before going to Japan, Sean worked in a market. Sean was twenty-eight years old when she arrived at Narita airport in December 1992, and was sent to work at a snack bar in Kofu. "I worked in a 'dating snack' and had to 'date clients' in order to pay off my debt of 120 bai [1.2 million yen; US$11,000[220]]. Each month, another 3 bai [30,000 yen; US$270] was added to the debt for the apartment and all other expenses, such as food and clothing. The Japanese owner also added 3 bai per month to my debt for having given me the job. My agent had told me I could pay off my debt in three to four months, but it took me nine months to pay off my debt."[221]

- Phan's mama paid for her apartment and food, but Phan said she had to cover all of her other expenses, including birth control pills: "I tried to buy all the extra things I needed with my tip money so it wouldn't be added to my debt."[222]

- When Miew arrived in Japan in early 1999, she was told that each month she had to pay 50,000 yen (US$430[223]) protection money, 50,000 yen (US$430) for

---

[219] Human Rights Watch and FOWIA interview, Bangkok, Thailand, March 2, 1995.

[220] This dollar amount was calculated using the average yen-dollar exchange rate from 1993.

[221] Human Rights Watch and FOWIA interview, Nagano prefecture, Japan, May 24, 1995.

[222] Human Rights Watch and FOWIA interview, Chiang Rai province, Thailand, October 5, 1995.

[223] These dollar amounts were calculated using the average yen-dollar exchange rate during the first four months of 1999: 117 yen to the U.S. dollar. Due to rounding, the numbers do not add up precisely.

housing, and 30,000 yen (US$260) for food. These expenses, totaling 130,000 yen (US$1,100) a month, were added to her debt.[224]

- Sri, a Thai woman working as a mama at a snack bar in Kofu, told Human Rights Watch in 1995 that, though an abortion at a private hospital costs about 6-7 bai (60,000-70,000 yen; US$640-740), if a hostess becomes pregnant while in debt, snack bar employers may charge her up to 30 bai (300,000 yen; US$3,200) for an abortion and then add this amount to her debt.[225]

With fees and other expenses imposed at their mama's discretion, women often found it impossible to keep track of their debt repayment calculations. And, even when they tried, they found that their efforts were fruitless, as they were forced to defer to their mamas when calculations differed:

- Faa was told she owed 120 bai (1.2 million yen; US$9,000[226]). "I paid off this debt in five months. I served at least one client a night and at most three. The snack paid for room and board, but I had to pay for my birth control and my own health care and personal needs. But I didn't really know exactly how the debt worked or what I owed for what. I just waited to be told my debt was paid."[227]

- Pot recalled, "In all, I worked for eight months to pay back my debt and I had calculated that I must have paid it back long ago, but the mama kept lying to me and said she didn't have the same records as I did. . . . I tried to keep track of my own records quietly, but I didn't know all the additional expenses that the mama was adding to my debt. And I did not want the mama to know I was keeping track for fear that she would get angry."[228]

---

[224] Human Rights Watch interview, Tokyo, Japan, April 16, 1999.

[225] Human Rights Watch and FOWIA interview, Osaka prefecture, Japan, May 26, 1995.

[226] It was not clear from Faa's testimony whether she arrived in Japan in 1991 or 1992, so this dollar amount is calculated using the average exchange rate for those two years, 131 yen to the U.S. dollar.

[227] Human Rights Watch and FOWIA interview, Chiang Mai province, Thailand, October 3-4, 1995.

[228] Human Rights Watch and FOWIA interview, Ibaraki prefecture, Japan, June 1, 1995.

Even in cases where women were released from debt within the promised time frame, the discretion that their employers exercised over the conditions of their employment, as well as over the debt repayment calculations, often qualified the arrangement as debt bondage. While in "debt," women had no power to negotiate the nature or conditions of their work and could not take sick days or rest days without permission. They could not refuse clients or clients' demands, making them highly vulnerable to violence and other abusive treatment. They furthermore received no compensation for their labor, and while the women we interviewed were typically allowed to keep tips from clients, in some cases even that was not allowed. An advocate who worked on a hotline for foreign women told Human Rights Watch about a Thai woman whose mama demanded that hostesses hand over their tips: "So she rolled the tips in saran wrap and put them in her vagina to escape detection by her mama. Then she mailed the money home, but it was stolen along the way and never got there, so it was all for nothing."[229] And a Thai woman who had been arrested for murdering her mama wrote the following in a letter composed from prison in 1993:

> The mama took all the money I got by engaging in sex with dirty-minded men, but she did not pay anything to me. . . . Moreover, she charged us food, rent, and other things as well, and our debt to her went up—although we never really borrowed from her. . . . When [the other hostesses] saw me get tipped, they threatened that they were going to tell the mama that I got a tip unless I gave them some. So I gave them some. I thought that giving some to them was better than having it all taken away by the mama.[230]

Interviewees explained that their indebtedness was consistently used as a justification for the strict control that mamas exercised over all aspects of their lives, which included the confiscation of their passports, strict isolation, constant surveillance, and the threat and use of violent punishments for disobedience. The debt itself also provided a strong incentive for hard work and obedience. Women came to Japan with the primary objective of sending money back to Thailand, so when they learned that they had to repay a debt before they could keep their earnings, their top priority became repaying their debt (or having it repaid) as quickly as possible. This meant staying on good terms with the mama, who had

---

[229] Human Rights Watch interview with Teruko Enomoto, Kyoto, Japan, April 11, 1999.

[230] Letter written from Tsuchiura Prison, Ibaraki prefecture, October 14, 1993 (original translated from Thai to Japanese by Yuriko Fukushima).

ultimate control over calculating debt repayment and even reserved the right to "resell" women into higher levels of debt and/or worse working conditions. Finally, the lack of wages obstructed women's access to outside assistance and increased their dependency on their employers for food, medical care, housing, and other necessities.

Dr. Suriya Samutkupt, a Professor of Anthropology at the Suranaree University of Technology, in Thailand, spent several months in Japan in the mid to late 1990s, interviewing Thai women who were working as sex workers in Ibaraki prefecture. These women had arrived in Japan in debt bondage, but had successfully paid off their debts and were now sending money home to Thailand each month. Samutkupt recalled their descriptions of the period of debt bondage, emphasizing that "these were women who had 'made it' in Japan, so their experiences were not as bad as many others":

> They didn't really understand the finances or the accounting, but they knew that cooperation and obedience would get them through. If they cooperated with the boss and the clients, their chances of getting tips and getting free were much, much better. They prayed to be bought out of their contracts [by clients] and they tried to stay away from drugs and drink. They said that the younger women would get into trouble by getting involved in drugs and alcohol and by disobeying. Then they would be beaten or resold. But they explained that "as long as you do your job, the gangsters aren't too bad and will take care of you when you're sick." They also explained that if you're young and pretty you have a better chance.[231]

Fines

The system of debt bondage provided snack bar managers with punishments that could be used to exact strict obedience from women without resorting to the explicit threat or use of physical force. Strict rules were imposed regarding matters such as punctuality, weight gain, and failure to fully satisfy clients, and mamas fined women for minor infractions, thus prolonging their period of indebtedness. Women also reported facing fines if any of their customers complained, thus encouraging them to yield to all customer demands.

---

[231] Human Rights Watch interview, Suranaree University of Technology, Nakhon Ratchasima, Thailand, April 27, 1999.

- At Kaew's snack bar, "women were fined for coming back late, fighting with each other, or not agreeing to sit with a client, so," Kaew explained, "I did what I was told."[232]

- Chan explained, "I could eat anything I wanted, but I was penalized if I ever weighed more than 54 kilograms [119 pounds]."[233]

- Lee, who had left her two-year-old twins with her family in Samut Sakhon Province to come to Japan in 1991, when she was twenty-three years old, explained that her mama added a 10,000 yen (US$75) fine to the debt of a woman who gained even one kilogram.[234]

- Noi was twenty-one when she arrived in Japan. She described her mama as nervous, and sometimes cruel, and said women were "fined if they were fat or gave bad service to clients."[235]

- Miew was fined 500,000 yen (US$4,300[236]) for giving the snack bar's telephone number to her parents. She explained that "Women also got fines for asking customers to help them escape [if the customer told on them] or for not satisfying the customer."[237]

"Resale"

Many women reported being faced with the threat or actuality of having their debt renewed by being "resold" to another snack bar. In a clear demonstration of the slave-like status of indebted women, procurers considered it their right to "sell" a woman, this time acting as her broker, or to return her to her original broker. Many women were resold, or threatened with resale, into higher levels of debt and worse working conditions as a punishment for disobedience or "causing trouble." Women also explained that being found HIV positive was considered grounds for "resale":

---

[232] Human Rights Watch interview, Chiang Rai province, Thailand, April 25, 1999.
[233] Human Rights Watch and FOWIA interview, Bangkok, Thailand, March 2, 1995.
[234] Human Rights Watch and FOWIA interview, Chiba prefecture, Japan, May 20, 1995.
[235] Interview by M. N., Chiang Rai province, Thailand, September 8, 1997.
[236] This dollar amount was calculated using the average yen-dollar exchange rate from the first four months of 1999.
[237] Human Rights Watch interview, Tokyo, Japan, April 16, 1999.

• Chan said that she served three to four clients every night and explained that she and the other hostesses "weren't exactly forced to take clients but we were pressured, and if we didn't cooperate our lives could be made very difficult. So everyone learned to do as we were instructed. I had to take clients from the first day. I had never done this type of work before, and I had to serve about three or four clients every night. The mama said we had to work hard to pay off our debt within five months, or she would sell us again."[238]

• Kaew said she "saw lots of women who tried to run away from their debt, but were caught and resold, even caught back in Thailand."[239]

• According to Miew, she had to be careful in asking clients to help her escape, because "if I asked a customer to help me escape and he told my mama, I would be sold to another place with double debt."[240]

• Janya was resold after more than a year of working to repay her debt because her boss, a Thai woman, owed heavy gambling debts and wanted to return home to Thailand. It then took her another year to repay her debt to the second snack bar.[241]

Samutkupt's discussions with Thai sex workers in Japan confirmed that "indebted women could be resold, because they were under contract. They might be resold for misbehavior, or for some other reason, such as because their boss was in debt, or because the club owners changed."[242]

Tactics to prevent escape

Passport Deprivation
   One of the ways in which brokers and employers prevented women from attempting escape was by confiscating their passports and other documentation. None of the women Human Rights Watch interviewed were allowed access to their passports while in debt, and in some cases women could not get their passports back even after their debt was paid. Khai's mama kept her (fake) passport while she was

---

[238] Human Rights Watch and FOWIA interview, Bangkok, Thailand, March 2, 1995.

[239] Human Rights Watch interview, Chiang Rai province, Thailand, April 25, 1999.

[240] Human Rights Watch interview, Tokyo, Japan, April 16, 1999.

[241] Human Rights Watch interview, Tokyo, Japan, March 14, 1994.

[242] Human Rights Watch interview, Suranaree University of Technology, Nakhon Ratchasima, Thailand, April 27, 1999.

in debt, and then, when Khai finished paying off her debt in 1992, demanded a fee for its return. Khai was told to pay 50 bai (500,000 yen; US$4,000) and, since she didn't have the money, she never saw her passport again.[243] Without their passports and other papers, women were left without any proof of their identity, making it difficult for them to arrange transportation back to Thailand. A Japanese man who has helped many Thai and Filipina women escape from debt bondage in snack bars explained that, when he attempts to rescue women, most of them are very concerned about their passports. Their employers have told them that they cannot go home without a passport or identification, and the women believe them.[244] Furthermore, foreigners in Japan are required to carry their passports with them at all times. Failure to produce a passport upon demand by a police or immigration official is punishable by a fine and often leads to detention as a suspected illegal immigrant. Thus, if a woman leaves the snack bar without her passport, she faces the risk of being placed into detention by police or immigration officials. Pot explained that "the mama had my passport so I never dared to run away or even consider running to the police. Without my documents I was sure I would be arrested and jailed. I never got my passport back from the mama even after my debt was paid."[245]

Restrictions on movement and communication

Snack bar employers also used strict supervision and restrictions on women's freedom of movement and communication to limit opportunities for successful escapes. Virtually all of the women interviewed by Human Rights Watch complained that every aspect of their lives, during both working and non-working hours, was controlled by the mama while they were in debt. They were housed in apartments with other snack bar hostesses under the supervision of the mama, and they could not go out of the apartment without an escort, if at all. Communication was also tightly controlled. Women were often forbidden to speak in Thai, and one woman reported that though she could send and receive letters, both incoming and outgoing mail was opened and read.

- Nat worked in a bar with a Singaporean mama. "The mama had lived in Japan for twenty-four years and had been employing Thai women. Because she often

---

[243] Human Rights Watch and FOWIA interview, Osaka prefecture, Japan, May 27, 1995.

[244] "Chapter 2: Questions to Japan," *Today's Japan,* April 26, 1994, p. 21.
In reality, women can return home with Certificates of Identity issued by the Thai Embassy, but obtaining such documentation can be a prolonged and difficult task.

[245] Human Rights Watch and FOWIA interview, Ibaraki prefecture, Japan, June 1, 1995.

traveled to Thailand, she spoke fluent Thai and knew well how to scold in Thai. The mama managed the women very strictly. She watched our every move from her house. Video cameras were set up for this purpose at the snack bar and in the room on the second floor where we lived. All doors made a sound when opened or closed and we could not go anywhere.[246]

- Miew lived next door to the snack bar and was watched all the time. "There was a motion sensitive light that went on if anyone went up or down the stairs to the apartment. I don't know who was watching us, but someone was."[247]

- Rei called home about once a month for thirty minutes and was also able to send and receive letters. But she explained that none of the women were allowed to go out alone.[248]

- Pong worked at a snack bar with eight other Thai women. "I lived with the mama in the same apartment, and I had no freedom to go out. I was watched and controlled all the time. When somebody went out to buy food, another woman had to go with her. Mama ordered the Yakuza to watch the women to prevent escape. Mama told us that if anybody escaped from here, she would be killed." Pong's communication with family members in Thailand was also strictly limited. "I could send letters to my family in Thailand, but I could not receive any letters from my family because I was prohibited from telling our address to anybody."[249]

The extreme isolation many women are subjected to was described in wrenching words in a letter written by one Thai woman, who has since disappeared, to her father:

I live without hope. What I do everyday is just have customers. I cannot go out. There are more than ten Yakuza here. This letter must be hidden from them. If they find it, I will be beaten. If I try to run away from here, I will be killed, and my body will be thrown to the sea. . . . I do not know where I am now. All of us do not speak. There are lots of Thais and Filipinas. I am prohibited to talk to them. . . . The Yakuza are always

---

[246] Interview by M. N., Chiang Rai province, Thailand, September 3, 1997.
[247] Human Rights Watch interview, Tokyo, Japan, April 16, 1999.
[248] Human Rights Watch and FOWIA interview, Bangkok, Thailand, January 17, 1995.
[249] Human Rights Watch interview, Chiang Rai province, Thailand, April 24, 1999.

watching me carefully. I am forced to stay at the place where Yakuza live. The restaurant where I work is located on an island. The Yakuza are threatening me. . . . Living here is like living in hell. Yakuza sometimes take us somewhere in order for us to get customers. They pack us into a truck without windows. I cannot look outside.[250]

Violence/Intimidation

Finally, many women reported that brokers and employers used physical violence and threats of violence to frighten women into submission. Women were beaten for failing to please their clients, for failing to prevent a coworker's escape, or for other acts of disobedience.

- Khai complained that the clients would not use condoms, and "if I tried to get a client to use one and he told the mama, I would get in trouble. If I did anything that did not please the client and he complained I would get beaten." She also said that the mama beat the women at the snack bar if they asked clients for any tips or favors.[251]

- Jaem explained that she was beaten often by her employers because "I wouldn't say I was wrong when I hadn't done anything wrong."[252]

- Phon arrived in Japan in 1993 at age eighteen and was "sold" to a snack bar owner named Yoko. When two of her coworkers escaped from the snack bar, the boss "beat and kicked me and another woman, asking if we knew something about the two women's escape."[253]

Threats and intimidation were commonly used to prevent women from trying to escape, and women often heard stories of others who were severely punished, and even killed, for fleeing before they were released from their debt. Rei told Human Rights Watch about an eighteen-year-old woman who was caught trying to escape: "they took the girl back and the mama sold her to the Yakuza. Now she has to work

---

[250] The father who received this letter went to Japan to look for his daughter and could not find her. An international NGO assisted him and translated this letter from Thai into English. On file with Human Rights Watch.

[251] Human Rights Watch and FOWIA interview, Osaka prefecture, Japan, May 27, 1995.

[252] Interview by M. N., Phayao province, Thailand, September 1997.

[253] Interview transcript provided by a staff member at a women's shelter in Japan, who worked with Phon in April 1993.

for them in a Yakuza brothel, or 'black jail,' indefinitely with no pay. . . . Some women who try to escape are killed."[254] Another woman, Miew, explained that "a friend of mine working at the same snack told me about a woman who had tried to escape. The first time she was caught and returned to the snack and then, when she tried again, she was killed and found dead in the forest. My friend said that if a woman escapes, she is killed and thrown away in the forest or the ocean."[255] Suriya Samutkupt told Human Rights Watch that in his conversations with Thai women who had been released from debt bondage in snack bars in Japan, he also "heard of many others who had disappeared, either resold or killed by the Yakuza. . . . The women had heard stories of women being thrown into the sea or into the forest for disobeying their bosses." He went on to explain, "I don't know if these stories were true or if they were just threats used as a control tactic," but regardless of their accuracy, they were effective in eliciting obedience. Despite the terrible conditions that they described, none of the women Samutkupt met had ever tried to escape.[256]

Some employers also told women that if they left the snack bar before their "debts" were repaid, their family members would face violent retaliation back in Thailand. Korn, for example, whose successful escape from debt bondage is described below, told Human Rights Watch, "even though we [Korn and one of her coworkers] escaped, we will not return to our families in Thailand because our agents know where we are from and might seek revenge. My mama threatened to kill my mother and older sister if I ever ran away."[257] Human Rights Watch was unable to determine whether such retaliation was commonly carried out in practice, but according to shelter staff and other advocates whom we interviewed in Tokyo, Kyoto, and Bangkok, these threats are credible, and the fear generated by such threats serves as a significant deterrent against escape attempts and other acts of disobedience.[258]

---

[254] Human Rights Watch and FOWIA interview, Bangkok, Thailand, January 17, 1995.

[255] Human Rights Watch interview, Tokyo, Japan, April 16, 1999.

[256] Human Rights Watch interview, Suranaree University of Technology, Nakhon Ratchasima, Thailand, April 27, 1999.

[257] Human Rights Watch and FOWIA telephone interviews, Kanagawa prefecture, Japan, May 1995.

[258] Human Rights Watch interview with Rutsuko Shoji, Director, HELP Asia Women's Shelter, Tokyo, Japan, April 8, 1999; Human Rights Watch interview with Rieko Aoki, Kyoto YWCA, Kyoto, Japan, April 11-13, 1999; Human Rights Watch interview with Sumalee Tokthong, Foundation for Women, Bangkok, Thailand, April 23, 1999.

Excessive hours

Nearly every woman Human Rights Watch interviewed was forced to work seven days a week while in debt, without days off for rest or, in some cases, even for illness.[259] Typically, the women were taken to the snack bar at 6:00 or 7:00 p.m and worked until at least 2:00 or 3:00 a.m. They provided sexual services for two to four clients each night and often performed other tasks as well, including cleaning, washing dishes, serving food and drinks, and entertaining clients by singing or playing games with them at their tables:

- Rei explained that she tried to work hard to pay off her debt as fast as possible. "If I was sick I could rest for two or three days and mama gave me medicine (the cost of which was added to my debt). But I rarely stopped, even when sick, and the mama pushed me to work." Rei said her mama insisted that she serve at least two clients a night, and most nights she served three.[260]

- In one of the snack bars where Nuch worked, she was woken up every morning at 9:00 a.m. to clean the house and the snack bar before lunch. After lunch, she and the other women from the snack bar had to work in a field behind the bar where the owners grew vegetables and rice. They worked there until dinner-time, and they were closely supervised to make sure they did not steal any produce; anything they wanted to eat from the fields had to be purchased with their tip money. After dinner Nuch went to work in the snack bar, serving clients from 6:00 p.m. to 3:00 a.m. as she struggled to repay her debt.[261]

- Lai was twenty-three when a friend in southern Thailand recruited her to go to Japan in 1993. Once there, she was forced to work every day from 7:00 p.m. to 2:00 a.m., without any compensation or days off. Her clients paid 20,000 yen (US$180) for two hours or 30,000 yen (US$270) for an overnight stay, but the money went straight to the snack bar owner.[262]

---

[259] An exception is Nung, who was given two days off each month and was not forced to work when she was sick (Interview by M. N., Chiang Rai province, Thailand, August 6, 1997).

[260] Human Rights Watch and FOWIA interview, Bangkok, Thailand, January 17, 1995.

[261] Human Rights Watch and FOWIA interview, Bangkok, Thailand, March 1995.

[262] Interview transcript provided by a staff member at a women's shelter in Japan, who worked with Lai D. during 1993.

Several women reported taking contraceptive pills without any days off (to allow for menstruation), so that they could go out with customers every day of the month. Some women said their mamas "forced" them to take pills daily; in other cases, they felt compelled by the urgent need to pay back their debt as quickly as possible:

• Khai told us that her mama made her pay for her own birth control and take it without any days for menstruation: "I bought the birth control pills on the black market for 2,500 yen [US$20[263]] per month. I didn't have my period for one and a half years. Then when I stopped taking birth control I bled every day for one and a half months."[264]

• Kaew had been sterilized so she did not need to take birth control pills for contraceptive purposes. But, she said, I took the pill daily so that I wouldn't get my period and could work every day. The mama said to me, 'don't let your period come, or you'll never finish paying your debt.'"[265]

One woman we interviewed was able to avoid taking birth control pills without regular breaks by sitting on ice to clot her blood when she was menstruating, so that she could still serve clients.[266]

Abuse by clients

Women's inability to turn down customers meant that they were often forced to tolerate even the most abusive clients. Many of the women we interviewed explained that some of their clients were sadistic and violent:

• Khai told us, "I was beaten by clients several times. One client even burnt me many times with a cigarette." But Khai was never allowed to refuse clients.

---

[263] This dollar amount was calculated using the average yen-dollar exchange rate from 1992.

[264] Human Rights Watch and FOWIA interview, Osaka prefecture, Japan, May 27, 1995. The Senior Medical Consultant to Physicians for Human Rights, Vincent Iacopino, M.D., PhD., explained that if contraceptive pills are taken without days off for menstruation, a woman's uterus lining builds up beyond what is normal, so excessive menstrual bleeding would be expected when she stopped taking the pills. (Human Rights Watch telephone interview, Nevada, United States, September 8, 1999).

[265] Human Rights Watch interview, Chiang Rai province, Thailand, April 25, 1999.

[266] Human Rights Watch and FOWIA interview, Bangkok, Thailand, January 17, 1995.

"The clients could do whatever they wanted to me. There were times when I was bruised all over by the clients and still the mama made me go with them for as long as the client was willing to pay. . . . One Thai woman who worked with me was beaten by a client and when she returned to the snack bleeding the mama stilled yelled at her and blamed her for not pleasing the client. The mama kept saying it was her fault for not pleasing him."[267]

• Rei also reported having to accept every client and fulfill all of their requests. "The client could do anything they wanted with me and could ask me to do anything and I couldn't refuse. The only thing the mama said to the clients was 'these women belong to the Yakuza so be careful with them.'"[268]

• According to Jo, "Some clients were violent with us. Once we went out with a client, we had to follow his instructions and satisfy him."[269]

A volunteer staff member at a Japanese women's shelter told Human Rights Watch that, during the year and a half that she worked there, from early 1998 to mid-1999, nine Thai women escaped to the shelter from snack bars and two escaped from brothels. Several women reported traumatic experiences with clients, including one woman who was forced to have sex in the snow, and was then left in the snow by her client when she fainted. She was rescued by her mama, who went to find her when the client returned with only the woman's clothing.[270]

Risks to physical and mental health
    Women working in debt bondage in Japan's sex industry face serious risks to their physical and mental health. These include the risk of contracting sexually transmitted diseases (STDs)—including HIV/AIDS—from their clients. Several women interviewed by Human Rights Watch explained that they were unable to negotiate or insist on condom use, especially while they were still in debt. Kaew said she tried to use condoms during oral sex "but some of the clients refused to use the condoms."[271] Nam explained, "I could not refuse clients, and very few clients

---

[267] Human Rights Watch and FOWIA interview, Osaka prefecture, Japan, May 27, 1995.

[268] Human Rights Watch and FOWIA interview, Bangkok, Thailand, January 17, 1995.

[269] Interview by M. N., Phayao province, Thailand, October 8, 1997.

[270] Human Rights Watch interview with shelter staff, Tokyo, Japan, June 11, 1999.

[271] Human Rights Watch interview, Chiang Rai province, Thailand, April 25, 1999.

used condoms."[272] We also spoke to a Thai mama, Sri, who told us that while she tried to convince clients to use condoms with the women who worked for her, she did not insist on it; if clients refused to use a condom, the women had to follow their clients' wishes or it would be bad for the snack bar.[273] A staff worker at MsLA, a women's shelter and hotline and counseling center in Yokohama, corroborated the testimony of Human Rights Watch interviewees regarding condom use: "Thai women are very concerned about STDs. They ask for condoms but ten out of ten customers refuse. Condoms are a common form of birth control in Japan, but it is something to be used with wives. Men feel that since they have paid for the services of a prostitute, they should be able to do whatever they want."[274]

Women's limited access to medical testing and treatment exacerbated the health risks they faced from sexually transmitted diseases. Restrictions on women's freedom of movement meant that they could not visit a doctor without their mama's approval, and, typically, her accompaniment. Language barriers—coupled with a lack of interpreters in Japanese hospitals and clinics—compounded the problem, making it impossible for women to communicate directly with health care providers. Indebted women also lacked the funds to pay for exams and medication, and their undocumented immigration status served to exclude them from nearly all government health care subsidies, including government-subsidized HIV/AIDS treatment. Not only did this mean that women's access to medical care depended on their mamas' decision to pay for it, it also meant that visits to the doctor could prolong their period of indebtedness, as all health care costs were added to their debt.

---

[272] Human Rights Watch interview, Chiang Rai province, Thailand, August 4, 1997.

[273] Human Rights Watch and FOWIA interview, Osaka prefecture, Japan, May 26, 1995.

[274] Human Rights Watch interview, Kanagawa prefecture, Japan, March 17, 1994.
A survey of (non-indebted) Thai female sex workers in Japan conducted in 1994 found similar results. The Thai women interviewed for this study explained that when they worked as sex workers in Japan, many of their clients preferred not to use condoms. The study indicated that the majority of Thai female sex workers were aware of the risk involved in unprotected sex and made some attempt to protect themselves, but that due to clients' reluctance to use condoms, unprotected sex was common. Sex workers reported being afraid to even suggest condom use to some of their clients, for fear of disappointing them, and they explained that if they insisted on condom use, they risked being punished by their managers for failing to satisfy their clients. (Nigoon Jitthai, "HIV in Japan: in Relation to Foreign Female CSWs," presented at the 12th World Congress of Sexology, Symposia on "HIV, AIDS, STD" in Yokohama, Japan, August 15, 1995.)

The result was that, while in debt, women's access to testing and medication for STDs and other illnesses was strictly controlled by their mamas. Some women were never tested. Pong, for example, explained that she was never checked for STDs, even though very few clients used condoms.[275] Other women were given blood tests, but the results were provided to their mamas—in violation of their right to privacy—while being withheld from the women themselves. Providing medical test results to the women's managers constitutes a serious breach of the principle of doctor-patient confidentiality. Still other women were given the results, but could not afford to pay for the medication they needed. And those who did receive treatment saw their debts increase as a result:

- Rei told Human Rights Watch that while she was working as an indebted snack shop hostess, she and her coworkers went to the hospital once a month for blood tests to check for STDs and HIV/AIDS. The cost of the health visits were added to the women's debt, and the test results were given to the mama. Rei knows that she had syphilis twice, but she does not know whether she has HIV/AIDS because her mama never told her.[276]

- Soi worked at a snack bar in Chiba prefecture for two months and then was transferred with her mama to a snack bar in Mie prefecture. During the four months that she worked without compensation, from October 1990 to January 1991, she and the other hostesses were taken to the doctor for blood tests twice a week, but the doctor discussed the results only with their mama. In Soi's words, "The doctor checked us for diseases by taking out blood and listening to our chests with a stethoscope. The mama paid the doctor. The doctor never told us our diagnosis. He would tell the mama. . . . The mama said she would tell us if we were sick."[277]

- When Khai had her blood checked, the health center told her that she "had too many white cells"—meaning she was HIV-positive—but her mama refused to give her money for medication.[278]

---

[275] Interview by M. N., Chiang Rai province, Thailand, August 2, 1997.

[276] Human Rights Watch and FOWIA interview, Bangkok, Thailand, January 17, 1995.

[277] Human Rights Watch interview, Japan, March 1994.

[278] Human Rights Watch and FOWIA interview, Osaka prefecture, Japan, May 27, 1995.

• Ooi saw a doctor once while she was at the snack bar. "The doctor took my blood and examined my vagina. It took a week for me to find out my results. I was told I did not have syphilis. But I was not told anything else. The mama made me see the doctor. One of the clients asked the owner to bring the women for medical check-ups because some diseases can be transmitted. So the owner told the mama to take the girls to the doctor because if the client got a disease, then he might take back his money. The mama paid the doctor's fee. After I got back to the apartment, the mama told me that my debt would be increased. . . . One month before I was arrested, I was taken to a hospital for a check-up. The doctor gave me a month's supply of medicine. I did not know what the medicine was for."[279]

Based on her conversations with Thai women, a staff member at MsLA observed,."Half the women get regular checkups and the medical fees are added to their debt. The other half have no way of knowing if they have any disease."[280]

There is also some evidence that women trafficked from Thailand into the Japanese sex industry are at risk of developing serious mental health problems as a result of the abuses they suffer. Though there are no statistics estimating the extent of mental disorders among undocumented female migrants from Thailand in Japan, such problems have been identified by physicians who treat foreign patients in Japan as one of the major medical problems facing Thai women. Takashi Sawada, a physician at the Minatomachi Medical Clinic, told Human Rights Watch that, in his experience, acute psychosis and substance abuse are prevalent among Thai women working as entertainers or sex workers in Japan.[281] Human Rights Watch spoke to several women who appeared to be suffering from addictions and/or serious mental health problems after working in debt bondage in Japanese snack bars. A few of their stories are related below, though we do not have sufficient information or expertise to reach definitive conclusions about how or why their problems developed:

• When we met Khai, she had escaped from debt bondage in a snack bar and was working on the streets in Osaka. She was living with a Japanese boyfriend, and explained that she was trying to stop working, but without the work she gets bored and has no money of her own. "I am still addicted to the drug 'U' and

---

[279] Human Rights Watch interview, Japan, March 18, 1994.

[280] Human Rights Watch interview, Kanagawa prefecture, Japan, March 17, 1994.

[281] Electronic mail communication, October 11, 1999. See also Human Rights Watch interview, physician at the Minatomachi Medical Clinic, Yokohama, Japan, June 2, 1995.

so I need some money. I get angry with myself sometimes and beat myself by sticking needles in my arms and banging my head against the wall hard. If I am drunk or on drugs I feel better. I often have severe headaches."[282]

• Bee was working at a bar in Bangkok that served primarily Japanese clients when a friend of hers asked her to go to Japan. Bee agreed, but when she got to Japan and was sold to a snack bar in Ibaraki prefecture, the conditions proved unbearable. She began consuming large amounts of cough syrup and drugs, and then had problems with her nerves. "I became crazy and then the neighbors reported me." It is not clear whether her neighbors called the police or the hospital, but Bee was taken to a mental hospital, where she was treated and then turned over to the police.[283]

• Four months after her baby was born, Faa began having temper tantrums. She was eventually sent to a psychiatric hospital in Japan and then transferred to Thailand. When we spoke to Faa at the psychiatric hospital in Thailand, she did not remember her temper tantrums or know why she had been committed to hospitals in Japan and Thailand. The hospital staff believed that her mental disorders were probably a result of her addiction to medicated cough syrup during the nearly four years she was in Japan.[284]

Japan's public health system provides for free treatment to undocumented migrants whose cases are so severe that they are considered at risk of physically harming themselves or others and are in need of emergency intervention. But for women with less extreme problems, the high cost of treatment can deter them from seeking assistance. The fact that there are few Thai-speaking psychiatrists in Japan means that effective care is often unavailable even in emergency cases.[285]

Snack bar hostesses may also suffer from a range of illnesses or injuries, particularly given the excessive work hours and the prevalence of physically abusive clients and/or employers. Again, Human Rights Watch found that the risk to their health was heightened by their dependence on their employers for access to medical care and medication: they needed permission from their mama to see a doctor, as well as a "loan" to pay for the visit and any necessary medication. And

---

[282] Human Rights Watch and FOWIA interview, Osaka prefecture, Japan, May 27, 1995.

[283] Interview by M. N., Chiang Rai province, Thailand, September 12, 1997.

[284] Human Rights Watch interviews with Faa and with hospital staff, Chiang Mai province, Thailand, October 3-4, 1995.

[285] Takashi Sawada, e-mails to Human Rights Watch, October 9, 11, and 16, 1999.

again, the cost of any medical care that women did receive was added to their debts and thus could prolong their period of debt bondage. Joy reported, "We had to work even if we were ill or menstruating. And as long as we were in debt, we were not allowed to go to the doctor, even if we were sick."[286] Wanna described her mama as a "cold-hearted woman," and complained that "when I was ill I had to take clients."[287] Nuch said that when she developed a rash and fever, her mama bought her medicine, but did not take her to see a doctor and the cost of her medicine was added to her debt.[288]

Women continue to face problems in obtaining affordable health care after being released from debt. Excluded from government health benefits on the basis of their immigration status, the high cost of medical care could prevent women from even seeking treatment. Rei told Human Rights Watch that, while she was working as a sex worker on the streets, after paying off her debt in a snack bar, a client took her to an apartment and threw her down a flight of steps. Despite her resultant injuries, she did not go to a doctor: "I had no health care insurance and no money." Instead, she simply stayed at home for a month without working.[289] Women who successfully obtain medical care find themselves saddled with expensive medical bills. Most found the money to cover their bills, but those without the resources to pay could be forced into excruciating choices. Nid explained that, when she was pregnant in 1995, her inability to pay her medical expenses, which totaled 800,000 yen (US$8500), nearly led her to give up her unborn children to a woman who offered to cover her hospital bills in return.[290] Fortunately, staff members from the Japanese NGO Saalaa intervened and assisted Nid in arranging both child care and a hospital payment plan.[291]

In 1994, a staff worker from OASIS, a Japanese women's association that was set up in 1983 to help foreign workers in Japan, noted that "Japanese authorities reported that twenty Thai girls died in 1993 after working in the snack bars or brothels because of various 'illnesses.' The illnesses were caused by the fact that they were forced to work too hard and because they had no time to rest and no money to see a doctor."[292] In interviews with Human Rights Watch in 1999, Thai

---

[286] Interview by M. N., Chiang Rai province, Thailand, September 1997.

[287] Interview by M. N., Chiang Rai province, Thailand, August 5, 1997.

[288] Human Rights Watch and FOWIA interviews, Bangkok, Thailand, March 10 and 26, 1995.

[289] Human Rights Watch and FOWIA interview, Bangkok, Thailand, January 17, 1995.

[290] Human Rights Watch and FOWIA interview, Tokyo, Japan, May 20, 1995.

[291] Human Rights Watch and FOWIA telephone interviews, Tokyo, Japan, 1995.

[292] Jiraporn Jarerndej, "What Price Freedom?" *Bangkok Post,* January 29, 1994.

officials, including the First Secretary of the Royal Thai Embassy in Japan and the Japan Desk Officer at the Consular Affairs Department of the Ministry of Foreign Affairs, cited similar mortality rates for Thai women in Japan, stating that about fifty Thai nationals die in Japan each year, and the majority of the deceased are women. They did not, however, provide any information about the causes of death.[293]

Release from debt

"Dat tact"

In some cases, a woman's release from debt bondage was expedited by a client who paid off her outstanding debt. Women referred to this as "dat tact"[294]:

• Soi had spent two months working in a snack bar without compensation, when one of her clients, Mr. Takashi,[295] paid her boss to release her. "He came to the snack for the first time in December 1990. He met me there, bought me [for the night], and then bought me about ten times after that. Then he proposed to me. I did not understand what he was saying so the mama interpreted for me. He asked me to stop working at the snack and to live with him. He paid 1.5 million yen [US$11,000] to my boss to set me free. I left the snack in January 1991 and started living with Mr. Takashi and his eighty-two-year-old ailing mother. I got a job and worked illegally at a button producing factory. I worked there for a year and a half. In November 1993, Mr. Takashi and I went to the ward office to get married. I went to the office with my real passport, which I had brought to Japan with me [though she entered Japan on a Malaysian passport]. It had no 'entry' stamp for Japan, but the ward office said I could get married if I had my real passport." When she spoke to Human Rights Watch in March 1994, Soi had applied for a visa as a spouse of Japanese national and hoped to receive it within the year.[296]

---

[293] Human Rights Watch interview with Nopporn Ratchawej, First Secretary, Royal Thai Embassy, Japan, April 15, 1999; Human Rights Watch telephone interview with Maliwan, Japan Desk Officer, Division for the Protection of Thai Nationals Abroad, Consular Affairs Department, Ministry of Foreign Affairs, Bangkok, Thailand, April 30, 1999.

[294] "Tact" is an abbreviated term for the English word "contract" and "dat" means "cut," so "dat tact" refers to breaking the contract.

[295] This name has been changed to protect the identity of the man and Soi H.

[296] Human Rights Watch interview, Japan, March 1994.

- While Kaew was working to repay her debt at a snack bar in Nagano prefecture in 1992, she met a man who was a friend of the owner. "He came to the snack bar often, but he never took women out, he just talked to them. I had to talk to him, and at first I was upset because I knew he wasn't going to pay to take me out, but then he gave me tips just to sit and talk. He told the owner that he liked me and asked to buy out my contract, and the owner agreed since it was his friend. Usually, they didn't allow men to buy women out. So he paid the 130 bai [1.3 million yen; US$10,000] that I owed [she had already repaid 250 bai (2.5 million yen; US$20,000)] and set me up in an apartment. He gave me money, and I also continued to work at the same snack bar, but I wasn't in debt so I earned money."[297]

Samutkupt found that it was common practice for clients to "buy" women out of debt in the snack bars and then take them as mistresses. The women he met with in Ibaraki prefecture explained that while they were in "debt," "they dreamt of getting out of their contract, and their goal was to be bought out of debt." Many of the women he interviewed had been "bought out" by Japanese men, who then rented apartments for the women, gave them spending money, and visited them once or twice a week.[298]

Women preferred "dat tact" to remaining in debt bondage, but they were also vulnerable to being exploited by the person who had purchased their "release" and thus felt entitled to demand services and obedience. Furthermore, the women continued to live in fear of deportation and became dependant on their "boyfriend" for protection against the authorities and access to housing, medical care, and other necessities. We interviewed one woman who was "released" from debt by her "boyfriend" while she was working at a snack bar in 1985, only to be told that she owed him a debt of 80 bai (800,000 yen; US$3300):

- Sri had been working in Japan for five months when her Japanese 'boyfriend' paid off the rest of her debt—she never found out how much that was — and took her to live with him. Then he brought her to Kofu, where he had just opened a snack bar of his own. "He told me I was to work there and pay off another debt of 80 bai [800,000 yen; US$3300]. He then bought another ten Thai girls for 180 bai [1.8 million yen; US$7500] each, and each of these girls had to work off a debt of 300-350 bai [3-3.5 million yen; US$12,400-14,500]. The girls' debt varied according to their age and beauty, the younger and more

---

[297] Human Rights Watch interview, Chiang Rai province, Thailand, April 25, 1999.
[298] Human Rights Watch interview, Suranaree University of Technology, Nakhon Ratchasima, Thailand, April 27, 1999.

beautiful they were, the higher their debt. I was told that my debt was less because I was to be the mama in that snack."[299]

"Finishing" the debt

Most women worked until they were told that their debt was "finished." While the amount of time it took women to repay their debts varied greatly, most of the women whose cases Human Rights Watch documented were released within a year:[300]

- Joy was "sold" to a snack bar in Gumma prefecture in 1991, where she was held in debt bondage and forced to work every day to repay a debt of 350 bai (3.5 million yen; US$26,000). She described her mama as "mean and malicious." "If we [Joy and her coworkers] didn't listen to the mama, she reported us to the Yakuza. We had to work even if we were ill or menstruating. And as long as we were in debt, we were not allowed to go to the doctor, even if we were sick." But after two and a half months, Joy had repaid her debt, and she went to work at a factory, earning about 130,000 yen (US$1000) a month after taxes.[301]

- When Pat went to Japan in 1990 at age twenty-four, she said, "I understood that I owed a debt of 2.3 million yen [US$16,000] and what type of work I would do. But I didn't know how long I had to work, and in the end I spent more than a year finishing my debt because I was resold to other snack bars several times." After her debt was "finished," she moved in with her forty-three-year-old Japanese boyfriend, whom she later married.[302]

- Lee agreed to come to Japan in 1991. "The agent told me I would work serving drinks in Japan. I did not know until after I arrived that I had to pay off my debt of 400 bai [4 million yen; US$30,000] through prostitution. That time was very difficult. I was sent to a snack bar, and it took me seven months to pay off my debt. I had one regular customer who came every other night which

---

[299] Human Rights Watch and FOWIA interview, Osaka prefecture, Japan, May 26, 1995.

[300] In some cases, the likelihood of eventual release from debt, coupled with the unpredictable length of the debt repayment period, provided another incentive for women to endure the terrible conditions and hope for a relatively early release, rather than take the dangerous risk of trying to escape.

[301] Interview by M. N., Chiang Rai province, Thailand, September 1997.

[302] Interview by M. N., Phayao province, Thailand, October 1997.

helped, but besides him I had to serve any client who wanted me and I couldn't refuse." Lee stayed at the snack for several months after repaying her debt, until she had saved enough money to move. Then she got a job at a snack bar near Narita airport in Chiba prefecture, and worked there for more than a year.[303]

After they were released, most of the women continued to work in Japan, either in sex work or other types of employment. These women were finally able to collect wages for their work, and many women sent significant amounts of money home to their families in Thailand. Non-indebted hostesses in the snack bars had more choices about where they worked, when they worked, the types of services they performed, and the clients they accepted. However, some women reported that their mamas continued to exercise abusive levels of control, even after their debt was repaid. In some cases, women found themselves with no choice but to continue working at the same snack bar, because they did not have enough money to leave:

- Phan spent five months paying off a debt of 400 bai (4 million yen; US$30,000) after she arrived in Japan in January 1991. Then she agreed to enter into a second debt. "The mama asked me if I wanted another contract. I was not allowed to earn the money I made and save it along the way—the mama explained that according to her system, you had to take the advance and then worked it off. So I agreed to extend my contract by 100 bai [1 million yen; US$7,500], which I sent home to my family. The mama said that for 100 bai I would have to pay off a debt of 200 bai [2 million yen; US$15,000], and I agreed. During the second debt, a client offered to 'dat tact' [pay off the rest of Phan's debt to have her 'released'], but the mama wouldn't allow it. I never went out of the apartment or snack because I was afraid of the mama's temper and also because I knew I was illegal and could be arrested. Then after I paid off the second 'tact' [contract], I took 150 bai [1.5 million yen; US$11,000] advance to send to my family and worked off a third debt of 300 bai [3 million yen; US$22,000]. In all I worked in this snack for the Taiwanese mama for more than a year. Once I paid off my third debt [in early 1992], I worked to get an extra 20 bai [200,000 yen; US$1,600] to leave. . . . The mama warned me that once a woman leaves her snack she has to leave the town of Kofu. This is because the mama is afraid that if the woman goes to work at another snack, her clients will follow her and take the mama's business away. So I went to

---

[303] Human Rights Watch and FOWIA interview, Chiba prefecture, Japan, May 20, 1995.

work in an 'awk kaek' snack in Shinjuku, Tokyo." Two months later, however, Phan decided to return to Kofu because her friends and regular customers were there. "When the mama from the snack I had worked at found out I was back in town, she threatened me, telling me to either work for her or to leave town. I refused. Then the mama with her older sister, a friend and two Yakuza members (who were also taxi drivers) took me out of town and beat me up." Phan left again, and this time stayed away for almost a year, until her Japanese boyfriend in Kofu offered to pay off the Yakuza to allow her to return.[304]

• Khai said that while she was in debt in 1992, her mama yelled at her, telling her that if she did not work harder to please the clients it would take at least a couple years for her to pay off her debt of 340 bai [3.4 million yen; US$27,000]. "But, I worked hard and actually paid off my debt in six months. I paid off my debt faster than any other woman in that snack. Then the mama told me I had to work for an additional two months at the snack, but I didn't have to take clients if I didn't want to. I still had to go with clients in order to get some money to leave the snack with, but I did not have to take as many clients as before. After these two months, I didn't have enough money saved to leave, and I didn't know where to go. But the mama told me I had to pay her 50 bai [500,000 yen; US$4,000] a month to continue working there. She also told me she would give me the (fake) passport that I traveled to Japan with, if I gave her 50 bai. I told her I had already paid off my debt and had the right to get my passport back. However, the mama insisted on the 50 bai and so I said 'forget it.' Soon after that, the mama sold me to another snack. I left with very few clothes or possessions. This snack was run directly by the Yakuza. I was told I was again in debt; this time for 200 bai [2 million yen; US$16,000]."[305]

Escape

The testimonies of women who escaped from debt bondage provide important insights into the difficulties and dangers of such attempts. Unfamiliar with Japan and far from their friends and family, women did not know where to go or who to turn to for help. Many resisted turning to Japanese authorities. Unable to communicate in Japanese, aware of their illegal status, and believing—in at least some cases correctly—that their employers had connections to the police, they

---

[304] Human Rights Watch and FOWIA interview, Chiang Rai province, Thailand, October 5, 1995.
[305] Human Rights Watch and FOWIA interview, Osaka prefecture, Japan, May 27, 1995.

feared being arrested and punished as illegal aliens or returned to their employers. Moreover, while all of the women Human Rights Watch interviewed about their escape attempts were successful, there is evidence that others are not so fortunate. As related above, Human Rights Watch heard stories of women being caught and killed or otherwise punished for trying to escape before their "debts" were repaid. We were not able to verify these accounts, but the fear they instilled in trafficked women was potent and real.

Human Rights Watch spoke to one woman who was returned to her snack bar owner by the police after she voluntarily surrendered to them in an attempt to get home. Sri recalled,

> When I arrived in Japan [in 1985] I was first sent to a snack bar in Ibaraki prefecture. I worked there for only one month. Then there was a fire at the snack, and the police came to the snack and asked who wanted to go home. I said I wanted to go home and asked to be arrested. The police took me and two other Thai women who also wanted to go home to the police station. We were separated at the police station and questioned by the police, but only about the fire. When the questioning was done the police released us the same day to our snack bar owner. The owner sold us to another snack in Ibaraki for 80 bai each [800,000 yen; US$3300].[306]

In a widely reported incident in the early 1990's, two police officers were forced to resign after releasing two Thai women in their custody to a former Yakuza member. An advocate who later assisted these women provided some of the details of the case to Human Rights Watch:

> On May 24, 1991, in Suzuka city, Mie prefecture, three Thai women were arrested. One Japanese man was with the women. There was some trouble and the police hit the man, and the man later said he would sue the police. He had gotten a doctor's certificate as proof of his injuries. The police negotiated to return the women to him if he would drop the charges. . . The police arranged with the man to release the women to him at Nagoya station on their way to Nara city. The police would

---

[306] Human Rights Watch and FOWIA interview, Osaka prefecture, Japan, May 26, 1995.

pretend that the women had escaped while going to the toilet. It turned out that the Japanese man was a former member of the Yakuza and was at Nagoya station with a current member of the Yakuza. Of the three women, two were thus returned to the Yakuza. The other one was taken to Tokyo Immigration. This case was widely reported in the media in the end of July. The police chief of Mie prefecture was transferred. The top officer from Suzuka city was forced to resign, with pension. He was the one responsible for investigating the case. The two police officers from Suzuka city who had directly negotiated with the man were also forced to resign on July 25, 1991, but were not charged with any crime. These two were members of the crime prevention unit that deals with bars, gangsters, and so on.[307]

An attorney working with a women's shelter in Tokyo explained to Human Rights Watch that "there are many cases in which women are returned by the police to snack bars because they cannot speak Japanese." She recounted one case in which a Filipina woman went to the police after being assaulted at the snack bar where she was working: "She was pushed down a flight of stairs and went to the police for help. The police returned her to the bar. She ran away twice and eventually went to [the shelter]."[308]

Women were also reluctant to turn to Japanese or Thai authorities because when officials assisted women in escaping, the women were deported as illegal aliens without any opportunity to seek back wages or other compensation for the violations they had faced. Still, Human Rights Watch interviewed four women who successfully relied on the assistance of Japanese or Thai government officials in their attempts to escape from debt bondage in snack bars (Miew, Korn, Gaew, Chan), and we received testimonies of two more cases from staff at Japanese women's shelters (Lai, Phon).[309] These women preferred to return to Thailand,

---

[307] Human Rights Watch interview with Sugiura, International Network of Engaged Buddhists, Aichi prefecture, Japan, March 22, 1994. See also "Mie Police Admit Their Secret Trade: Disposition of Suzuka Police Chief and a Lieutenant," *Yomiuri Shimbun*, July 25, 1991 (translated from Japanese).

[308] Human Rights Watch interview with Yukiko Oshima, Tokyo, Japan, March 17, 1994.

[309] Human Rights Watch also interviewed one woman, and received an interview transcript of another, who had escaped from debt bondage in Japanese brothels (Thip, and Hom, respectively). Both had escaped with assistance from Thai or Japanese authorities and were interviewed in women's shelters in Japan.

even empty-handed and fearing retaliation from their traffickers, rather than continue to face the abuses of their bosses and clients.[310]

- Chan had been working in debt bondage for three months when a client left her to take a taxi back to her apartment alone. Instead, she took the taxi to Tokyo and asked how to get to immigration. Immigration officials were not very helpful. "My mama's husband had followed me to the Japanese immigration office, but neither the Thai translator nor the immigration staff would help me hide from him." Finally, the Thai translator called a travel agent to help arrange Chan's trip back to Thailand, and the travel agent referred her to a nearby guesthouse for the night. The next day, Chan went to the Thai Embassy and, after spending one night there, she was sent to stay at a women's shelter until she was deported later that month, in February 1994. After Chan was deported, an agent followed her to her home in Korat asking for the rest of the debt. "I was afraid, so I left my family's home and came to Bangkok. I am still afraid they are following me even though it is one year later. I am afraid that if they catch up with me they will kill me. When I was in Japan, I heard that that is what they do to those who don't repay their debt. That is why very few women dare to escape. Everyone I knew stayed and finished their debt."[311]

- Miew's mama was very concerned about preventing escape attempts. "The mama told us [Miew and her coworkers] that if we tried to escape we would be followed and found by the Yakuza or police. She also took a pornographic photo of me to prevent me from escaping." Furthermore, one of Miew's friends at the snack bar told her about a woman who was killed for trying to escape. Still, Miew began thinking about ways to escape as soon as she realized the conditions under which she had to work to repay her debt. After about three months, in April 1999, she succeeded in escaping. "I asked many customers to help me escape. It was difficult at first because I didn't know who I could trust and I didn't speak enough Japanese to explain what I wanted

---

[310] It is likely that a disproportionately high percentage of the women interviewed for this report escaped (as opposed to completing their "contract"). Women who escape with the help of Thai Embassy officials or Japanese authorities are generally placed into privately run women's shelters, and in three of the eight escape cases described here, the interviews were conducted at such shelters (Lai, Phon, and Miew) Furthermore, two of the other five women who escaped (Korn and Gaew) were contacted through staff at a women's shelter where the women had stayed after their escape from debt bondage.

[311] Human Rights Watch and FOWIA interview, Bangkok, Thailand, March 2, 1995.

to my clients. Also, if I asked a customer to help me escape and he told my mama, I would be sold to another place with double debt. Finally, a customer that really liked me agreed to help me escape. I was lucky to get a regular customer who liked me. He contacted the Thai Embassy and got them to make up a CI paper [a CI paper, or "Certificate of Identity," is a temporary travel document that permits a Thai national who lacks a valid passport to reenter Thailand] for me (to prove my nationality, my family sent my house registration documents to the Embassy from Thailand). One day when the CI was ready, the client and I planned my escape. According to our plan, he drove down the street next to the apartment when I went to take the garbage out, and I jumped into the car. I was afraid of being seen so I laid down on the floor of the car while we drove away." Miew stayed at a women's shelter in Tokyo while awaiting her return to Thailand. While she was there, she told her story to the police. "At first I was afraid of the police, because I thought they might tell someone where I was staying. But the shelter staff told me not to worry about that. So I gave all of the information to the police because I was angry at my boss and mama, who told me I owed heavy debts. Also, some other women at the snack wanted to escape."[312]

• In 1995, Korn and Gaew accepted job offers at a snack in Chiba prefecture, but then found that they had been sold into debt bondage. According to Korn, "As soon as we realized we had been tricked, we tried to escape." Korn wrote to her brother in Thailand, who asked a journalist to help her. The journalist knew an official at the Thai Embassy in Japan, Udom Sapito, and sent him the photograph and telephone number of the snack, which Korn had given her brother. Sapito then referred the photograph and telephone number to a women's shelter that assists trafficking victims and other foreign women in Japan, and the shelter staff arranged a rescue attempt by Japanese men posing as snack bar clients. The rescue was successful and Korn and Gaew were taken to the women's shelter to await deportation. But as mentioned above, these women told Human Rights Watch that they would not return to their families because of the threats of retaliation made by their mama. [313]

When we spoke to the then recently-appointed First Secretary of the Thai Embassy, Nopporn Ratchawej, in April 1999, he told us that in his first three months at the Embassy, he had helped rescue four women who were being held

---

[312] Human Rights Watch interview, Tokyo, Japan, April 16, 1999.

[313] Human Rights Watch and FOWIA telephone interviews, Kanagawa prefecture, Japan, May 1995.

against their will in snack bars or brothels. He had arranged to meet them near their place of work or residence, took them back to the Embassy, and then placed them in privately-run Japanese women's shelters. And he had done this without the help of the Japanese police. He explained to Human Rights Watch that he did not have time to ask for their assistance: "One woman, for example, called at night and I had to meet her the next morning. She was working in [a Tokyo suburb], and she said she could get out when the mama was sleeping in the morning. So I told her to meet me at the subway station the next day."[314] Human Rights Watch later met this woman while she was staying at a woman's shelter awaiting her return to Thailand. She said that her agent in Bangkok had promised her a job as a waitress, but when she arrived in Japan she was forced to work in a brothel, serving numerous clients each day. So she called a relative in Thailand to get the Thai Embassy's phone number in Tokyo, and then managed to call the embassy one night when her employers were sleeping. "Fortunately," she said, "I spoke to an officer who understood my situation. He told me how to get to the train station and then he brought me to stay at [the woman's shelter]."[315]

Occasionally, women may escape from debt bondage without turning to government officials for assistance. The following women escaped from their initial employers and then continued to live and work in Japan for several years, despite threats of retaliation from their traffickers:

• Bee escaped from a snack bar in Yokohama without fully repaying her debt, but her agent, who was also one of her relatives, found out and threatened her family. "The agent went to my family and warned 'if Bee cannot pay her debt, I will take your land and house from you.' My family was shocked and they contacted me, saying 'there is a big problem, so send money to us immediately.'" So Bee sent them money to pay off the agent.[316]

• When Pong went to Japan with one of her sisters, she had an older sister who was already working there. Pong explained that she was able to escape because she had this older sister living in Japan whom her mama did not know about: "After two months, I called my older sister and ran away. I had argued with the mama before and told her that I would call the police, and she said to go ahead, that I had more to fear from them than she did. I wasn't afraid of the mama. She was also without legal status. She was from Laos, and she couldn't go out without her boyfriend's permission. When I left, I threatened to go to the

---

[314] Ibid.

[315] Human Rights Watch interview with Thip, Tokyo, Japan, April 16, 1999.

[316] Interview by M. N., Chiang Rai province, Thailand, September 12, 1997.

police, so the mama didn't dare do anything. But when I called the snack bar later to talk to one of the other women, the woman told me that the mama had sent the Yakuza to follow me.[317] But the Yakuza couldn't find me because I had gone to my older sister's. My other sister stayed at the snack for three more months. She was afraid to escape right away. When she left, she had been working for five months so she had one month of debt left."[318]

- Khai escaped with the help of a Yakuza member after being resold by her mama to another snack bar. She explained, "This snack was run by the Yakuza directly. I was told I was again in debt and this time for 200 bai. I paid off nearly 100 bai of this debt. Then I met a Thai woman who invited me to work in Osaka. I ran away from the snack with the help of a Yakuza member. I had to leave without anything and the Yakuza member gave me ten bai to go to Osaka."[319]

---

[317] Pong explained that she could call the snack bar because the owner there was not directly connected to her mama. Many mamas brought "their women" to this bar to work.

[318] Human Rights Watch interview, Chiang Rai province, Thailand, April 24, 1999.

[319] Human Rights Watch and FOWIA interview, Osaka prefecture, Japan, May 27, 1995.

VIII. DEPORTATION AS "ILLEGAL ALIENS"

Nearly all of the women trafficked to Japan eventually return to Thailand. Most voluntarily surrender to Japanese immigration officials after they have been released from debt and have decided to go home. Some turn to the authorities for assistance in their efforts to escape from debt bondage. And others are arrested during police or immigration raids. In all of these cases, the trafficked women are deported to Thailand as "illegal aliens," without any official acknowledgment of the coercive nature of their migration and employment in Japan. While Thai and Japanese officials sometimes facilitate the women's deportation, helping them obtain the necessary documentation and funds for the trip, neither government takes any steps to provide trafficked women with redress for the abuses they have suffered. Moreover, some women have reported abusive treatment by Thai immigration officials upon their arrival back in Thailand, and others have found themselves indefinitely barred from reentering Thailand due to their inability to provide proof of Thai nationality. Finally, trafficked persons who are arrested by Japanese officials are subjected to punitive treatment that is wholly inappropriate for victims of trafficking and, often, fails to meet minimum international standards for due process and treatment of detainees.

Voluntary surrender

In 1995, the Immigration Bureau estimated that about seventy percent of foreigners who overstay their visas in Japan eventually surrender to authorities voluntarily in order to return to their country of origin.[320] Human Rights Watch found that this was common practice among women from Thailand, and most of the women we interviewed returned to Thailand after voluntarily surrendering to immigration. Some had just escaped from the abuses of debt bondage, but most decided to return some time after their debt had been repaid in order to rejoin the families they had been working to support. Women who surrendered voluntarily were generally issued deportation orders by Japanese immigration officials and then allowed to await their deportation without being held in detention facilities. Those in need of shelter were referred by Japanese or Thai officials to privately-run women's shelters—government women's shelters do not accept undocumented migrants—where they stayed while travel arrangements were made. For women with the necessary documentation and funding for the return trip to Thailand, these arrangements could be completed within a few days.

---

[320] "Changes in deportation process planned," *Kalabaw newsletter,* no. 29, December 1995, p. 3.

Difficulties in obtaining the documentation and funds to return home

Other women, however, faced long delays as they tried to collect the identification and funds needed to return home. In some cases, Thai or Japanese officials facilitated women's deportation by contacting their employers and demanding their passports and/or travel money. Chan explained to Human Rights Watch that, after she escaped from her snack bar in 1994 without any identification or money to return home, "The Thai embassy called the mama for my passport. After talking with her for a long time, the bar owner sent the passport and 50,000 yen (US$490) for the air ticket."[321] A local government labor official in Tokyo confirmed that this is regular practice among Japanese immigration officials as well:

> I have heard that immigration officials try to get unpaid wages back themselves in some cases to pay for plane tickets. I understand that they do this because detainees don't have any money, but they should get back all of the wages, not just enough to cover travel expenses. Sometimes they will ask for more than just the travel expenses, but if the detainee has enough for the ticket already, they won't contact the employer at all.[322]

Attorney Yoko Yoshida, who has assisted migrant women in detention, confirmed this practice, though she described it somewhat differently: "The interest of immigration officials is to deport foreigners, and they don't want to use Japanese government money.[323] So they use the provision in the Immigration Act that prohibits employing illegal migrants as a threat to get travel money from employers. They are not interested in punishing the employers or collecting the women's wages. In some cases, they will enforce penalties for employing illegals, but only when the working conditions are very bad or there are many workers."[324]

Women who cannot produce a valid passport—either because they entered Japan on fraudulent papers or because their documents were confiscated by their brokers or employers and cannot be retrieved—must convince Thai Embassy officials that they are Thai nationals, in order to obtain a "Certificate of Identity" (CI paper) that allows reentry into Thailand. An officer at the Japan Desk of the

---

[321] Human Rights Watch interview, Bangkok, Thailand, March 2, 1995.

[322] Human Rights Watch interview, Tokyo, Japan, April 14, 1999.

[323] According to Japan's Immigration Control Act, "when an alien who has been issued a written deportation order determines to return to his/her country of origin via personal burden of expenses, an IDC warden or a chief Inspection officer may permit the alien to do so based on a petition for return submitted by the alien." (Article 52(4)). The law does not say who will cover travel expenses if the alien cannot.

[324] Human Rights Watch interview, Kyoto, Japan, April 13, 1999.

Thai Ministry of Foreign Affairs' Division of Consular Affairs in Bangkok told Human Rights Watch that she contacts family members of women who wish to return to Thailand to collect birth certificates, house registration, and other documents, and then sends these papers to embassy officials. The First Secretary of the Thai Embassy in Japan, Nopporn Ratchawej, said that he can also issue CI papers on the basis of a personal interview.[325]

The Thai Embassy will also assist women in collecting the necessary funds to return home by contacting friends in Japan or asking the Thai Ministry of Foreign Affairs to collect money from the women's relatives in Thailand. Eventually, if a woman is still unable to raise enough money for her airfare, the Thai government will give her a loan. The Japan Desk Officer at the Consular Affairs Department of the Thai Ministry of Foreign Affairs explained to Human Rights Watch that there is no deadline for repayment, but there is a ban on traveling abroad again until the loan has been repaid.[326]

Women who cannot produce any proof of identity, however, face a more intractable problem. In particular, women whose nationality was questionable—or undocumented—before they left Thailand can find it extremely difficult to prove their nationality after being trafficked to Japan. Human Rights Watch found that staff of Japanese NGOs have stepped in to help women in particularly difficult cases. Reiko Aoki, Secretary of the Kyoto YWCA, described the case of a Thai woman who was born in Bangkok, but whose birth was never registered: "This woman went to Japan and worked, and then she wanted to return to Thailand, but they wouldn't accept her because she wasn't registered as a Thai national. It took us six months to get in touch with the man she thought was her father, get him to go to the hospital where she was born, get the hospital to issue a birth certificate, and then finally get permission for this woman to return to Thailand."[327]

---

[325] Human Rights Watch telephone interview with Maliwan, Japan Desk Officer, Division of Protection of Thai Nationals Abroad, Consular Affairs Department, Ministry of Foreign Affairs, Bangkok, Thailand, April 30, 1999; Human Rights Watch interview, Royal Thai Embassy, Tokyo, Japan, April 15, 1999.

The Thai Embassy's policy of issuing CI papers has greatly facilitated the repatriation of thousands of Thai migrants, including victims of trafficking and debt bondage. Embassy statistics for the period from January 1996 through March 1999 indicate that CI papers are issued to more than 2500 Thai nationals each year; of these, about sixty percent were issued to women.

[326] Human Rights Watch interview, Royal Thai Embassy, Tokyo, Japan, April 15, 1999; Human Rights Watch telephone interview with Maliwan, Japan Desk Officer, Division of Protection of Thai Nationals Abroad, Consular Affairs Department, Ministry of Foreign Affairs, Bangkok, Thailand, April 30, 1999.

[327] Human Rights Watch interview, Kyoto, Japan, April 11, 1999.

Other women have found themselves barred indefinitely from reentering Thailand. One woman interviewed by Human Rights Watch in Japan explained that she wanted to return to Thailand, but had no way to prove her identity. Khai grew up in Thailand, but she has no idea where she was born. At age four she was taken to Bangkok to live with a family as their maid. She was never allowed to go to school because she had no official papers, and she was always told that she was a refugee. When Khai was about sixteen years old—she is not sure of her exact year of birth—she went to see the doctor who had arranged her placement in this family's home:

> I insisted he tell me where my mother was. The doctor told me my mother had remarried and had two more kids so I should not make things difficult for everyone. Then I went back to the home of the family who raised me. I tried to swallow enough medicine to kill myself because no one cared about me. I was so lonely and everyone was disgusted by me, even the other kids. It was like I wasn't human. The family even referred to me as an animal, rather than a person. I was taken to the hospital where I was treated for one month for the overdose. During that time no one came to see me and the staff treated me so badly.
>
> When I was released I went to the house to get my belongings and left to find a job. The son of the family I was living with rented me an apartment and brought me clients to prostitute myself. I was a prostitute just as I was beginning to get breasts and before I even started menstruating. I worked for this "brother" for quite some time.[328]

Khai was trafficked to Japan in December 1991. After working for eight months to pay off her debt in one snack bar, and then being resold to another, Khai escaped. When we interviewed her in 1995, she had been working independently at snack bars and on the streets since her escape, sending her earnings to a friend in Thailand who she thought would help her get a Thai ID card. As she explained, "I sent all my money to my friend's account in Thailand. I recently learned that my friend spent all my money and didn't save it for me as she had promised. So, now

---

[328] Human Rights Watch and FOWIA interview, Osaka prefecture, Japan, May 27, 1995.

I have no savings at all. I gave my friend so much money believing she would help me get a Thai ID card. I would like to go back to Thailand."[329]

In our conversations with activists and lawyers in Japan, Human Rights Watch learned of numerous cases in which women were denied the right to return to their homes and families in Thailand. Rutsuko Shoji, the Director of HELP Asian Women's Shelter in Tokyo, told Human Rights Watch about three cases that HELP was pursuing at the time of our interview. The women concerned had traveled from Thailand to Japan through trafficking networks, who provided them with false passports, handled their travel arrangements, and then delivered them into debt bondage labor in Japan. Two of the women were hilltribe people and the third was a third generation Vietnamese "refugee" from Thailand.[330] The Vietnamese woman was born and raised in a designated refugee camp in Thailand and had lived in Thailand continuously until leaving for Japan at age sixteen. Her family members were later accorded Thai citizenship under legislation that was adopted after she had left the country. The two hilltribe women grew up with their families on the Thai-Burma border. Their births were not officially registered, and they did not possess official Thai citizenship, though one had a hand-written letter from a village leader in northern Thailand stating that she was born in December 1968 in his general vicinity.

When we interviewed Shoji in April 1999, these three women were living in a state of legal and social limbo. They had been denied permission to reenter Thailand, despite their strong links to the country, as evidenced through their family ties, place of birth, language, and long-term residency in the country. The Japanese authorities, on the other hand, had issued them orders of deportation; while they were allowed to reside outside of detention facilities, they did not have the right to work and could not access any of the health or social services that are reserved for Japanese citizens and long-term (or permanent) legal foreign residents.[331]

The women first realized that they were "stateless" after they surrendered voluntarily to Japanese immigration officials, expecting to be issued CI papers by the Thai Embassy and repatriated. The Thai Embassy, however, refused to recognize them as Thai nationals and denied them permission to reenter the country. The women then turned to HELP for assistance. HELP staff members tried without success to convince Thai officials to allow the women to reenter Thailand. They also lobbied the Japanese government to regularize the women's status by granting

---

[329] Ibid.

[330] Thailand's treatment of hilltribe people and refugees will be discussed in greater detail in the "Thai Government Response" chapter.

[331] See the "Japanese Government Response" chapter for a further discussion of these policies.

them special residency permits. They hoped that if the women had permission to reside in Japan, the Thai government would provide them with at least temporary visitor visas for Thailand. But Japanese officials also dragged their feet. Under pressure from the Tokyo bar association, the immigration bureau eventually agreed to accept the women's applications for permits, but many months passed before the women were called in for interviews to complete the application process.

When Human Rights Watch followed up on the women's situation in March 2000, they were still in Japan, but progress had been made. With persistent efforts on the part of HELP staff members, as well as pressure from local protection officers of the United Nations High Commissioner for Refugees, two of the women had been issued one-year Japanese residency permits with reentry permission. In response, the Thai government had agreed to issue them visitor visas for Thailand. The third woman could probably have gotten a permit as well, but HELP staff members had lost touch with her. She left Tokyo when it seemed she had little chance of ever being able to return to Thailand, and HELP staff members were unable to locate her to tell her about the progress they had made with Japanese officials.[332]

Human Rights Watch interviewed one woman who managed to return to Thailand from Japan despite her lack of citizenship. Her testimony demonstrates how the Thai government's unyielding policy provides criminals and corrupt government officials with opportunities for profit:

> Phan was born in Burma, but moved to Thailand with her family as a young teenager. Her experiences of being trafficking into Japan and then working under conditions of debt bondage are described in the previous two chapters. About four years after arriving in Japan, Phan decided that she wanted to return to Thailand. She had repaid her debt, saved some money, and was pregnant with her Japanese boyfriend's child, and she wanted to have the baby in Thailand where it would be less expensive and her extended family would be there to support her. Phan recalled, "When I told my friends I wanted to go home, they told me about 'Y.' They said he could help to get me home. 'Y' told me I would either have to buy an illegal Thai house registration or else agree to go back to Burma. So I bought a fake Thai house

[332] Human Rights Watch interview with Rutsuko Shoji, Director, HELP Asian Women's Shelter, Tokyo, Japan, April 8, 1999. Information supplemented by e-mail, facsimile, and telephone communication to Human Rights Watch by Rutsuko Shoji and her staff over a several month period from August 1999 to March 2000.

registration for 30,000 baht [US$1,200] plus another 6,000 baht [US$240] to get it and send it to me. When I received the documents I went to the Thai embassy with 'Y.' I gave them the documents and four photos and received my CI. . . . I returned to Thailand in 1995. When I arrived at Don Muang airport I just walked off the plane and a Thai immigration officer asked me 'are you the young Burmese girl?' I said 'yes.' The same friend who had arranged for me to get a fake Thai house registration had also arranged for me to get through immigration. I paid the immigration office 15 bai [150,000 yen; US$1,600] in Japanese yen. I had also bought three bottles of whiskey—one for the immigration officer and one for [my friend's] relative and the other for my father."[333]

Abusive treatment of deportees

Once they obtain the necessary funds and paperwork for their return to Thailand, trafficked women are deported by the Japanese government as illegal aliens. In accordance with Japan's usual deportation procedures, fines and jail terms for immigration offenses are typically waived or suspended, but a temporary ban on reentering Japan is imposed on the basis of the women's alleged immigration offenses (until February 18, 2000, this penalty was one year; it has since been increased to five years).[334] Human Rights Watch recognizes states' right to control their borders. However, Japan's application of this punitive measure when repatriating victims of trafficking is symptomatic of the government's generally inappropriate response to the problem of trafficking. Far from being treated as victims of serious human rights abuses, trafficked women are held responsible for violations of Japanese immigration laws that have resulted directly from their being trafficked. In addition, for women who have started families in Japan—and seek to return to Thailand so that they can reenter Japan legally on spousal visas—this penalty has meant long family separations.

After women arrive in Thailand, those traveling on CI papers have to submit to a special interview with Thai immigration officials at the airport: Human Rights Watch was told that officials often try to extort money from the women returning from Japan. Nung told us that when she surrendered to Japanese immigration authorities, an officer warned her that she might have trouble with the immigration officials at the airport in Thailand. Later, when she arrived at Don Muang airport,

---

[333] Human Rights Watch and FOWIA interview, Chiang Rai province, Thailand, October 5, 1995.
[334] Immigration Control Act, Article 5(9).

"an officer who knew I had returned from working in Japan asked me to pay 10,000 yen [US$84[335]]. At that time, I had only 1000 baht [US$40] in my purse, and he took 500 baht [US$20] away. My friend had 5000 yen [US$42] taken away by officers."[336] Another woman, Pong, explained how she avoided giving money to immigration officials when she arrived in Thailand in 1991. Since she was traveling on CI papers, "I had a long interview with immigration officers in the airport here. They asked me whether I made a lot of money, and when I said 'no' they didn't bother me. Usually, if you say you made lots of money, they ask for some."[337]

Arrest, detention, and deportation

Though most women voluntarily surrender to authorities, many others are deported after being arrested by police or immigration officials for their undocumented immigration status. Human Rights Watch found that their treatment routinely violates international standards. Victims of trafficking are subjected to arbitrary and sometimes prolonged detention, without sufficient judicial oversight. They are not informed of their rights, including their right to consular assistance, and there is a strong presumption of guilt in the determination of their cases. Human Rights Watch also found evidence of substandard, and even abusive, detention conditions, as well as excessive restrictions on—and censorship of—detainees' communication.

Arbitrary arrest of trafficking victims

During raids on snack bars and other establishments where undocumented migrants are employed, trafficking victims are routinely arrested and then detained until their deportation date. Police even arrest and detain women who are clearly working under coercive conditions at the time of the police raid. This treatment is inappropriate, as women who have been deceived into entering the country illegally; placed into debt bondage upon their arrival and forced to remain in the country until after their visas have expired; or forced to perform activities "outside their visa status" are not guilty of the associated immigration offenses.

Human Rights Watch interviewed two women who were arrested for immigration violations and received detailed testimonies from four others. At least four of these women were victims of trafficking; the other two did not provide enough information about the circumstances of their travel or initial job placement

---

[335] It is unclear from her testimony what year she returned to Thailand, so this dollar amount has been calculated using the average exchange rate over the nine year period from 1990 through 1998.

[336] Interview by M. N., Chiang Rai province, Thailand, August 6, 1997.

[337] Human Rights Watch interview, Chiang Rai province, Thailand, April 24, 1999.

to determine whether or not they were trafficked. One of the women we interviewed was arrested before her debt had been repaid:

- Nuch was arrested in 1993 when police officers raided the snack bar where she was being forced to work off a debt of 380 bai (3.8 million yen; US$34,000). According to Nuch, the police came at 9:00 a.m. before anyone had gotten up, and, when the mama's daughter opened the door, she was faced with numerous police officers and police cars. The officers included three Japanese women who spoke Thai. Nuch recalled, "they asked me and the others in Thai whether we wanted to go home, and said if so, to get our clothes. Only myself and one other woman got our clothes, but everyone was arrested: the mama, her husband, his two Taiwanese friends, and the seven Thai women [who worked in the snack bar]. One Thai woman had just finished paying off her debt after two years and was about to be paid for the first time for twenty clients. She was especially upset. We were all taken to the police station in the town. There we were asked for all of the details about what had happened to us."[338]

Nuch was then detained in three different jails over the next few months before being transferred to an immigration detention center, and finally returning to Thailand.

In another case we documented, seventeen Thai women who were working in debt bondage in Kofu were arrested and deported for overstaying their visas. The mama of the bar, Sri, insisted that she treated the women well, but she also described coercive conditions amounting to forced labor. Her boyfriend, the snack bar owner, "bought" the women and forced them to repay a debt of approximately twice their purchase price. Sri paid the Yakuza each month for services which included following any of the women who ran away. When the snack was raided in 1992, all of the women were detained and deported, but the snack bar owner spent only twenty days in jail. As Sri recalled:

> The snack was raided and all seventeen girls working there were arrested; only I managed to escape. I think the snack next door reported us because they were jealous of our business. My boyfriend was arrested and had to pay 500 bai [5 million yen; US$39,500] and spend twenty days in jail. Afterwards he was on probation for three years and was not allowed to operate another

---

[338] Human Rights Watch and FOWIA interview, Bangkok, Thailand, March 1995.

snack during that time. The seventeen girls were detained as overstayers and deported back to Thailand.[339]

Newspaper accounts of raids on snack bars and other entertainment venues also consistently indicate that Japanese officials arrest foreign women for immigration violations, such as failure to carry their passports, overstaying their visas, or working without proper work visas, even when they find clear evidence of coercion on the part of their employers.[340]

Arbitrary and prolonged detention

Persons detained for immigration offenses are almost always kept in detention until their day of deportation. Human Rights Watch conducted interviews with (or received detailed interview transcripts from) six women who recounted their arrests for immigration violations. Orn, who was seven months pregnant, was allowed to reside at a women's shelter in Tokyo while she awaited her deportation date.[341] But the other five women were forced to remain in detention while arrangements for

---

[339] Human Rights Watch and FOWIA interview, Osaka prefecture, Japan, May 26, 1995.

[340] In a recent example, seventy people were arrested in early 1999 in a major crackdown on the trafficking of Colombian women into the Japanese sex industry. The Metropolitan Police Department in Tokyo also obtained arrest warrants for several brokers in Colombia, and they classified the illegal brokers into three sectors: those who recruit women in Colombia; those who accompany the Colombian women to help them enter Japan; and those who coerce the women to work in prostitution clubs and striptease theaters. Despite officials' seeming understanding of the coercive practices involved in the operations, however, they also arrested fourteen Colombian women who were working as prostitutes or strippers. Moreover, reports indicated that the three brokers who were arrested in the crackdown were charged on suspicion of violating the prostitution prevention law and the immigration control law; there was no mention of charges related to the abuse they inflicted on the women. ("70 held in move to stem prostitution," *Asahi Shimbun* (English edition), June 17, 1999.)

For other examples of arrests, see: "Nagoya Immigration Control Bureau accosted 6 foreign women," *Asahi Shimbun* (Japanese edition), July 10, 1999; "Date club owner arrested in Yokohama," *Kanagawa Shimbun* (Japanese edition), June 15, 1994; "Prosecution in Yokohama," *Kanagawa Shimbun* (Japanese edition), November 13, 1993; "Police Arrest Two Japanese Accused of Trading Women," *Yomiuri Shimbun,* October 9, 1992. Note that these articles do not always provide enough information to determine whether or not the women were working in coercive conditions.

[341] Interview transcript provided by a staff member at a women's shelter in Japan, who worked with Orn during 1993.

their deportation were being made, even though at least three of them had been trafficked into Japan.[342]

International human rights standards provide that detainees have the right to prompt judicial review of both the initial detention decision and any continuance of detention.[343] The strong presumption towards continued detention in immigration proceedings, and the lack of either periodic review or time limits for continued detention, suggests a violation of the right to fair legal procedures for the review of detention decisions. Japanese immigration law provides that suspects may be held for up to sixty days before a deportation determination is made,[344] and indefinitely once deportation orders have been issued.[345] The law does not explicitly mandate the continued detention of all suspects, but internal guidelines prepared by the Immigration Bureau state, "As regards the deportation procedures, though there are no explicit provisions stipulating that all suspects should be detained, it is understood that the Act provides for a so-called 'detention always comes before deportation' ('detention in principle') policy."[346] The Immigration Control Act

---

[342] See interviews with Nuch, Kaew, Jo, Ane, and Gap.

[343] According to the ICCPR, Article 9(1,4): "No one shall be deprived of his liberty except on such grounds and in accordance with such procedure as are established by law. . . . Anyone who is deprived of his liberty by arrest or detention shall be entitled to take proceedings before a court, in order that court may decide without delay on the lawfulness of his detention and order his release if the detention is not lawful." Prolonged detention without judicial review is also contrary to the standards enunciated in the United Nations Body of Principles for the Protection of All Persons under Any Form of Detention or Imprisonment, which demands that all detainees be afforded prompt judicial review of their cases, as well as judicial review for the continuance of detention (Principles 11, 37).

[344] The period of detention for accused is generally limited to thirty days under Article 41 of the Immigration Control Act, but it may be extended for another thirty days if "a Supervising Immigration Inspector finds that there are unavoidable circumstances." There is no discussion of what does and does not qualify as "unavoidable," and there are no checks on the SII's power to make this determination.

[345] According to Article 52, a deportee shall be deported without delay, but if this is not possible, then an Immigration Control Officer may detain him in an Immigration Center, detention house, or other places designated by the Minister of Justice or by a Supervising Immigration Inspector commissioned by the Minister of Justice until such time as deportation becomes possible." There is no elaboration of the valid or invalid reasons why "a deportee cannot be deported immediately," and there are no limits put on the time that can pass before "deportation becomes possible."

[346] Quoted in Immigration Review Task Force (IRTF), "The Actual Status of the Deportation Procedures and Immigration Detention Facilities in Japan," Japan, 1998, p. 3. Note that as explained above, foreigners who voluntarily surrender to immigration authorities are exempted from this policy.

allows for provisional release of persons detained under written detention or deportation order,[347] but in practice such release is rarely granted. The Immigration Review Task Force (IRTF) found that only one of forty applications for provisional release is accepted, and concluded that release is generally granted only to "those who are prepared to leave at their own expense and are married to Japanese nationals."[348] Attorney Yoko Yoshida similarly explained, "Provisional release, even on bail, is never granted to overstayers unless they are married to a Japanese person. A detainee can ask for provisional release, but they will be refused unless they have a connection to a Japanese person, like a Japanese husband."[349] Rieko Aoki, who assists foreign women through her work with Asian People Together (APT) at the Kyoto YWCA, told Human Rights Watch about a migrant woman who was detained for immigration violations when she went to the police after being raped by an assailant armed with a knife:

> We tried to get provisional release for her. This woman was suffering from injuries she had sustained when she was raped by an assailant who was armed with a knife, and so she was suffering in detention. . . . We asked the immigration officials and the judge to release her, but they refused, saying that because she was an overstayer she had no address. We offered to be responsible and to use the YWCA's address, but they still refused. So she was detained until she was deported.[350]

According to local advocates in Japan, it is not unusual for the period of immigration detention to exceed six months.[351] Human Rights Watch interviewed one woman, Kaew, who spent only five days in the Tokyo IDC before returning to

---

[347] Article 52 allows ICOs to detain deportees until deportation becomes possible, but it also allows IDC Directors and SIIs to release such persons "under conditions deems necessary such as restrictions on place of residence and area of movement and duty of appearing at a summons."

[348] IRTF, "The Actual Status of the Deportation Procedures and Immigration Detention Facilities in Japan," pp. 14-15.

[349] Human Rights Watch interview, Kyoto, Japan, April 13, 1999.

[350] Human Rights Watch interview, Kyoto, Japan, April 13, 1999.

[351] Human Rights Watch interview with Rutsuko Shoji, Director, HELP Asian Women's Shelter, Tokyo, Japan, April 8, 1999. See also Attorney Tadanori Onitsuka, *The situation of Alien Deportation Procedures in Japan* (1995), p. 5. See also Human Rights Committee, "Concluding observations of the Human Rights Committee : Japan," November 19, 1998 (CCPR/C/79/Add.102).

Thailand. "I didn't have to stay long," she explained, "because I had my passport and enough money for the trip home." But she also noted, "Many women had been in the IDC for a long time."[352] As explained above, the deportation of trafficked women is often delayed by the difficulties they face in obtaining the necessary documents and funding to return home. In at least one case in the early 1990s, a woman from Thailand was held in detention for nearly two years while her nationality was in dispute.[353] The Immigration Review Task Force has reported that detention pending deportation is also commonly prolonged because detainees cannot afford to pay for the trip back to their country of origin.[354] The Japanese government does provide some money to cover foreigners' deportation costs, but this funding is used at the discretion of immigration officers; there is no mechanism for detainees to apply for or request these resources.[355]

Detention becomes arbitrary when immigration detainees are held indefinitely and do not know when they will be released.[356] To protect against the arbitrary or capricious detention of undocumented migrants, all efforts should be made to minimize the period of detention. Human Rights Watch believes that when initial attempts to secure the funding and documentation for a person's deportation from Japan fail, a review system should be in place to assess the need for continued detention on the basis of specified conditions; if detention is continued, it should be subject to periodic review.

Violations of due process in deportation procedures

Our research also indicated that deportation procedures fail to uphold the rights of those detained and make it virtually impossible for them to understand, let

---

[352] Human Rights Watch interview, Chiang Rai province, Thailand, April 25, 1999.

[353] Human Rights Watch interview with Rutsuko Shoji, Director, HELP Asian Women's Shelter, Tokyo, Japan, April 8, 1999. See also Onitsuka, *The situation of Alien Deportation Procedures in Japan*, p. 5.

[354] IRTF, "The Actual Status of the Deportation Procedures and Immigration Detention Facilities in Japan," p. 15.

[355] Onitsuka, *The situation of Alien Deportation Procedures in Japan*, p. 5. As will be discussed below, this money has been used in at least two incidences to expedite the deportation of detainees who had filed civil suits against the government for compensation for abuses suffered in detention.

[356] Arbitrary detention has been defined not only as contrary to law but as including elements of inappropriateness, injustice and lack of predictability (*Van Alphen v. Netherlands* (U.N. Human Rights Committee, Communication No. 305) 1988. See also discussion in Human Rights Watch, "Locked Away: Immigration Detainees in Jails in the United States," *A Human Rights Watch Report,* vol. 10, no. 1, September 1998, pp. 24-26).

alone challenge, the proceedings. International human rights standards guarantee detainees the right to be presumed innocent until proven guilty, the right not to testify against themselves, the right to an attorney, adequate opportunities to communicate with and receive visits by legal counsel and family members, and the right to be informed of their rights and of the charges against them promptly and in a language they understand. Foreign detainees should also be given the opportunity to communicate with representatives from their country's embassy or consulate.[357] Japanese immigration procedures fall far short of these guarantees. They are characterized by a presumption of guilt, highly restricted access to legal counsel, and a failure to adequately explain or translate charges and procedures.

The Immigration Control Act provides that a person accused of entering Japan without a valid passport—an offense which carries penalties of up to three years of imprisonment—"shall prove for himself" that s/he is not guilty.[358] It is unacceptable to place the burden of proving innocence on the defendant. Moreover, immigration procedures make it nearly impossible for the accused to mount an effective defense. Critical decisions are made behind closed doors with little opportunity for suspects to present a defense. Both the initial determination of guilt by the Immigration Inspector and the review of suspects' objections by the Minister of Justice are made without the benefit of any type of hearing or trial. The only opportunity for the accused or her representative to produce evidence and cross-examine witnesses is during the hearing (if the accused requests one), and even these procedures are heavily restricted and controlled by the Special Inquiry Officer (SIO). Only one of the suspect's relatives or friends may be admitted to the hearing, and even then only with the SIO's permission; although the suspect may request that certain witnesses be ordered to come forward and testify, it is up to the SIO's discretion whether to call the witnesses.[359]

Immigration officers routinely interrogate suspects to establish grounds for deportation without making any effort to inform them of their right not to

---

[357] These non-binding, but authoritative standards are established by the Body of Principles for the Protection of all Persons under Any Form of Detention or Imprisonment and the United Nations Standard Minimum Rules for the Treatment of Prisoners. They apply to *all* individuals in detention for any reason.

[358] Article 46.

[359] Article 48, which refers to Article 10(3-5).

incriminate themselves or their right to an attorney.[360] Access to attorneys is strictly limited and monitored throughout the period in which detainees are held and determinations regarding their deportation and/or punishment for immigration violations are made.[361] There is no provision for appointing legal counsel for those who cannot afford to retain a lawyer themselves.[362] Virtually all proceedings are conducted entirely in Japanese without the presence of an interpreter, including the written summary record of interrogations, which the suspect is asked to sign to establish its truthfulness.[363] In 1995, Immigration Review Task Force members went to the Philippines and interviewed ten persons who had recently been arrested,

---

[360] Japanese law does not guarantee immigration detainees the right to not to testify against themselves or the right to counsel, despite the protections established under the Japanese Constitution. Article 38-1 of the Constitution states: "No person shall be compelled to testify against himself;" and Article 34 provides: "No person shall be arrested or detained without being at once informed of the charges against him or without the immediate privilege of counsel." The Constitution makes no distinction between different types of detention, indicating that these protections should apply to detainees in both immigration and criminal cases, but immigration laws and regulations do not make any reference to such rights. A Japanese court ruled on May 26, 1960 that, while the right to counsel applies to criminal procedures, it is not guaranteed during immigration procedures. In reference to this ruling, a Japanese immigration attorney noted that: "Constitutional law scholars have concluded that this provision is applicable to administrative procedures where by such procedures entail the prolonged physical confinement of an individual. In this sense, such administrative confinement differs only very slightly from arrests and moreover poses little conflict to the need for administrative expediency." (Onitsuka, *The Situation of Alien Deportation Procedures in Japan*, p. 4.)

[361] According to IRTF, "Even if a lawyer is appointed, he or she is not considered a formal representative under the immigration procedures. Communication with the appointed lawyer by telephone or mail is restricted; documents from the lawyer are censored; and guards often monitor meetings between detainees and their lawyers." (IRTF, "The Actual Status of the Deportation Procedures and Immigration Detention Facilities in Japan," p. 5.) One member of IRTF explained to Human Rights Watch that while the criminal procedure code states that lawyers "can meet" with clients without the attendance of guards, even this weak "guarantee" does not apply under immigration law and guards typically attend all lawyer-client meetings. (Human Rights Watch interview with Toru Takahashi, member of IRTF, Tokyo, Japan, April 8, 1999.)

[362] Human Rights Watch interview with Toru Takahashi, member of IRTF, Tokyo, Japan, April 8, 1999.

[363] Exceptions may be made for persons with absolutely no knowledge of Japanese. See IRTF, "The Actual Status of the Deportation Procedures and Immigration Detention Facilities in Japan," p. 19; Onitsuka, *The situation of Alien Deportation Procedures in Japan*, pp. 2-3.

detained, and deported from Japan. In every case, they found that "no interpreter nor adequate translation of procedural information or legal rights was given by immigration authorities. All interviewees felt they could not fully understand the charges against them, what they were being interrogated about nor what their legal status or rights were."[364] Finally, while Human Rights Watch did not document any cases in which detainees specifically requested diplomatic assistance and were refused, the First Secretary at the Thai Embassy explained that Japanese immigration officials only contact the embassy regarding Thai detainees after deportation orders have been issued.[365]

Abusive conditions in immigration detention facilities

In addition to procedural violations, immigration detainees regularly face conditions that could amount to ill-treatment in custody, ranging from physical and verbal abuse to substandard sanitary conditions and insufficient opportunity for exercise.[366] Nuch recounted conditions of overcrowding and poor sanitation as she described her experience in immigration detention in 1993: "We all slept on the floor with thin mattresses that we rolled out each night. There were about thirty Thai women in each room. Each room was about the size of a three car garage. There were thousands of illegal immigrants in this place. There was one toilet in each cell. Each cell was taken to shower once a week and we all had to fight over time allotments for showers as everyone wanted to take longer showers than allotted and the others were afraid the time would be up before they got their shower in."[367] Nuch also told us that the food was so bad that the women usually bought instant noodles to eat, despite their limited funds.[368] Gap said that when she was detained at the Osaka immigration facility in 1997, she was only allowed to shower once or

---

[364] Immigration Review Task Force (IRTF), "Fact-finding Mission on Human Rights Violations against Foreign Nationals by Japanese Immigration Officers, 26-31 Manila, Philippines," July 31, 1995.

[365] Human Rights Watch interview, Tokyo, Japan, April 15, 1999.

[366] International standards provide that prisoners be allowed under necessary supervision to communicate with their family and reputable friends at regular intervals, both by correspondence and by receiving visits; that prisoners have at least one hour of suitable exercise in the open air daily if the weather permits; and that medical care be provided, including psychiatric services, pre-natal and post-natal care and treatment, and other medical services.

[367] Human Rights Watch and FOWIA interview, Bangkok, Thailand, March 10, 1995 and March 26, 1995.

[368] Ibid.

twice a week,[369] and Kaew confirmed that at the Tokyo immigration detention facility, only one shower was permitted each week: "I didn't get to shower while I was there because showers were on Monday, and I was arrested on a Wednesday and then left on Monday before shower time."[370]

When the Immigration Review Task Force (IRTF) interviewed women from the Philippines about their experiences in Japanese immigration detention, they received similar accounts of substandard conditions. Not only were women limited to one or two showers per week, each shower was limited to five to ten minutes, and the shower room was unsanitary with body hair and mold on the floor and walls. Women also complained about the lack of outdoor exercise; in the Tokyo IDC, detainees were not allowed outdoors at all, and, in Ushiku, detainees were allowed outside only once a week.[371] Continuing investigation by IRTF has revealed that this problem persists. In 1996, a Chinese woman, her seventy-three year old mother, and her infant child were held in detention pending deportation in the Nagoya Immigration Detention Center for thirty-six days.[372] During this time, the family was allowed outside exercise only once.[373]

Human Rights Watch also heard allegations that the Immigration Bureau tolerates degrading and abusive treatment by immigration officials in detention facilities, including violence and sexual assault, as well as excessive application of severe disciplinary measures such as solitary confinement with physical restraints. While the women we interviewed did not report such abuse, credible accounts documented by foreigners' rights advocates point to a serious problem. In October 1994, a group of lawyers established a telephone hotline to investigate rights abuses of foreigners. In the first two months, they received calls from thirty-five detainees, identifying themselves as Thais, Iranians, Peruvians, Americans, Argentinians, Myanmarese, Bangladeshis, Sri Lankans, and others, who claimed to be victims of

---

[369] Interview by M. N., Chiang Rai province, Thailand, October 1997.

[370] Human Rights Watch interview, Chiang Rai province, Thailand, April 25, 1999.

[371] IRTF, "Fact-Finding Mission on Human Rights Violations against Foreign Nationals by Japanese Immigration Officers, 26-31, Manila, Philippines."

[372] The prolonged detention of a small child is particularly intolerable. According to the Convention on the Rights of the Child, "The arrest, detention or imprisonment of a child shall be in conformity with the law and shall be used only as a measure of last resort and for the shortest appropriate period of time" (Article 37(b)).

[373] IRTF, "The Actual Status of the Deportation Procedures and Immigration Detention Facilities in Japan," p. 12.

violence at the hands of immigration and police officials.[374] IRTF member Toru Takahashi explained to Human Rights Watch that some efforts had been made to improve the human rights situation in immigration facilities in response to the widespread accounts of abuse that were publicized during the early nineties. "But," he concluded "these efforts did not last long," and abuses have continued.[375]

Lack of access to immigration detention facilities makes it difficult to obtain information about abuses. Unable to interview detainees in Japan, members of the Immigration Review Task Force have traveled to detainees' countries of origin to obtain their testimonies after their deportation. When the Immigration Review Task Force went to the Philippines in 1995 to interview Filipinas who had been held in the immigration detention house in Kanagawa prefecture, they received numerous accounts of verbal and physical sexual abuse. Young women described being taken to private rooms by immigration officers who proceeded to verbally assault them with sexual innuendoes, stories, jokes, and questions and to fondle them with their hands. One interviewee said that male immigration officers would often spy on the women taking showers, and another complained of a male officer who walked around her cell and watched her at night, keeping her from being able to sleep.[376] In 1994, a female detainee in TRIB, the Tokyo immigration facility, described the harrowing incidents of sexual harassment and rape that she endured there:

---

[374] "More detainees claim abuse by officials," *The Japan Times,* December 30, 1994, p. 3. See also Kalabaw, "Record of Human Rights Abuses Against Aliens by Immigration Control, Police and Courts of Justice," in Women's Research and Action Committee [ed.], *NGOs' Report on the Situation of Foreign Migrant Women in Japan and Strategies for Improvement* (1995); Onitsuka, *The situation of Alien Deportation Procedures in Japan,* p. 7; Toru Takahashi [translated by Masumi Azu and Elson Boles], "Violence at Japan's immigration detention centers," *Women in Action,* DATE?, p.58; Toru Takahashi, "Violence Against Female Detainees by the Immigration Control Bureau Officers," in Women's Research and Action Committee [ed.], *NGOs' Report on the Situation of Foreign Migrant Women in Japan and Strategies for Improvement* (1995), p. 47.

[375] As evidence, he cited the death of an Iranian national in the Tokyo Regional Immigration Control Bureau Detention Center (TRIB) in August 1997. Mousavi Abarbekouh Mir Hossein died from a dislocation of the cervical vertebra after receiving a hard blow to the head. The circumstances surrounding his death have never been explained. (Human Rights Watch interview, Tokyo, Japan, April 8, 1999; IRTF, "The Actual Status of the Deportation Procedures and Immigration Detention Facilities in Japan," pp. 2 - 3.)

[376] IRTF, "Fact-finding Mission on Human Rights Violations against Foreign Nationals by Japanese Immigration Officers, 26-31 Manila, Philippines."

During my stay there, I was raped by several officers. First, a female officer brought me to another room where one male officer waited for me. The female officer bowed to him and left the room. The male officer compelled me to take off all my clothes, and when I became naked, four to five officers entered the room and raped me for many hours. When I tried to resist, they hit me. The rape incidents occurred regularly towards female inmates inside the facility. My female roommates, Persian, Korean, Filipina, Thai, were subjected to this violence as well.[377]

In December 1994, allegations of routine physical abuse of detainees were confirmed by a former immigration official, Takeshi Akiyama, who explained that he had resigned from his position as a guard in a Tokyo immigration detention house because he could not stand the treatment of the detainees. He estimated that about ten percent of the immigration officers in the Kita Ward where he worked used violence under the guise of "taming" or "punishing" detainees, and he explained, "Violence against detainees who didn't listen to what they were told was a daily occurrence."[378] Some guards, he said, would threaten detainees who failed to follow instructions saying "I will kill you" or "Do you want to go home in ashes?" and they would continue to kick and punch them even after they had collapsed on the ground.[379] Akiyama further asserted that his superiors ordered guards not to beat prisoners in the face, where injuries would be more obvious, and he quoted one of his colleagues as saying, "Even if they die we can just handle it by saying it was an accident."[380] During the week following the press conference, more than twenty people called *The Japan Times* supporting Akiyama's claims.[381]

Perhaps even more disturbing than these allegations was the muted response of the Japanese government. Officials downplayed the seriousness of the accusations, denied any wrongdoing, and continued to deny advocates access to

---

[377] Takahashi, "Violence Against Female Detainees by the Immigration Control Bureau Officers," *NGOs' Report on the Situation of Foreign Migrant Women in Japan and Strategies for Improvement*, p. 46.

[378] "Ex-Japanese guard: Immigration officials beat alien detainees," *Bangkok Post,* December 25, 1994, p. 4.

[379] Naomi Hirakawa, "Assaults on detained foreigners denied by officials," *Mainichi Daily News*, December 23, 1994.

[380] "Ex-Japanese guard . . .," *Bangkok Post,* p. 4.

[381] "More detainees claim abuse by officials," *The Japan Times,* December 30, 1994, p. 3.

detention facilities. On December 20, 1994, Masaki Kazawa, chief of the immigration bureau's enforcement division, announced that officials had investigated Akiyama's claims over the weekend, interviewing several officials who had been assigned to detention centers in Tokyo, Osaka, and Fukuoka at the time of the alleged incidents, and found no evidence or reports of such actions. One ministry official told reporters, "It is a groundless report." Kazawa admitted that officers reprimanded detainees who would not follow instructions, but he denied that they used threatening or violent words. He also said his ministry did not plan to conduct hearings with detainees currently in custody because the newspaper reports did not mention complaints from them.[382] Reports of abuse in immigration detention have slowed since the mid-1990s, but incidents of violence continue to occur and immigration authorities continue to evade accountability. In August 1997, for example, when an Iranian man died in custody at the Tokyo Kita-ku Immigration Detention Center, immigration officials insisted that he had fallen down and banged his head. After a forensic report concluded that the man's death was the result of a severe beating, the police investigated and eight immigration officers were charged with assault, but the prosecutor dropped the case and the officers were never indicted.[383]

In one highly unusual case, a Chinese woman, Tao Ya Pin, successfully sued for compensation after being beaten to the point of unconsciousness by immigration officials in the Second Tokyo Regional Immigration Bureau (TRIB) detention house. Her success was possible only as a result of exceptionally strong evidence coupled with immediate and concerted action on the part of lawyers, who persisted in pursuing Tao's case after she was deported. Tao was arrested along with eight of her coworkers in a joint immigration and police raid on October 31, 1994. During her interrogation, she was brutally beaten in the presence of several immigration officers, none of whom sought to intervene.[384] In Tao's words:

---

[382] Hirakawa, "Assaults on detained foreigners denied by officials," *Mainichi Daily News.*

[383] See Amnesty International, "Japan's human rights record must be challenged," October 27, 1998 (Available: http://www.amnesty.org.uk/news/press/releases/27_october_1998-1.shtml. June 2000); and Stephanie Coop, "Detention Abuses," *The New Observer,* February 1999.

[384] Attorney Tadanori Onitsuka and Attorney Ayako Mizuno, "Summary Report on the Physical Abuses and Assaults by Immigration Control Enforcement Officers against Foreign Nationals in Japan at Various Stages of Compulsory Deportation Procedures, with Legal Commentary," Tokyo, March 1995, p.3; Takahashi, "Violence Against Female Detainees by the Immigration Control Bureau Officers," *NGOs' Report on the Situation of Foreign Migrant Women in Japan and Strategies for Improvement,* pp. 44-45.

I was punched an incredible number of times while my hands were handcuffed behind me ... They disregarded my answers, and they grabbed my hair, pushed down my face, then hit me over and over again in succession. I lost my strength and became nauseous. Suddenly, I vomited blood. When the man saw this, he started hitting me again ... Did I commit a crime to deserve this treatment? If I committed a crime, I should be punished by the law. I simply overstayed my visa.[385]

Tao complained of shortness of breath and head pain and asked to be taken to a hospital, but her request was denied until the late afternoon of the following day, November 2, in order that the questioning could continue. As a result of this interrogation, the immigration officer determined that Tao should be officially detained.

While Tao's interrogation at TRIB was underway, immigration officials released a few of her former coworkers who had witnessed Tao's abuse. When they reported what they had seen, an attorney visited Tao in detention and verified her injuries, and Tao later filed a law suit for damages against the state as well as a criminal case against the immigration enforcement officer who assaulted her.[386] Photographs of Tao's badly swollen face while she was in detention prompted an unprecedented admission from immigration officials that force had been used, and Tokyo Immigration Control Authorities reprimanded one of the officers for using violence during the interrogation.[387] However, charges that unnecessary force had been used were denied; immigration authorities explained that "only one immigration enforcement officer in charge assaulted Tao . . . she was hit only twice in the interrogation room and twice in another room . . . and this was done so as to stop her from acting violently or trying to kill herself."[388] Immigration officials furthermore worked to obstruct Tao's access to justice by deporting her to China

---

[385] Takahashi, "Violence Against Female Detainees by the Immigration Control Bureau Officers," *NGOs' Report on the Situation of Foreign Migrant Women in Japan and Strategies for Improvement*, p. 45.

[386] Onitsuka and Mizuno, "Summary Report on the Physical Abuses and Assaults by Immigration Control Enforcement Officers against Foreign Nationals in Japan at Various Stages of Compulsory Deportation Procedures with Legal Commentary," pp. 3-4.

[387] "Assaults on detained foreigners denied by officials," *Mainichi Daily News,* December 23, 1994.

[388] Onitsuka and Mizuno, "Summary Report on the Physical Abuses and Assaults by Immigration Control Enforcement Officers against Foreign Nationals in Japan at Various Stages of Compulsory Deportation Procedures with Legal Commentary," p.4.

on December 3, 1994, a month after her allegations were made. Departing from usual practice, the Japanese Immigration Department covered all of her travel expenses, in an apparent effort to remove Tao from the country quickly and thereby induce her to abandon her charges against TRIB.[389]

The attitude and actions of Japanese immigration authorities—even in the face of substantial evidence of abuse—reconfirms the general situation of impunity with which immigration officers can violate the rights of detainees. According to IRTF, investigations of cases of injury and even death in Japanese immigration detention facilities are regularly handled by immigration authorities behind closed doors.[390]   There are no established procedures for filing complaints about mistreatment during detention in immigration facilities or prisons in Japan, and, while some complaints have been brought to court, these cases have generally proven unsuccessful.[391]

Excessive restrictions on communication

One of the factors facilitating abuse of those held in immigration detention facilities is that heavy restrictions are placed on detainees' ability to communicate either with outsiders or with each other, restrictions that Human Rights Watch understands to exceed the "reasonable conditions and restrictions" on communication allowed by the Body of Principles for the Protection of All Persons under Any Form of Detention or Imprisonment.[392] Furthermore, these restrictions

---

[389] Takahashi, "Violence at Japan's immigration detention centers," *Women in Action,* pp. 58-59; IRTF, "The Actual Status of the Deportation Procedures and Immigration Detention Facilities in Japan," p. 15.

Tao's lawyers pursued her case in absentia, seeking six million yen in compensation for the abuse she suffered at the hands of the immigration officers, and in July 1996 a settlement was finally reached for damages of one million yen (US$9200). (National Network in Solidarity with Migrant Workers-Japan, "The Rights of the Migrants and their Families in Japan and the ICCPR: A Report Concerning the Rights of the Migrants and their Families in Japan for the Consideration of the Fourth Periodic Report Submitted by Japan in Accordance with Article 40 of the ICCPR," 1998, p. 24.)

[390] IRTF, "The Actual Status of the Deportation Procedures and Immigration Detention Facilities in Japan," pp. 2, 4.

[391] See IRTF, "The Actual Status of the Deportation Procedures and Immigration Detention Facilities in Japan," pp. 10, 15; Takahashi, "Violence Against Female Detainees by the Immigration Control Bureau Officers," *NGOs' Report on the Situation of Foreign Migrant Women in Japan and Strategies for Improvement,* p. 47; Luke Thomas, "Immigration vs. Foreigners: Abuses in Need of Solutions," *Tokyo Underground,* no. 2, February 1995, p. 2.

[392] Principle 19. See also Principles 16 and 18.

are coupled with very limited access to detention facilities and detainees by monitors and other advocates.[393] When three members of the Japanese Diet were permitted to inspect immigration detention centers in 1994, even they were only granted permission to observe the facilities and not to interview detainees independently.[394]

Regulations governing immigration detainees' communication allow wide latitude to individual directors. The Immigration Control Act provides that a Director of the Immigration Center or Regional Immigration Bureau may, when "he considers it necessary for security or sanitation purposes," "inspect communications the detainee dispatches and receives" and "prohibit or restrict the dispatch and receipt of communications."[395] The more-detailed "Regulations for the Treatment of Detainees" states:

> When a detention center/prison warden deems that the contents of correspondence written by a detainee serves to obstruct the security of the penal institution, the warden may make the detainee correct and/or delete the sentence(s) in question. Further, if the detainee refuses to oblige the warden in making such corrections/deletions, the written correspondence then becomes the property of the penal institution. The above is applied to written correspondence received by the detainee as well.[396]

Citing the need to protect institutional security, the Immigration Bureau has refused to further clarify the rules and guidelines governing the censorship of correspondence, so the actual standards being employed remain obscure.[397]

While the high degree of discretionary power granted to individual directors and wardens leads to variations between institutions, Human Rights Watch and others, including the Immigration Review Task Force, have found that detainees consistently report that tight controls are exercised over all written and verbal communication. Visits are highly restricted and all conversations must be

---

[393] When Human Rights Watch conducted an investigation of Japanese prison conditions in 1994, we were unable to visit any immigration detention facilities and only permitted extremely limited access to select prisons. (Human Rights Watch/Asia and Human Rights Watch Prison Project, *Prison Conditions in Japan* (New York: Human Rights Watch, 1995), p. viii.)

[394] "MP Inspect IDC," *Mainichi Shimbun,* December 8, 1994.

[395] Article 61-7(4, 5).

[396] Article 37; quoted in Onitsuka, *The situation of Alien Deportation Procedures in Japan*, p. 8.

[397] Onitsuka, *The situation of Alien Deportation Procedures in Japan.*

conducted in a language understood by the guards. Kaew S. explained to Human Rights Watch that her boyfriend was allowed to visit her while she was in the immigration detention center in Tokyo, but "[w]e could only speak in Japanese, so others who didn't know Japanese couldn't talk at all."[398] Telephone calls and written communication are also strictly limited. At TRIB, detainees are forbidden from making or receiving any telephone calls; if a detainee needs to make a phone call, an immigration officer has to make the call on the person's behalf. And officials there have essentially forbidden all written correspondence with family members, friends, and even legal counsel. The only correspondence they allow is letters aimed at securing funds for deportation. At Ushiku Detention Center, regulations regarding telephone use are less strict, but detainees are prohibited from discussing complaints about mistreatment.[399] And a detainee at Ushiku who tried to describe his mistreatment in letters written to Japanese Diet members in November 1998 was ordered to cross out statements, such as "after that I was immediately locked up together with the existing criminals and overstayers in their detention rooms," before the letters could be mailed.[400]

Mistreatment in the criminal justice system

Human Rights Watch found that Thai women who come into contact with the Japanese criminal justice system outside of the deportation context also face serious violations of due process, as the inadequacy of general due process protections in Japan is exacerbated by the women's lack of Japanese language skills and unfamiliarity with the Japanese legal system. As in the immigration system, these procedural problems prevent women from effectively challenging, or even understanding, the charges against them. Some practices in the Japanese criminal justice system violate the minimum guarantees provided for criminal suspects under international human rights law, which requires that all persons facing criminal charges have the right to legal assistance (free of charge, if the accused does not have sufficient means to pay for it), the right to be informed of the right to legal assistance, and the right not to be compelled to testify against oneself or to confess guilt. The ICCPR also explicitly provides that anyone charged with a criminal offense has the right "to be informed promptly and in detail in a language which he understands of the nature and cause of the charge against him" and "to have the free assistance of an interpreter if he cannot understand or speak the language used in

---

[398] Human Rights Watch interview, Chiang Rai province, Thailand, April 25, 1999.

[399] Onitsuka, *The situation of Alien Deportation Procedures in Japan*, p. 8.

[400] Lawyers Group for Burmese Asylum Seekers - Japan, "Censorship in Immigration Detention Center: Violation of the right of freedom of expression," *Migrant Network News,* no. 11, January 1999, p. 1.

court."[401] Concerns about persistent rights violations against both foreigners and Japanese nationals have been voiced by the Japan Civil Liberties Union, the Japan Federation of Bar Associations, and other Japanese advocates.[402] Such concerns were also noted by the United Nations Human Rights Committee in its review of Japan's compliance with the ICCPR in 1998.[403]

Nuch told Human Rights Watch that she spent months in prison without ever understanding why she was being held. When she and the other women from the snack bar were brought to the police station, "we were asked all the details about what had happened to us. The Japanese women who could speak Thai translated. The Japanese translators told me and the others that we didn't have to talk unless we wanted to. I told everything. The police and translators told me they would help me go home." But instead, Nuch was kept at the station for the next ten days, then transferred to another police station for two more days, and then moved to a jail where she spent the next two or three months. During this time, Nuch was repeatedly questioned about her experiences, but she did not have a lawyer, and she was never provided with a statement of any charges against her, nor of any judgements on her case.[404]

The Japanese NGO Hand-in-Hand Chiba reported that foreign detainees are hardly ever informed of their rights to request a lawyer, and, even when they are informed of this right, police discourage them from exercising it by stressing the costs of lawyers' fees. Lawyers are also barred from attending police interrogation sessions during suspects' initial period of detention.[405] One Thai woman whom we

---

[401] Article 14(3).

[402] See Japan Civil Liberties Union, *1998 Report Concerning the Present Status of Human Rights in Japan* (Third Counter Report), October 1998; Japan Federation of Bar Associations, "A Report on the Application and Practice in Japan of the International Covenant on Civil and Political Rights," April 1993.

[403] Human Rights Committee, "Concluding observations of the Human Rights Committee: Japan," November 19, 1998 (CCPR/C/79/Add.102).

[404] Human Rights Watch and FOWIA interview, Bangkok, Thailand, March 1995.

[405] Toako Matsushiro (Hand-in-Hand Chiba), "Problems in Legal Procedures: The Murder Trial of Trafficked Thai Women," in Women's Research and Action Committee [ed.], *NGOs' Report on the Situation of Foreign Migrant Women in Japan and Strategies for Improvement* (1995), p. 42.
The initial period of police detention, before to a suspect's indictment, is called *daiyo kangoku*. It can last up to twenty-three days, and questioning is always conducted without the presence of a lawyer, even though the primary purpose of the interrogation is to obtain a confession. Both the Japan Civil Liberties Union and the Japan Federation of Bar Associations have identified the daiyo kangoku period as "a hotbed" of violence and coerced confessions. (Japan Civil Liberties Union, "1998 Report Concerning the Present Status of

interviewed was arrested by police as an overstayer in early 1997 and held in police detention for twenty days before being transferred to an immigration detention facility. She was interrogated every day during her detention, without ever seeing a lawyer.[406] According to NNSMW-Japan, foreign detainees have reported the following statements made by police after their arrest: "There are no lawyers in Japan"; "If you sign the investigation report, a lawyer will come"; "A lawyer can do nothing. You are just throwing money away, and then what will you do? If you admit to the crime we will let you go"; and "Even if you get a lawyer, you will still never be released because lawyers are powerless."[407]

In the criminal trials of several Thai women arrested on murder charges in the early amd mid-1990s, these problems were compounded by inadequate translation and interpretation services. Without such assistance, women were unable to clearly understand the charges against them, accurately communicate their testimonies, or follow the proceedings as their cases progressed. Staff members of Hand-in-Hand Chiba, who closely monitored these trials, concluded that inadequate interpretation during the investigation at the Public Prosecutor's Office led to repeated incidents of misunderstanding during the trials and that insufficient interpretation during trial proceedings led defendants to accept the court ruling before they were able to fully understand it.[408] Hand-in-Hand Chiba tried to assist the defendants by voluntarily translating all of the statements of the prosecutors and the court decisions into Thai using their own time and resources.[409]

One of these cases, which became known as the "Shimodate Incident," involved the arrest of three Thai women for murdering and robbing their mama at a snack bar in September 1991. A team of volunteer lawyers was assembled to present their defense, and according to one of these lawyers:

Human Rights in Japan (Third Counter Report)"; Japan Federation of Bar Associations, "Prisons in Japan," October 1992.)

[406] Interview by M. N. with Gap, Chiang Rai province, Thailand, October 1997.

[407] National Network in Solidarity with Migrant Workers - Japan, "The Rights of the Migrants and their Families in Japan and the ICCPR: A Report Concerning the Rights of the Migrants and their Families in Japan for the Consideration of the Fourth Periodic Report Submitted by Japan in Accordance with Article 40 of the ICCPR," 1998, p. 16.

[408] Toako Matsushiro (Hand-in-Hand Chiba), "Problems in Legal Procedures: The Murder Trial of Trafficked Thai Women," in Women's Research and Action Committee [ed.], *NGOs' Report on the Situation of Foreign Migrant Women in Japan and Strategies for Improvement* (1995), p. 41.

[409] Ibid., pp. 41-42.

The three accused women were arrested and held for three days before they got a lawyer. They were held in police lockups for twenty days, during which time they were questioned everyday by the police without the presence of their lawyers. The police took a statement, including a confession, from each of the women. A police interpreter assisted with the statement. The women claim that they never received a Thai translation of their statement in writing, only a verbal translation which did not mention anything about conspiracy to commit murder or robbery. Although the women claim that they never admitted to any premeditation nor an intent to commit robbery,[410] either the translation was messed up or the police put in a different version of what happened because the final statement said both. The women claim that they did not plan to murder the boss, that they only wanted to take back their passports, not any money or jewelry, and to escape.[411]

At the trial, the defense attorneys argued that the police statements were flawed and the interpreters had been incompetent, noting that "even the judge had to ask an interpreter to speak more clearly because her Japanese was so bad."[412] But the judge dismissed these claims and sentenced the women to ten years of imprisonment each.[413] Upon appeal, the women's sentences were reduced to eight years, but the judge refused to acknowledge any problems in interpretation or translation and maintained the conviction for murder for robbery.[414] While there have not been any arrests of Thai women on such serious charges in the last several

---

[410] Murder with the intent to commit robbery is a more serious crime than simply murder.

[411] Human Rights Watch interview with Attorney Kazuko Kawaguchi, Japan, March 9, 1994.

[412] Abigail Haworth and Kyoko Matsuda, "Flesh and Blood: part two," *Tokyo Journal*, August 1994, p. 37. See also "The Shimodate Incident: From an interview with Takahashi Hiromichi," *AMPO Japan-Asia Quarterly Review*, vol. 25, no. 2, 1994, p. 4.

[413] See Haworth and Matsuda, "Flesh and Blood: part two," *Tokyo Journal*; and "Thai women get 10-year jail for murder in Japan," *The Nation* (Bangkok, Thailand), May 23, 1994.

[414] Yuriko Saito, "Shimodate Case: Judgement of Appeal Hearing," 1996; Yuriko Saito, "Trafficking in women: the Shimodate case and human rights abuses," *Tokyo Kaleidoscope* (weekly online journal), July 22, 1996. Available: http://202.239.42.30/topics/0094p01e.html. June 2000.

years, the advocates who followed those cases remain concerned as the criminal justice system has not acknowledged or addressed these issues.

As in immigration detention facilities, detainees in the criminal justice system also face strict restrictions on all forms of communication.[415] These controls make it difficult for detainees to communicate with their lawyers while investigations and trials are proceeding, and impede detainees' ability to discuss abuses they may have suffered at the hands of prison officials. The rules have a particularly heavy impact on foreign detainees without Japanese language skills, as conversations with visitors must be conducted in a language that guards understand, and all foreign language correspondence must be translated, at the detainee's expense, before it can be sent or received.

A Thai NGO worker interviewed by Human Rights Watch recounted her experience of trying to visit a female Thai prisoner in Japan in 1997:

> I went to Japan two years ago for six weeks, and while I was there I tried to visit a Thai woman in jail. But I was not allowed to speak in any language except Japanese, so I was not able to say anything - because I don't speak any Japanese. I went with a Japanese NGO that visits prisoners every week and brings them Thai language books and other things. They are allowed to leave these books as long as they explain what they are and the guards approve them. I just wanted to say "sawadee-ka" [hello] but I couldn't. So the Thai woman and I sat looking at each other with a window separating us and couldn't even say hello. A guard was there the whole time too, and recorded everything that was said [by the Japanese NGO staff] with a tape recorder.[416]

---

[415] As in immigration facilities, regulations governing conditions in prisons and detention houses are vague, giving individual prison directors wide discretion to formulate and implement internal rules regulating the day-to-day operations of the prison, and these internal rules are kept secret, ostensibly in the interest of protecting the institution's security. The abusive conditions in these facilities have been widely publicized and criticized, both by domestic and international human rights organizations. See Japan Civil Liberties Union, "1998 Report Concerning the Present Status of Human Rights in Japan (Third Counter Report)"; Japan Federation of Bar Associations, "Prisons in Japan"; Human Rights Watch/Asia and Human Rights Watch Prison Project, *Prison Conditions in Japan*; and Amnesty International, *Japan: Abusive Punishments in Japanese Prisons,* June 1998.

[416] Human Rights Watch interview, Catholic Commission on Migration: Women's Desk, Bangkok, Thailand, April 30, 1999.

Sister Ando, a Japanese woman who is also fluent in Thai, confirmed that when she visited a Thai woman in prison, in principle they could only speak in Japanese, "though sometimes the guard would allow us to speak in Thai if I translated right away into Japanese for the guard."[417]

During the trial of the three Thai women arrested in the "Shimodate Incident" described above, even conversations with simultaneous interpretation were prohibited. Members of the support group that had organized on the women's behalf tried to visit the defendants in detention to discuss their cases, but were told that all conversation in Thai was prohibited in order to allow "the trial to progress smoothly." The group offered to bring a court-approved legal interpreter to the meeting, but their request was still denied.[418] Questioned about this policy, a Ministry of Justice spokesperson said that meetings could be held in a language not understood by detention center officials if the meeting is regarded as "important" by the detention center and a "reliable" person is available to translate the conversation, such as a diplomat from the detainee's country.[419] Denied the ability to discuss their cases orally, the defendants described their recollections of the snack bar, the day of the murder, and the manner of their arrest and interrogation in letters addressed to their lawyers. But these letters could only be sent after being translated and censored by the detention house. Not only did this constitute a breach of lawyer-client confidentiality, it also delayed correspondence, as a Thai translator only came to the detention center once or twice a month. In a letter to a support group member, one of the defendants wrote, "A letter arrived from Thailand the other day, but the translator is busy so I cannot read it."[420]

The common use of solitary confinement in Japanese prisons further isolates detainees. Human Rights Watch interviewed a Thai woman who was arrested during a police raid on a snack bar where she was working in debt bondage. The woman, Nuch, was kept in solitary confinement during the entire two to three month period that she was detained in prison before being transferred to an immigration facility in 1993. She described the extreme isolation and otherwise abusive treatment that she was subjected to:

> I was allowed out to exercise every few days for one hour. I was taken out alone and was never allowed to meet or talk with

---

[417] Human Rights Watch interview, Kyoto, Japan, April 12, 1999.

[418] "Chapter 2: Questions to Japan," *Today's Japan,* April 26, 1994, p. 29.

[419] Forum on Asian Immigrant Workers, "Citizen's Report on the Human Rights of Foreign Workers in Japan (with a special emphasis on male workers)," April 17, 1993, p. 29.

[420] "Chapter 2: Questions to Japan," *Today's Japan,* pp. 30-32.

others. I was not allowed to write. I was only allowed to look at Japanese books. I was not allowed to sleep or lie down during the day. I had to sit up and read Japanese books or find something else to do in the little room. I had my meals alone in my room. . . . Once during my stay, I was taken to a big court with four other women from my snack bar. We were handcuffed with a rope around our waists tied to a guard at the end of the rope, like criminals. . . . When I saw the others I tried to speak to them. The guards kept forbidding us, but we kept sneaking in conversation with each other.

Nuch was never told why she was separated from other detainees, but she believes it was because she was HIV positive.[421]

---

[421] Human Rights Watch interview, Bangkok, Thailand, March 1995.

Subjecting a detainee to solitary confinement without cause—and/or without informing the detainee of the cause—contravenes the Standard Minimum Rules for the Treatment of Prisoners (Articles 27, 29, 30).

IX. RESPONSE OF THE JAPANESE GOVERNMENT

Undocumented foreigners are entitled under international law to the same basic human rights protections as all other individuals. These rights include the right to be free from slavery-like practices and forced labor, the right to be free from torture and other cruel or degrading treatment, the right to a fair trial, and the right to freedom from discrimination. These rights are also guaranteed under the Japanese Constitution and reflected in domestic legislation. Yet, in practice, women trafficked from Thailand into Japan's sex industry are rarely afforded such protections. High-ranking Japanese officials have acknowledged trafficking as a persistent and large-scale problem, but the government has yet to make a serious effort to address the abuses connected with it.

Trafficking in persons typically involves multiple actors and a range of abuses. Efforts to combat it must be designed to respond to each of the human rights abuses and to provide victims with strong incentives to come forward, report crimes, and cooperate with law enforcement officials. The Japanese government lacks policies designed specifically to respond to trafficking and has yet to aggressively enforce existing laws against forced labor, forced prostitution, illegal confinement, coercive job placement, and other severe abuses committed against trafficked women by traffickers and employers. Indeed, instead of guaranteeing the safety of trafficked persons and ensuring their access to compensation and redress, the government all too often effectively penalizes them for abuses that have occurred as a result of their having been trafficked.

Human Rights Watch found that while brokers and snack bar employers were sometimes charged with employing illegal aliens, failing to properly register their business under the Entertainment Businesses Law, or procuring prostitutes for customers, evidence of more serious crimes was rarely investigated. Furthermore, victims of trafficking and debt bondage were deported as illegal aliens without any opportunity to seek compensation for the abuses they had suffered, and no government resources were provided for their shelter, medical care, travel expenses, or other necessary services.

Response to Trafficking in Persons — Rhetoric without action

There is a growing willingness among Japanese officials to acknowledge and discuss the problem of trafficking in persons, but serious efforts to address the issue are still lacking. When the United Nations Committee on Human Rights observed in 1998 that "traffic in women and insufficient protection for women subject to trafficking and slavery-like practices remain serious concerns" in

147

Japan,[422] the director of the human rights and refugee division of Japan's Foreign Ministry agreed that women who entered the country through brokers were "frequently forced into prostitution in their workplaces in entertainment businesses."[423] Despite this seeming understanding of the slavery-like nature of the offense, the Japanese delegation pointed to a recent amendment to the Law on Control and Improvement of Amusement Businesses (hereinafter: Entertainment Businesses Law) as the government's primary effort to address the problem. This amendment, which went into effect in April 1999, prohibits anyone engaged in operating an entertainment business from either imposing an unreasonably high debt (relative to the debtor's ability to repay it) that must be repaid at the time that the debtor leaves (or tries to leave) his/her job, or confiscating the identification normally needed to apply for a job (including a passport) from an employee upon whom an "unreasonably" high debt has been imposed.[424] Although any legal measure designed to address the tactics used to control trafficked women represents a step forward, the usefulness of this provision is unclear. It is narrowly written, and no criminal penalties are provided; a business found to be in violation would only have its license revoked. As of March 2000, the National Police Agency reported that the new provision had not yet been used.[425]

---

[422] Human Rights Committee, "Concluding Observations by the Human Rights Committee: Consideration of Reports Submitted by States under Article 40 of the Covenant, Japan," November 5, 1998, paragraph 29.

[423] Transcript of the 1714th meeting of the Committee on Human Rights to consider the Fourth Periodic Report of Japan, October 28, 1998.

[424] Entertainment Businesses Law, Article 18-2, paragraph 1 provides that a person who runs an entertainment business shall not:"(1) charge an unreasonably high debt . . . to the employees engaged in the service of entertaining the customers (hereinafter called the "employees entertaining the customers") in consideration of their ability to repay on condition that the outstanding debt becomes due and payable immediately upon their ceasing to be the employees entertaining the customers. (2) hold in custody or to have a third party hold in custody the passports . . . (or other documents designated by a government order as the documents which employers would normally request the job seekers to display for their identification) of the employees entertaining the customers who have been charged with an unreasonably high debt in consideration of their ability to repay." Article 31-3 specifies that this article should apply to persons who run "non-store type sex entertainment businesses." See discussion of the Entertainment Businesses Law below for a definition of this term. (Note that the English translation of the amended Entertainment Businesses Law used here and below was provided to Human Rights Watch by Fumie Saito, Legislative Aide to Senator Mizuho Fukushima, Member of the House of Councilors, Japan.)

[425] Fumie Saito, Legislative Aide to Senator Mizuho Fukushima, Member of the House of Councilors, Japan, e-mail to Human Rights Watch, March 16, 2000.

At a seminar organized by the Thai Embassy in Tokyo in September 1999, Japanese officials reiterated their understanding of the problem of trafficking and their concern for the victims. The seminar was designed to identify the problems faced by Thai sex workers in Japan and to discuss possible solutions. Toshikino Itami, director of the enforcement division of Japan's Immigration Bureau, explained that many women from Thailand are "sold" to sex business operators for more than four million yen, and then are forced to repay this amount before they can begin earning money for themselves. He also noted that in most of these cases, the women's passports are confiscated by their employers.[426]

In January 2000, Japan's Ministry of Foreign Affairs sponsored its own conference on trafficking, the "Asia-Pacific Symposium on Trafficking in Persons." The Senior State Secretary for Foreign Affairs, giving one of the key-note statements, acknowledged the seriousness of the problem of trafficking and cited Japan's participation in international efforts to frame responses to the issue as evidence of his government's concern.[427] But neither the President of the International Criminal Police Organization (Interpol), Toshinori Kanemoto, nor the Director-General of the Immigration Bureau, Yukio Machida, pointed to any concrete efforts to combat trafficking beyond investigating and prosecuting traffickers for facilitating illegal migration, a charge that scarcely begins to address the range of abuses perpetrated against trafficking victims. Moreover, Machida expressed doubts about whether there really is a significant trafficking problem in Japan, claiming that incidents of coercion are rare and the majority of so-called "trafficking victims" are merely illegal migrants with crime syndicates "behind them." A similar attitude was evident during Kanemoto's comments; as evidence of Japan's efforts to combat trafficking, he cited statistics for the number of "stowaways" arrested on charges of entering the country illegally and the number of foreign women arrested on charges of prostitution, indecency, or violating the Entertainment Businesses Law. No statistics were provided regarding the arrests of traffickers or employers of undocumented migrants.[428]

---

[426] Sanitsuda Ekachai, "Conference seeks help for Thai victims: These women are not criminals-envoy," *Bangkok Post,* September 28, 1999; "Govt, NGO officials meet on Thai women's problems," *The Daily Yomiuri,* September 28, 1999.

[427] These efforts will be described further in the "International Response" chapter.

[428] According to Kanemoto, 1,360 "stowaways" were arrested for illegal entry in 1997, 1,023 in 1998, and 770 in 1999. He also explained that in 1998, 1,522 foreign women were arrested for violations of the Prostitution Prevention Law, of the laws against indecency, or of the Entertainment Businesses Law. Broken down by nationality, the foreign women who were arrested on such charges included 497 Koreans, 342 Thais, 277 Filipinas, and 122 Colombians. The only other arrest statistic he cited was the number of persons

These comments suggest that Japanese law enforcement authorities continue to target the victims of trafficking, rather than the traffickers themselves. They also disregard the forms of coercion commonly employed by traffickers and employers of trafficked women, such as debt bondage and threats of injury to women and their families. When Human Rights Watch met with a panel of Japanese government officials, including representatives from the National Police Agency, the Immigration Bureau of the Ministry of Justice, and the Criminal Affairs Bureau of the Ministry of Justice, in April 1999, we asked whether there had been any attempt to train police to identify trafficking victims and the abuses they may have suffered. The only person to respond, Police Inspector Akio Koshikawa, answered by explaining that the police were cooperating with the Thai Embassy, NGOs, and others to arrest traffickers.[429]

Existing legislation that could be used to punish trafficking and debt bondage
There are several laws already on the books in Japan that could be used to punish persons who traffic in women, such as the penal code and Japanese "special" laws regarding prostitution, the entertainment industry, labor standards, and immigration. These laws include many provisions that could address the slavery-like practices involved in the recruitment and employment of women from Thailand and elsewhere and that could provide compensation to victims.[430]

Penal Code
The physical confinement and violent threats that brokers and employers use to control indebted women could be prosecuted under articles 220 and 222 of the Penal Code (Law No. 45). Article 220 proscribes restrictions on freedom of

---

arrested for child prostitution or child pornography in the two months since Japan's new legislation against these practices came into force in November 1999, but it was not clear whether any foreign victims were involved in these cases. (Presentation at the Asia-Pacific Symposium on Trafficking in Persons, Tokyo, Japan, January 20, 2000.)

[429] Human Rights Watch interview, Tokyo, Japan, April 15, 1999.

[430] Also note that victims can get compensation in both civil and criminal cases in Japan. While victims must initiate a civil case to actually sue for damages, judges and lawyers in criminal cases regularly encourage the defendant to offer some compensation to the victim as an indication of remorse. The amount of compensation is then one of the considerations that judges take into account during sentencing. Judges will even extend trials in certain cases until the defendant is able to pay more money. Though there is no provision for this practice in the criminal procedure code, attorney Yoko Yoshida explained that it is common and is implied by the wide range of fines and prison terms specified in the penal code, which give judges broad discretion in sentencing. (Human Rights Watch interview, Kyoto, Japan, April 13, 1999.)

movement: "A person, who illegally arrests or confines another, shall be punished with penal servitude for not less than three months nor more than five years."[431] Article 222 prescribes penalties of up to two years' imprisonment or a five hundred yen fine for anyone who threatens to injure the "life, person, liberty, reputation, or property" of a person or his/her relative. The penalty is steeper, up to three years in jail, if the intimidation causes the victim to perform an act which he/she is not bound to perform.[432]

Articles 225 and 227 of the Penal Code forbid kidnapping "by force or allurement for the purpose of profit, obscenity or marriage" and "receiv[ing] a person having been kidnapped or sold" for the purpose of profit or obscenity. Maximum penalties are ten years and seven years, respectively. Brokers in Japan who "receive" women from their agents and/or escorts, hold them by force or threat of force, and then deliver them to snack bar employers for a profit without giving the women the option of selecting or refusing their placement, violate both of these provisions. Employers who "procure" women without their consent also violate the anti-kidnapping provision.

Recognizing the additionally aggravating consequences when victims are transported across international borders, Japan also has legislation in place that explicitly targets the kidnaping, buying, and selling of persons for the purpose of transporting them out of Japan.[433] Strikingly, however, the Japanese Diet has not passed legislation to cover cases in which persons are transported *into* Japan, as some Japanese opponents of this trade in people have advocated. Human Rights Watch would support the introduction of such legislation, which should explicitly target those involved in the transport, sale, or purchase of persons for the purpose of placing them into debt bondage or forced labor in a country not their own (whether or not "kidnapping" in the country of origin can be proven).

---

[431] "The Penal Code of Japan," EHS Law Bulletin Series, EHS Vol. II (Tokyo: Eibun-Horeisha, Inc., 1992). All excerpts from the Penal Code below are also taken from the EHS Law Bulletin Series.

[432] Article 223, Law No. 124, June 30, 1947.

[433] Article 226 of the Penal Code states: "A person, who kidnaps another by force or allurement for the purpose of transporting the same out of Japan, shall be punished with penal servitude for a limited period of not less than two years [and not more than fifteen years].

The same shall apply to a person who buys or sells another for the purpose of transporting the same out of Japan, and to a person who transports out of Japan another having been so kidnaped or sold."

There are other more general penal code provisions that could be applied against traffickers. The physical abuse of women by brokers, employers, employers' associates, and clients is punishable under Japan's assault laws, which prescribe penalties for inflicting injury and encouraging the infliction of injury.[434] Prison sentences are also prescribed for acts of sexual assault and rape. Using violence or threats to commit an indecent act is punishable by a minimum of six months and a maximum of seven years' imprisonment, and the offense of rape, involving violence or threat, is punishable by two to fifteen years of imprisonment.[435] Further, the confiscation of women's passports, wages, tips, and other belongings could be prosecuted under provisions against theft.[436]

Anti-Prostitution Laws

Prostitution is defined by the Prostitution Prevention Law (Law No. 118) (hereinafter, PPL) as "sexual intercourse with an unspecified other party for compensation or for a promise of compensation."[437] The law covers only vaginal sexual intercourse and does not purport to deal with exchange of other sexual services for pay. While being a prostitute or a client of a prostitute is prohibited under this law, there are no penalties provided for the act of prostitution itself; rather, penalties are provided for a range of activities associated with the business of prostitution. "Prostitutes" are prohibited from publicly soliciting clients, an offense which carries a penalty of up to six months' imprisonment or up to a 10,000 yen fine. The rest of the PPL's provisions are targeted at brokers and employers in the sex industry (there are no penalties provided for clients of prostitutes), and contain prohibitions on:

• procuring a prostitute for someone else;
• deceiving or influencing someone to prostitute;
• using violence or the threat of violence to force someone to prostitute;

---

[434] Articles 204 through 208 of the Penal Code, which were last amended by Law No. 31, April 17, 1991.

[435] According to Article 177, rape carries a penalty of imprisonment for a limited period of no less than two years, and Article 12 of penal code provides that "a limited period" shall mean no less than one month, but less than 15 years. Sexual assault is prohibited under Article 176.

[436] Article 235: A person who steals the property of another shall be guilty of the crime of theft and be punished with penal servitude for not more than ten years.

[437] "Prostitution Prevention Law," EHS Law Bulletin Series, EHS Vol. II (Tokyo: Eibun-Horeisha, Inc., 1991). All excerpts from the Prostitution Prevention Law below are also taken from the EHS Law Bulletin Series.

- receiving or demanding compensation for someone else's act of prostitution;
- giving an advance with an intent to make someone prostitute;
- concluding a contract to make someone prostitute;
- knowingly furnishing a place for prostitution;
- engaging in the business of furnishing the place for prostitution; and
- engaging in the business of making a person live in a prostitution place and prostitute herself.

The maximum penalties for these offenses range from two to ten years' imprisonment and/or 50,000 to 3 million yen in fines.[438] Punishments for the use of force to compel women to engage in prostitution are relatively mild. A maximum penalty of three years' imprisonment or a 100,000 yen fine is provided for "any person who threatens or uses violence towards a person and makes her prostitute."[439] The same penalties are prescribed for compelling someone to engage in prostitution by deception, embarrassment, or taking advantage of kinship ties.[440] These penalties are substantially less than the up to ten years' imprisonment prescribed for forced labor under Japanese labor laws, which will be discussed in more detail below.[441]

In addition to the Prostitution Prevention Law, a new law prohibiting child prostitution and pornography was passed in 1999. The Legislation on Punishment for Child Prostitution and Child Pornography covers sexual intercourse and/or similar acts performed by adults with any person under the age of eighteen by offering or promising compensation to him/her. It includes penalties for clients as well as for third parties involved in facilitating child prostitution. It is also extraterritorial in scope, so that it can be applied to Japanese perpetrators whether they have committed their crimes in Japan or abroad.

---

[438] Under the Child Prostitution and Pornography Act, which was adopted by the Japanese Diet in May 1999, clients who engage in prostitution with girls under age eighteen can be penalized.

[439] Article 7(2). This penalty is increased to a maximum of five years imprisonment or a 200,000 yen fine if the offender receives or demands compensation from the act of prostitution (Article 8(1)).

[440] Article 7(1). This penalty is increased to a maximum of five years imprisonment or a 200,000 yen fine if the offender receives or demands compensation from the act of prostitution (Article 8(1)).

[441] As another point of comparison, the punishments for forced prostitution in the PPL are actually slightly *less* severe than those in the Immigration Control Act for entering the country illegally or overstaying one's visa.

Entertainment Businesses Law

The Law on Control and Improvement of Amusement Businesses (Law No. 122) (hereinafter, the Entertainment Businesses Law) regulates the sale of sexual services that do not constitute "prostitution" under the Prostitution Prevention Law. That is, the sale of any sexual acts excepting vaginal sexual intercourse, is not illegal as long as it is done in accordance with the regulations of the Entertainment Businesses Law. This act specifies licensing, zoning, and other types of regulations for a variety of entertainment venues. Under the law, entertainment businesses are divided into two main categories, entertainment businesses and sex entertainment businesses, each of which has two sub-categories. Entertainment businesses include restaurants that provide non-sexual entertainment, such as cabarets and dance halls, as well as other amusement businesses, such as mah-jong clubs and pinball parlors. Sex entertainment businesses include "store form" businesses, in which sexual entertainment is provided on the premises, such as strip clubs, sex shops, "soap lands," and private video rooms; and "non-store form" businesses, which arrange for sexual services to be conducted elsewhere, such as telephone escort services and mail order adult video services; and transmittable visual sex entertainment businesses — internet pornography.

In principle, "dating" snack bars, in which customers pay to take women out of the bar for sexual services, are subject to strict reporting requirements under the law as non-store form sex entertainment businesses. Such businesses are also prohibited from employing people under the age of eighteen or from having clients under the age of eighteen, and are subject to the new provisions against excessively high debts described above.[442] These provisions could be used to penalize snack bar owners and managers, although the maximum penalties are light — typically a fine and/or a prison term of no more than six months.

Labor Laws

Japanese labor laws, and particularly the Labor Standards Law (LSL) and the Employment Security Law (ESL), establish minimum acceptable labor standards and provide for a range of employment protections against abuses by employers and job brokers. These laws make no distinction between workers on the basis of immigration status. Under the LSL, employers who "force workers to work against their will by means of violence, intimidation, imprisonment, or any other unfair restraint on the mental or physical freedom of the workers" are liable for penalties of one to ten years' imprisonment or fifty thousand to one million yen.[443] Wages

---

[442] Articles 31-2, 31-3, 18-2.
[443] LSL, Article 5. See Chapter XIII, Penal Provisions, Article 117 for penalties.

must be paid "at least once a month at a definite date," "in cash and in full directly to the workers,"[444] and all forms of indebted labor are prohibited, whether or not the practice rises to the level of debt bondage.[445] The law requires employers to clarify working conditions, including wages, working hours, and other conditions, and it sets minimum requirements for these conditions. The LSL also establishes minimum standards for dormitory living, not only requiring that employers provide adequate facilities, but also prohibiting them from "infring[ing] on the freedom of the personal lives of workers." Finally, the Labor Standards Law provides detailed requirements for medical compensation in cases of work-related illnesses and injuries, prohibits dismissal due to injury, and outlines procedures for complaining about employer response to illnesses and injuries.[446]

Japanese labor laws also contain numerous provisions that could be used against those who place women into forced labor conditions. Until 1999, the ESL forbade fee-charging employment placement projects in nearly all industries, and while recent revisions have loosened this restriction, a permit from the Minister of Labor is still required.[447] Furthermore, the ESL prescribes steep punishments for coercive or otherwise egregious types of illegal job placement activities.[448] The Workers Dispatching Law, which regulates businesses involved in the employment placement of temporary workers, provides similar penalties for "a person who has dispatched a worker with an intention of having workers do work injurious to public health or public morals."[449]

Japanese labor laws are enforced by a network of labor offices. Primary responsibility rests with the central government's Ministry of Labor. Its Labor Standards Bureau and Employment Security Bureau have local offices throughout

---

[444] Article 24.

[445] Article 17: "The employer may not offset wages against advances of money or advances of other credits made as a condition for work. In other words, may not deduct wages to collect money that is advanced on condition of labor (may not automatically deduct debt from a salary)."

[446] Labor Standards Law, Articles 19, 75-77; Enforcement Ordinance.

[447] "Labor mobility key to employment," *Yomiuri Shimbun,* July 1, 1999.

[448] Article 63 of the Act prescribes penalties of one to ten years imprisonment or a fine of fifty thousand to one million yen for: "(1) a person who has carried on or engaged in employment placement, labor recruitment or labor supply by means of violence, intimidation, imprisonment or other restraint on mental or physical freedom; (2) a person who has carried on or engaged in employment placement, labor recruitment or labor supply with an intention of having workers do work injurious to public health or public morals."

[449] Article 58. Violating this provision carries penalties of one to ten years penal servitude or a 20,000 to 3 million yen fine.

the country tasked with addressing violations of the Labor Standards Law and Employment Security Law, respectively. Tokyo and several prefectures, such as Kanagawa, Osaka, and Nagano, also have local government labor offices. A local government labor official in Tokyo told Human Rights Watch that only the Tokyo and Kanagawa labor offices are empowered to handle migrant workers' cases.[450] Labor offices generally negotiate settlements in disputes between employers and employees without recourse to the courts. However, the Labor Standards Inspection Offices also have the authority to send cases directly to the public prosecutor, while Employment Security Offices and local government labor offices can send difficult cases to the police.[451]

Immigration Law

The Immigration Control and Refugee Recognition Act (hereinafter, the Immigration Control Act) is the primary tool used by Japanese law enforcement authorities to prevent and punish the unauthorized entry, residence, and/or employment of foreigners. It is under this law that all illegal entrants, visa overstayers, foreigners engaging in "activities outside of their visa status," and holders of false travel documents are prosecuted and/or deported. While most of its provisions are targeted at the illegal aliens themselves, a new provision was enacted in 1990 providing penalties for persons involved in the job placement and employment of undocumented migrants. This provision carries the same maximum prison term — three years — as illegally entering the country or overstaying one's visa, with higher maximum fines.[452]

---

[450] Human Rights Watch interview, Tokyo, Japan, April 14, 1999.

[451] Ibid.

[452] Article 72-3: "Any person subject to any of the following items shall be punished with penal servitude not more than 3 years or a fine not more than 2 million yen, or shall be punished with both prison and a fine.
    (1) A person who has had an alien engage in illegal work in relation to business activities;
    (2) A person who has placed an alien under his control for the purpose of having the alien engage in illegal work;
    (3) A person who has repeatedly mediated either the procurement of an alien to engage in illegal work or the act specified in the preceding item."
Penalties on the illegal migrants themselves were maintained and somewhat increased: the maximum period of imprisonment remained three years, but maximum fines were increased from 100,000 yen to 300,000 yen (Article 70). In 1998, additional revisions added stiff penalties — up to ten years imprisonment and a ten million yen fine — for those involved in transporting "collective stowaways," defined as "aliens in groups who have intention to land onto Japan without obtaining landing permission . . . or with obtaining landing

Lack of due diligence in enforcing existing laws against trafficking and forced labor abuses

Despite the battery of laws described above, traffickers and employers continue to exploit migrant women with virtual impunity. Brokers and employers are sometimes targeted for their involvement in the illegal transport or employment of migrant workers, for violations of the Entertainment Businesses Law, or for procuring prostitutes for clients. According to Police Inspector Akio Koshikawa of the Community Safety Bureau, since at least the mid-1990s, several hundred people have been arrested each year for employing illegal aliens.[453] There is also some evidence that the Japanese authorities have stepped up their efforts to investigate and prosecute brokers of trafficked women for facilitating illegal migration. However, it seems that disproportionately few brokers or employers are investigated, prosecuted, or punished for the abuses they inflict on trafficked women. Though we asked every advocate and government official with whom we met for statistics or examples of brokers or employers who had been investigated or punished for abusing migrant women, Human Rights Watch was only able to identify a few cases. Morover, it appeared that even the rare instances we identified were possible only with an enormous dedication of time and resources by volunteer lawyers and other advocates in Japan. As a result, the deception, coercion, violence, intimidation, illegal confinement, debt bondage, and forced labor to which trafficked women are subjected continues to go unpunished. This may be due partly to flaws in the laws, which were not designed specifically to address abuses of the trafficking and debt bondage suffered by foreign women. But it is primarily the result of a lack of political will and apparent indifference on the part of the National Policy Agency and the Immigration Bureau to the coercion and abuse suffered by women seen as "illegal aliens" and "prostitutes."

Attorney Tadanori Onitsuka, who has spent many years working on behalf of immigration detainees, asserted that foreign women are essentially excluded from legal protection due to their undocumented immigration status:

Investigations are initiated when a victim complains. And in most cases, when [undocumented migrant] women try to appeal to police, the police say you've broken the law and must go home. So when the women try to

---

permission . . . by a false representation or other illegal measures" (Articles 74 through 74-8). These provisions were added largely in response to the increasing incidence of smuggling in migrants by boat from China. (Here and below, excerpts taken from the English translation of the law on the Japanese Ministry of Justice website. Available: http://www.moj.go.jp/ENGLISH/IB/ib-19.htm. July 2000.)

[453] Human Rights Watch interview, Tokyo, Japan, April 15, 1999.

complain about their situation to the police, the police don't take them seriously, they just focus on the women's violation of the immigration law. It's arbitrary and up to the individual police officer. If that officer wants to investigate, they will. Otherwise, if NGOs, lawyers, and other advocates push a case then the police will have to investigate. But the key point is that they should always act, and they don't.[454]

And, in Onitsuka's experience, immigration officials are also generally uninterested in addressing abuses suffered by "illegal aliens." "The subject of immigration is the foreigners — the purpose is to interview the foreigners to find a reason to deport them. . . . Even if the immigration authorities know the employer's name and address they won't bring this information to the police, because that's not their objective."[455]

In their meetings with Human Rights Watch, Japanese lawyers, migrants' rights advocates, women's shelter staff, and government officials all supported the view that neither police nor immigration officials are interested in investigating or prosecuting those responsible for the abuses suffered by undocumented migrant women. In one meeting with a panel of officials from the National Police Agency, the Criminal Affairs Bureau, and the Immigration Bureau of Japan, Human Rights Watch was given a list of legal provisions that could be used to punish the human rights abuses committed by the traffickers and employers of women from Thailand. This list included the prohibitions in the Labor Standards Law against forced labor and indebted labor; the prohibitions in the Employment Security Act and the Workers' Dispatching Law against coercive job placement and placement into work injurious to the public health or morals; the provisions regarding kidnapping and receiving a person who has been kidnapped in the Penal Code; the Immigration Control Act's provision against employing illegal aliens; and a number of Prostitution Prevention Law provisions prohibiting involvement in the business of prostitution, including specific prohibitions against using violence or threat of violence to force someone to prostitute. However, with the exception of the immigration law, the officials failed to provide specific information about their implementation of these provisions.

Immigration officer Makiyoshi Uehara said that this was the responsibility of police: "We don't have the power to do anything about [the traffickers]. So we give the information to the police and sometimes work together to crack down." Police Inspector Koshikawa provided statistics for arrests under Article 73-2 of the

---

[454] Human Rights Watch interview, Tokyo, Japan, April 17, 1999.

[455] Human Rights Watch interview, Tokyo, Japan, April 17, 1999.

Immigration Control Act, prohibiting the employment of illegal aliens,[456] but he did not know whether any of those arrested also had been charged with non-immigration criminal offenses.[457] He explained candidly, "If a foreign woman asks the *koban* [police box] for help, we first see if she is legal or illegal. If she is legal then we fight against the broker. If she is illegal then we have to send her to immigration. But at the Immigration Detention Center, they will investigate what kinds of violence she has suffered."[458] However, the task of immigration officials, in the words of immigration officer Uehara, "is deporting the women who are staying here illegally,"[459] and the evidence suggests that they are largely unconcerned with investigating abuses suffered by the people they deport. Even when immigration officials actually locate abusive employers in order to claim money to cover a woman's deportation expenses, interviews Human Rights Watch carried out with trafficking victims, local advocates, and Japanese government officials indicate that immigration officials make no effort to hold these employers accountable for the crimes they have committed against the women — or to turn relevant information over to the police for investigation. According to one local government labor official in Tokyo, who Human Rights Watch met alone, "once a year or so, high level officials from the Ministry of Labor and the Immigration Bureau have a meeting to exchange information about the numbers of cases and maybe talk about very serious cases. But these are only high-ranking officials, not case workers, so they do not discuss details."[460]

During its meeting with Japanese law enforcement officials, Human Rights Watch asked why it had not heard of any cases in which the prohibitions against coercive job placement contained in the Employment Security Law had been applied against brokers who traffic in foreign women. In response, attorney Yutaka Matsumoto of the Ministry of Justice's Criminal Affairs Bureau said that the

---

[456]	number of cases	number of people arrested
1994	47	693
1995	326	422
1996	356	452
1997	488	627
1998	499	556

(Human Rights Watch interview with Police Inspector Akio Koshikawa, Consumer and Environmental Protection Division, Community Safety Bureau, National Police Agency, Tokyo, Japan, April 15, 1999.)

[457] Ibid.

[458] Human Rights Watch interview with a panel of Japanese government officials, Tokyo, Japan, April 15, 1999.

[459] Ibid.

[460] Human Rights Watch interview, Tokyo, Japan, April 14, 1999.

penalties under this law were quite severe, and he could not explain why the law was used so rarely.[461] A local government labor official told Human Rights Watch that the job placement regulations in the Employment Security Law are poorly understood, even by officials in the Employment Security Offices,[462] and thus rarely enforced. The official went on to explain that, "when police or labor inspectors send a case to the public prosecutor, they must specify which law should be applied and what the evidence is. The forms are very complicated, so they must really understand a law in order to use it. Therefore, they will usually just use a law they understand better."[463]

For migrant women who endure forced labor and other forms of exploitation in the Japanese sex industry, officials' indifference to the violations suffered by undocumented migrants is compounded by their reluctance to enforce provisions against abusive labor practices in that industry. Attorney Yoko Hayashi told Human Rights Watch that in her experience, it had been impossible to get police to file charges of forced prostitution under the Prostitution Prevention Law:

> To prosecute forced prostitution you must first prove prostitution, and to do this you are required to produce the specific names of the customers (police will ask for business cards) — so when I asked the police why they didn't arrest employers for forced prostitution involving foreigners, they explained that it was because the women can't recognize their customers' names. To prove that forced prostitution has taken

---

[461] Human Rights Watch interview with Yutaka Matsumoto, Attorney-at-Law, Public Security Division, Criminal Affairs Bureau, Ministry of Justice, Tokyo, Japan, April 15, 1999.

Immigration attorney Tadanori Onitsuka explained that since mediating in the employment of illegal aliens is now prohibited under the Immigration Control Act, this law would be applied instead. However, though there have been some arrests under this provision, it has not been applied on a consistent basis either. (Human Rights Watch interview, Tokyo, Japan, April 17, 1999.) Furthermore, the immigration law does not target the coercive tactics often involved in the job placement, or "sale," of migrant women and provides for maximum prison terms of only three years. This penalty is stiffer than that prescribed under the Employment Security Act for non-coercive job placement activities (which carries a maximum penalty of one year of imprisonment or a 200,000 yen fine), but significantly lighter than that prescribed for coercive employment placement (maximum of ten years of imprisonment or a one million yen fine).

[462] The Employment Security Law also covers a range of other issues, such as unemployment insurance and advance warnings for lay-offs.

[463] Human Rights Watch interview, Tokyo, Japan, April 14, 1999.

place, you must prove that the woman actually took clients and so she will have to provide clients' names. Then the police will ask the clients to come in and sign a statement admitting to buying sex—without the name there will be no investigation by police.[464]

A staff member at MsLA women's shelter in Kanagawa prefecture also alleged that police only detain suspects if they have several male witnesses; the word of a prostitute alone is not considered enough.[465] Yayori Matsui, Director of the Asia-Japan Women's Resource Center, said she was given a more cynical explanation when she asked a police officer why nothing is done about the forced prostitution of foreign women: "If we make a big effort to track guns or drugs, the media will report it and we will get lots of credit. But prostitution cases take so much time and effort to investigate, and then it is still not considered news and the media won't appreciate our efforts."[466] Attorney Yukiko Oshima asserted that in some cases, at least, police inaction is due to ties with snack bar owners. She pointed to one case in which a woman had run away from a snack bar in Sawara City: "A woman ran away to HELP. It turned out that the police were close to the owners of the snack bar and often used the bar. HELP called the police station [in Sawara]. The police didn't do anything. Then HELP found out that there was a close relationship. There are many cases like this."[467]

Advocates who had tried to facilitate the investigation and prosecution of abuses suffered by trafficked women recounted numerous examples of the frustration they met at the hands of Japanese authorities. In 1994, Human Rights Watch met with Kazuo Tanaka,[468] a Japanese man who has assisted many women in their efforts to escape from debt bondage and abusive employers. He told Human Rights Watch of his persistent frustration at trying to obtain the cooperation of the police. Tanaka has collaborated with MsLA and other Japanese NGOs to rescue foreign women and refer them to shelters and embassies for assistance. In some instances he has also tried to enlist the help of the police. In 1991, for example, when the three Thai women in the "Shimodate Incident," described above, were arrested for murdering their mama, Tanaka quickly formed the "Support Group for the Three Thais in the Shimodate Case" and recruited a lawyer, Attorney

---

[464] Human Rights Watch interview, Tokyo, Japan, April 17, 1999.
[465] Presentation at the Asian Women's Human Rights Conference, Waseda University, Tokyo, Japan, March 1994.
[466] Human Rights Watch interview, Tokyo, Japan, April 16, 1999.
[467] Human Rights Watch interview, Japan, March 17, 1994.
[468] This name has been changed to protect his identity.

Chinami Kajo, to defend them.[469] Two years later, while the women's murder trial dragged on, Tanaka tried to file charges of kidnapping and pimping against the snack bar manager, recruiter, and broker involved in forcing these women to work as sex workers. Tanaka recalled,

> In August 1993, I went to the Ibaraki prefectural police department to file charges against the management of the snack where the women worked, their recruiter, and the broker for kidnapping and pimping. The prefectural police responded by saying that they did not have enough people and therefore could not conduct an investigation. I was told to go to the local police. I then went to the Shimodate police station to file the charges and they responded saying, "there is not enough evidence to prove prostitution was going on. Bring the names of thirty people who have been customers."[470]

The police refused to conduct even a preliminary investigation into these charges, despite the shocking descriptions of coercion and abuse related in the women's police statements and court testimony during the murder investigation and trial.[471] A year later, Tanaka told us that the club was still operating under a new name.[472]

In another case, police only responded reluctantly to Tanaka's appeals for assistance in rescuing nine badly beaten Thai women, but they refused to conduct any investigation of their attackers. Tanaka had met six of the women in June 1993, when they were beaten by Yakuza members after a failed escape attempt. At the time they had been too afraid to run away, but they asked Tanaka for his phone number in case they changed their minds. In August 1993, he received a call:

> I took two other men with me to the snack. As soon as I sat down, a woman sat next to me and immediately said that she was afraid and showed me wounds around her neck. Because my team had only three people, we could only take three women out. We decided to take the three with the worst wounds and then come back to get the others. We got the women out of the snack at around 12 a.m. and went to the police station.

---

[469] Chitraporn Vanaspong, "A bad remedy for prostitution," *Bangkok Post,* August 18, 1996. See the previous chapter for more details about the murder trial.

[470] Human Rights Watch interview, Japan, April 2, 1994.

[471] Furthermore, there was already extensive evidence that the women worked as prostitutes in the police record from the murder investigation and trial. Still, the police agreed only to file his allegations as a "citizen's complaint."

[472] Human Rights Watch interview, Japan, April 2, 1994.

Initially, the women didn't want to go to the police, but I told them that I would make sure the police didn't arrest them, and that it was necessary to go to try to help the other women. When we arrived, only the police from the Traffic Bureau were there. We were told to come back the next day to see the Crime Prevention Bureau, which is in charge of dealing with the Yakuza. They refused to take a report. I returned to the police station with the three women at 8 a.m. the next morning. The Crime Prevention Bureau recorded the condition of the injuries. They located the snack bar on a map and confirmed the names of the managers. I asked the police not to arrest any of the women and to arrest and punish the management for assault and organized prostitution. But the police only agreed to the former. They said that if the management was indicted, the women would have to be witnesses, and the only way the women could stay [in Japan] is if they were arrested. Forty policemen and I went to the snack in four buses. We circled the snack, but because the police didn't have an arrest warrant, they couldn't go in. I went inside with my friends and got three women. I found out that three others were at a different location and also got them. The police said that the condition of the nine women was not enough evidence for a trial.[473]

According to Tanaka, "when the police 'investigate' a snack, they telephone the snack and ask for the boss. If they get an answer that the boss isn't there, that's where the investigation ends." He concluded, "There are police who move and police who don't move. The ones who move, move only halfway."[474]

Tanaka's experiences in Ibaraki prefecture were echoed by advocates in other parts of Japan. In 1999, Human Rights Watch met with the director of a women's shelter in Tokyo who has come into contact with numerous women escaping from debt bondage, domestic violence, and other abusive situations. She pointed to many cases in which she had reported incidents to the police or sought their assistance, but had received, at best, only a reluctant response. For example, she had sought police intervention when an increasing number of Colombian women had come to the shelter in 1998 and 1999, escaping from forced sex work, but had faced stiff resistance:

When Colombian women come here, they always name the same boss. So we go to the police and tell them to arrest him, and they say "yes, yes."

---

[473] Ibid.
[474] Ibid.

But then the next woman comes and says her boss is the same man, so we go back to the police and again they say "yes, yes." They don't give us any excuses, but they don't do anything either. On February 17 [1999], they finally arrested a main boss in the Colombian trade, but this was only because a journalist exposed him and there were articles about him in the *Tokyo Shimbun* and *Yomiuri Shimbun* [two large Japanese newspapers]. Also, he was only arrested for employing illegal workers and though he is in jail now, he will probably get only a 300,000 yen [US$2,500] fine.[475]

The police had also received information about this man from the Board of Directors of the Women's Christian Temperance Union of Japan (JWCTU), who lodged a complaint after several Colombian women escaped and identified the same Japanese man as their broker. The women described being taken to strip clubs and raped in front of customers, and accused the broker of brutally beating them if they tried to resist his instructions. Staff at the shelter where the women stayed after their escape collected testimonies of forced prostitution, trafficking in persons, and assault and battery, and presented this evidence to the Japanese authorities with the support of the Colombian Embassy. Nonetheless, when the police finally arrested the man, they charged him only with employing illegal aliens.[476]

In another example recounted by the women's shelter director, the police helped to rescue several Thai girls who had been brought to Japan through adoption procedures and then forced to sell sex, but no steps were taken against those responsible:

> We just got a girl here who was one of five fifteen-year-old Thai girls brought from the same village in Thailand this January [1999] as adopted daughters. Their families in Thailand sold them to different Japanese "families," who forced them to work as prostitutes. A customer tipped off the police, and the police helped to get the girls out and they've returned to Thailand. The one who came to help had been sold to the Japanese man by her grandmother. There have not been any charges filed against the agents or families. The police are not investigating and the girls are too afraid to push for prosecution. The scariest part is that when the girls were first brought here the adoption process was

---

[475] Human Rights Watch interview, Tokyo, Japan, April 8, 1999. The name of the shelter and the director have been withheld at the director's request.

[476] HELP Asian Women's Shelter, *Network News*, No. 35, May 1999, p. 3.

not complete, and if it is completed now they could still be brought back.[477]

The director said that in her experience, reporting abusive labor conditions to the police can even backfire on the women involved: "Sometimes the police will go to the club and arrest the women there for immigration violations. And we say no, we wanted you to arrest the boss, not the women. And occasionally they will arrest a small boss and be so proud of themselves."[478]

Human Rights Watch also spoke to Japanese lawyers who have devoted considerable resources to assisting migrant women in negotiating the Japanese legal system and seeking compensation for abuses. Attorney Yukiko Oshima, who has been working on migrant women's cases since the early 1980s, explained that in most cases she simply negotiates with bosses herself in her efforts to secure some compensation for women who have been held in debt bondage: "Cases usually do not go to court because the boss does not want trouble. Petitions signed by many people can also help to force snack bar owners to pay. . . . I do not bring many cases to the attention of the police because they will not do anything." In one case in which a woman had been assaulted, however, Oshima did go to the police. "I reported the case to the police and upon investigation, the police found that the batterer was a Yakuza member. The police questioned the woman about guns and drugs only. They interrogated her all day and gave her just one small sweet bun to eat. They were not interested in forced prostitution at all."[479] Another attorney, Yoko Yoshida, affirmed that police are reluctant to investigate allegations of abuse suffered by migrant women and explained that in her experience, this problem has been compounded by immigration officials' refusal to grant stays of deportation to migrant women who wish to participate in prosecutions.[480]

Reports in the Japanese press also indicate that even when police investigations reveal egregious slavery-like abuses, including the buying and selling of women and forced sex work, only immigration-related charges are filed. For example, in January 2000, police in Chiba prefecture arrested a Japanese man who, according to their reports, recruited a 20-year-old Thai woman and sold her to a pimp for 2.2 million yen (approximately US$21,000 at January 2000 exchange rates). Police explained that this man lived in Bangkok, where he and his co-conspirators recruited women for work in Japan, receiving about 2 million yen for each woman they sent. These women were then sold to bars and other establishments in Japan

---

[477] Human Rights Watch interview, Tokyo, Japan, April 8, 1999.
[478] Ibid.
[479] Human Rights Watch interview, Tokyo, Japan, March 17, 1994.
[480] Human Rights Watch interview, Tokyo, Japan, April 17, 1999.

for 4 million yen each. Despite the nature of these practices, the man was arrested only on charges of promoting illegal migrant labor in violation of the Immigration Control and Refugee Recognition Act.[481]

---

[481] "Bangkok resident arrested in recruitment of Thai women," Kyodo News International, January 24, 2000.
    In another recent example, the Public Safety Division of the Tokyo Metropolitan Police and the Nogata and Suginama branch officers announced in August 1999 that they had made fourteen arrests in connection with their investigation of foreign prostitution rings in the Kabuki-cho area of Tokyo. According to police, the suspects included three Thai brokers who were involved in sending women from Thailand to Japan, where they were placed under the brokers' supervision and forced to engage in sex work. During their investigation, the police found two women from northern Thailand who had been locked up in an apartment in Kabuki-cho and forced to pay off debts of 4.5 million yen (US$38,500) each through sex work. An article in the *Asahi Shimbun* reported, "The women, the police said, were essentially living in captivity under the control of the three brokers, sharing a room and working at night in the bar." The police charged the brokers with employing illegal aliens, in violation of the Immigration Control Act, and with placing workers into harmful and illegal work, in violation of the Employment Security Act. While the latter charge demonstrates some acknowledgment of the abuses the women faced, no charges of forced labor, forced prostitution, intimidation, or illegal confinement were filed. (See "Prostitution ring broken in Shinjuku," *Asahi Shimbun* (English edition), August 12, 1999; and "3 Thais arrested for arranging prostitution in Japan," *Japan Policy & Politics,* August 12, 1999. For a more complete description of the charges filed against the brokers, see "Metropolitan Police Arrest 14 People Suspected of Trafficking and Prostituting Thai Women," *Asahi Shimbun* (Japanese edition), August 12, 1999.)
    For a similar case involving Colombian women, see "The increase in Colombian prostitution," *Asahi Shimbun* (Japanese edition), June 22, 1999; and "70 held in move to stem prostitution," *Asahi Shimbun* (English edition), June 17, 1999. See also: "Date club owner arrested in Yokohama," *Kanagawa Shimbun* (Japanese edition), June 15, 1994; "Prosecution in Yokohama," *Kanagawa Shimbun* (Japanese edition), November 13, 1993; and "Police Arrest Two Japanese Accused of Trading Women," *Yomiuri Shimbun,* October 9, 1992.
    Ironically, while brokers are virtually never arrested for placing women into abusive and coercive working conditions, a newspaper report from 1998 indicates that on at least one occasion, Japanese police have actually arrested a broker on charges of defrauding a snack bar manager. The "broker," Masashiro Yasuzawa, went to Narita airport with two Thai women who had been living in Japan illegally for a year and a half. There he introduced the women to a snack bar manager, telling the manager that the women had just arrived from Thailand that morning. The manager paid him 3.8 million yen, and took the women back to his snack bar. They began working for the manager that night, but when they went out with customers, they never returned. Instead, they went back to Yasuzawa, who paid them each 500,000 yen. ("Lied about introducing Thai women — got 3.8 million yen

Laws and policies that exacerbate trafficking victims' vulnerability to abuse

The indifference of Japanese officials is reflected in — and compounded by — laws and policies that exacerbate trafficked women's vulnerability to abuse in the snack bars. Rather than providing women with an incentive to turn to authorities and report the violations they have suffered, Japanese policies and practices have targeted them as illegal aliens, excluded them from crucial labor protections, and denied them access to critical government services such as shelter and subsidized medical care.

Targeted and mistreated as "illegal aliens" and "prostitutes"

Japanese immigration policies are designed to eliminate illegal migration. No provisions are included in the Immigration Control Act to address the coercive and abusive tactics often employed by those who facilitate illegal migration and/or employ illegal migrants; the penalties prescribed for facilitating illegal migration and employment are of approximately the same severity as those for being an "illegal alien." A foreigner may be punished with to up to three years' imprisonment and/or a 300,000 yen fine for the crimes of illegal entry, overstaying one's visa, and — as of February 18, 2000 — an unlawful stay in Japan. The new crime of "unlawful stay" was created to counter the effects of the three year statute of limitations on immigration violations. Previously, while persons who entered Japan legally and then overstayed their visas were always liable for imprisonment and fines (as "overstaying" is an on-going crime), those who entered the country illegally could only be subjected to such penalties during the first three years after their entry (after three years had elapsed, such persons could still be deported with a temporary reentry ban, but they were not liable for imprisonment or fines). Establishing "unlawful stay" as an on-going crime eliminates this distinction.

In practice, when foreigners are arrested solely for violations of the Immigration Control Act, jail terms and fines are typically waived or suspended, but this relies on officials' discretion. No effort is made to identify victims of trafficking, who should be exempt from punitive treatment for immigration violations (though repatriation may be appropriate).[482] As described in the preceding chapter, women who are picked up in raids are forced to remain in immigration detention until they can prepare the documentation and funds to return home, even when their alleged immigration violations were a result of the coercive and deceptive actions of their traffickers and employers. Then, they are deported

---

by fraud," *Asahi Shimbun* (Japanese edition), September 23, 1998.

[482] While the Immigration Control Act explicitly excepts persons who qualify as refugees from penalties for the offenses of illegal entry and overstaying visas, no similar exceptions are made for victims of trafficking and forced labor.

as illegal aliens with punitive reentry bans, even when they have escaped from debt bondage and voluntarily surrendered to authorities. In sum, while trafficking abuses go largely unpunished, trafficking victims are subjected to punitive procedures that entirely fail to recognize or address the abuses they have faced.

This injustice is compounded by the anti-immigrant bias which is evident in both the writing and enforcement of the Immigration Control Act, with negative implications for all undocumented foreigners in Japan, including women victims of trafficking and debt bondage. The law discourages undocumented migrants from seeking assistance from government agencies or medical facilities by requiring civil servants to report to the immigration authorities any foreigner they know to be living in Japan illegally.[483] It facilitates prolonged and arbitrary detention of undocumented migrants through provisions allowing immigration officials to detain such persons indefinitely pending deportation.[484] It criminalizes the failure to carry one's passport at all times, without providing any penalty for passport confiscation.[485] And, though the law contains provisions for punishing persons involved in the transport, job placement, and employment of illegal migrants,

---

[483] According to Article 62(2), "Any official of the government or a local public entity shall inform the immigration authorities if he comes to have knowledge, in the performance of his duties, of an undocumented immigrant."

As will be discussed below, there have been modifications to this rule in response to concerns from the Ministry of Labor and the Ministry of Health, and reports indicate that labor official and medical professionals rarely turn undocumented migrants over to immigration officials. Still, the fear of being turned in can prevent migrants from accessing such services, and police commonly report suspected illegal aliens to immigration.

[484] According to Article 52, if a deportee cannot be deported immediately upon the issuance of a written deportation order, "an ICO may detain him in an Immigration Center, detention house, or other places designated by the Minister of Justice or by a SII commissioned by the Minister of Justice until such time as deportation becomes possible." There are no checks or limits on this power.

[485] In a highly unusual case in December 1997, a family of ethnic Japanese Brazilians sued their employer for refusing to return their passports when they wanted to return to Brazil following the Great Hanshin Earthquake in 1995. The Kobe District Judge ruled that it was illegal for employers to refuse to return the passports of migrant employees and ordered the defendant to pay 380,000 yen in compensation, in addition to 450,000 yen in unpaid wages, to the plaintiffs. However, the Judge also decided that it was not illegal for an employer to hold passports if requested to do so, despite the fact that Japanese immigration law requires that all foreigners carry their passports at all times. ("Kobe Court Ruling: Refusing to Return a Passport is Illegal," *The New Observer* (Tokyo, Japan), 1998.)

enforcement has focused disproportionately on the arrest, detention and deportation of undocumented migrants, rather than on those who exploit them.[486]

In the period just after the 1990 revisions were enacted, the immigration law was only weakly enforced. With Japan's economic boom and labor shortage, relatively few foreigners were arrested and deported. But as the Japanese economy slid into a recession in 1992, concern about illegal immigration mounted. In early 1993, a Workshop on Counterplans Against Illegal Workers was established by the National Police Agency, the Immigration Bureau of the Ministry of Justice, the Ministry of Labor, and the Management and Coordination Agency.[487] Immigration officials, in cooperation with the police, began to enforce laws against illegal migrants more vigorously, and, while fines and jail terms were still rarely enforced, arrests and deportations for immigration violations rose dramatically. Deportations nearly doubled in 1992, rising from 36,275 in 1991 to 66,892 in 1992, and then rose again to 69,136 in 1993.[488] These figures include 8,088 Thai nationals deported in 1992, and a record 13,283 Thais deported in 1993.[489] Since 1993, the number of deportations, like the number of estimated overstayers, has gradually decreased. In 1996, 52,550 persons were deported, more than 99.8 percent of them for violations of the Immigration Control Act.[490] At the same time, visa application procedures have been tightened in an effort to screen out applicants deemed likely to overstay their visas. Since Thai nationals account for a significant percentage of

---

[486] Kiriro Morita and Saskia Sassen, "The New Illegal Immigration in Japan, 1980-1992," *International Migration Review,* vol. xxviii, no. 1, 1993. As will be discussed below, 1990 revisions to the Immigration Control Act added punishments for recruiting and employing illegal immigrants, but the provisions against the migrants themselves are still more vigorously enforced.

[487] "Cracking Down of Foreign Workers; Government Exploits Recession Fears," interview with Kobayashi Kengo, *AMPO Japan-Asia Quarterly Review,* vol. 25., no. 1, 1994.

[488] Ministry of Justice, Japan, "Immigration: Deportation of Foreign Nationals; Illegal Work, Illegal Entry, Narcotics." Available: http://www.moj.go.jp/ENGLISH/IB/ib-11.htm. July 2000.

[489] "13,283 Thais deported from Japan last year," *Bangkok Post,* October 30, 1994.

[490] Ministry of Justice, Japan, "Immigration: Deportation of Foreign Nationals; Illegal Work, Illegal Entry, Narcotics." Available: http://www.moj.go.jp/ENGLISH/IB/ib-11.htm. July 2000. These were the most recent statistics available on the Japanese Ministry of Justice website when this report was being prepared.

"overstayers" in Japan, Thai women have been particularly affected by these efforts.[491]

The government also launched a mass media campaign criticizing foreigners and conducted high-profile mass arrests of foreigners in public places like parks.[492] During these raids, all foreigners who could not produce proper identification were detained and subjected to long interrogation sessions. Those found in violation of immigration regulations were sent to detention centers to begin deportation procedures.[493] The Ministry of Justice further contributed to the stigmatization of foreigners by publishing misleading statistics that portrayed migrant workers as increasingly criminally-inclined, despite the fact that the "crime" in question is typically not murder or theft, but simply residing illegally in Japan.[494]

Women working in the entertainment industry, including women working as hostesses in *baishun* snack bars,[495] have been specifically targeted by immigration crackdown efforts. In 1994, for example, the Immigration Bureau carried out a crackdown on illegal immigrants in Tokyo, Osaka, and Nagoya that concentrated

---

[491] Human Rights Watch interview with Attorney Tadanori Onitsuka, Tokyo, Japan, April 17, 1999. Note that according to Japanese Ministry of Justice statistics, in January 1997, fourteen percent of the 282,986 undocumented migrants in Japan were Thai nationals (Immigration Bureau, Ministry of Justice, "Change in Number of Illegal Stayers by Countries of Origin," March 9, 1997).

[492] Human Rights Watch interview with Toru Takahashi, Immigration Review Task Force member, Tokyo, Japan, April 8, 1999.

[493] Luke Thomas, "Beating on Foreigners: Victims of the Immigration Gulag," *Tokyo Underground*, Issue 1, January 1995.

[494] The Ministry of Justice's *1994 White Paper* included a section entitled "A Rapid Growth of Criminal Offenses Committed by Foreign Visitors." However, a careful reading shows that of all the foreign "criminals," 69.7 percent were prosecuted under the Immigration Control Act (Ministry of Justice, Japan, 1994 White Paper, 1995, p. 243). Similarly, in the *Summary of The White Paper on Crime 1998*, the discussion of foreign "special law offenders" fails to point out that these laws include the Immigration Control Act, so irregular immigration status is enough to qualify one as an "offender." Also, while the Ministry of Justice admits that the number of foreign penal code offenders fell in 1998, it is quick to point out that this figure is still seven times higher than it was in 1980 (Ministry of Justice, Japan, *Summary of The White Paper on Crime 1998*. Available: http://www.moj.go.jp/ENGLISH/RATI/1998/rati-08.htm. September 1999). For a more detailed analysis of Japanese officials' misleading use of arrest statistics to stigmatize foreigners, see Jens Wilkinson, "Gaijin Crime? A Look Behind the Statistics," *Tokyo Observer,* issue 22, 1996.

[495] *Baishun* means "prostitution," and "baishun snack bars" are snack bars that involve sexual exchanges.

on persons involved in prostitution and persons with forged passports or visas.[496] The campaign involved large-scale arrests without warrants and interrogations of foreigners, and included a well-publicized initiative in the Kabuki-cho district of Shinjuku Ward in Tokyo, an entertainment district in which a large number of foreign women are employed. This initiative was carried out under the auspices of the "Environmental Clean-Up Policy Headquarters," which had recently been established in the Shinjuku Police Headquarters.[497] In July of that year alone, these efforts led to the deportation of 2,686 foreigners, 520 of whom were Thai nationals.[498] Such crackdown efforts have continued. In May 2000, for example, immigration authorities carried out two sweeps of a total of twelve bars and nightclubs in Tokyo's Kabuki-cho district. According to officials, the first sweep, on May 16, was Japan's largest capture of illegal aliens in a single search: it resulted in the detention of 149 illegal aliens working in eight different bars. In all, 177 people who had either entered Japan illegally or overstayed their visas were taken into custody, and the majority of those detained were women working as hostesses. Immigration officials explained that while deportation procedures for the detained women were already underway, the firms who employed these women were unlikely to face criminal charges. "Since the intent of the search was to cleanse the environment of the area, it probably won't come to that (i.e., to charges against employers)," a Tokyo Regional Immigration Bureau official was quoted as saying.[499]

Foreign women have also been targeted in the enforcement of the Prostitution Prevention Law. Since at least the mid-1990s, most of the approximately one thousand arrests under the PPL for solicitation each year have been of foreign women. And women from Thailand have been particularly affected, accounting for approximately half of the foreign women arrested under the Prostitution Prevention

---

[496] "July raids send 2,700 illegals home," *Japan Times*, October 9, 1994.

[497] Thomas, "Beating on Foreigners . . ." *Tokyo Underground*, Issue 1.

[498] 1,611 men and 1,075 women were deported, and while the largest number of male deportees were from South Korea, the largest number of female deportees were from Thailand (Ibid.).

[499] "177 illegal aliens caught in two raids," *The Japan Times*, May 28, 2000.

Law each year.[500]   Once convicted of prostitution, women are deported with virtually no chance of ever being issued a visa to reenter Japan.[501]

In August 1999, the Diet adopted further revisions to the Immigration Control Act at the urging of the Immigration Bureau. These have worrisome implications for women from Thailand who are resident in Japan, though it is too early as yet to assess their effect in practice. The revisions, which took effect on February 18, 2000, establish "unlawful stay" as a crime and lengthen the ban on reentry after deportation from one year to five years.[502]   As explained above, the crime of "unlawful stay" essentially eliminates the three-year statute of limitations on the crime of illegal entry, making all undocumented migrants in Japan permanently liable for imprisonment and fines. Migrants and their advocates fear that the decision to enact this new provision signals the government's intention to seek jail terms and fines for immigration offenses more frequently; currently, such penalties are typically waived or suspended.

The extended ban on reentry means that a person who is deported from Japan for any reason will have to wait at least five years before even applying for a visa to reenter the country. Our research indicated that among women from Thailand, the reentry ban primarily affected those who wished to settle legally in Japan with Japanese husbands. These women often surrendered to immigration authorities, were deported to Thailand, and then applied for a legal visa to reenter Japan after one year, with a letter from their prospective husband. A five year reentry ban

---

[500] For overall statistics on arrests under PPL, see Research and Training Institute, Ministry of Justice, Japan, "Summary of the White Paper on Crime 1997." Available: http://www.moj.go.jp/ENGLISH/RATI/rati-65.htm. September 1999.

For statistics of foreign women arrested under PPL, see Human Rights Watch interview with Police Inspector Akio Koshikawa, Consumer and Environmental Protection Division, Community Safety Bureau, National Police Agency, Tokyo, Japan, April 15, 1999. Inspector Koshikawa provided the following statistics on arrests of foreign women under the Prostitution Prevention Law:

	total	Thai
1995	850	493 (58%)
1996	593	272 (46%)
1997	830	371 (45%)

[501] Human Rights Watch interview with Attorney Tadanori Onitsuka, Tokyo, Japan, April 17, 1999.

[502] See Nobuyuki Sato, "Point of View: It's time for Japan to guarantee foreigners' rights," *Asahi Shimbun,* May 27, 1999; Naoya Wada, Administrative Documentation Lawyer, Wada Legal Administrative & Translation Services, e-mail to Human Rights Watch, November 2, 1999.

could therefore result in longer separations of families (which often include children).

These revisions prompted immediate criticism from migrant support groups in Japan when they were proposed by the Ministry of Justice in late 1998. The National Network in Solidarity with Migrant Workers/Japan (NNSMW) issued a strong statement alleging that the revisions infringed on "the right of families to remain together by extending the waiting period for reentry following forcible repatriation," and disregarded the "acquired rights of residence" which migrants accrue through living normal, productive, and law-abiding lives in Japan.[503] Migrants' advocates also pointed out that these revisions demonstrated an increasing intolerance towards undocumented migrants. Toru Takahashi, a member of the Immigration Review Task Force of Japan, noted that lengthening the ban on reentry after deportation "doesn't make sense, because even now it is up to the Ministry of Justice to decide whether someone can reenter after that one year, and in reality it is usually very difficult and takes much longer than a year anyway."[504]

On the other hand, at the time that this report was being prepared in early 2000, there were also some indications that the Ministry of Justice's attitude towards undocumented immigrants was softening. In February 2000, for example, four Iranian families — a total of sixteen people — who had overstayed their visas were granted special permission to reside in Japan. Their petitions for residency had been submitted to the ministry with the support of the Asian People's Friendship Society, a Tokyo-based NGO that was established in 1989 to provide assistance to foreigners on a wide range of issues, including labor rights and marriage. The Ministry of Justice's decision reportedly took into account the fact that children in these families had grown up in Japan and would have difficultly adjusting to life in Iran.[505] Taking such a consideration into account was a welcome departure from usual practice. Human Rights Watch hopes that the ministry will work towards the systematic incorporation of concerns regarding foreigners' welfare and wellbeing in the design and implementation of immigration policy in the future.

Excluded from Labor Protections

Japan's labor laws could provide an important source of protection from — and compensation for — the abuses associated with trafficking and debt bondage. However, Human Rights Watch found that women victims of trafficking and debt

---

[503] NNSMW, "Stop! The 1999 Immigration Control Law Revision," *Migrant Network News,* Issue No. 12, March 1999, p. 3.

[504] Human Rights Watch interview, Tokyo, Japan, April 8, 1999.

[505] Hiroshi Matsubara, "Standards needed for granting residence status: rights activist," *The Japan Times,* February 21, 2000.

bondage in the Japanese sex industry were denied access to these protections as a result of their immigration status and occupation.

Lack of labor rights protections for undocumented immigrants

The protections established under the Labor Standards Law (LSL) apply regardless of workers' immigration status.[506] The LSL makes no distinction on the basis of immigration status and official orders — or *tsutatsu*[507] — issued by the Labor Standards Bureau to its staff in 1988 and 1990 explicitly instructed officials to deal strictly with violations of the labor standards laws even in cases involving "illegal" foreign workers. But these same orders also instructed officials to report illegal workers to immigration authorities, a requirement that must obviously

---

[506] Article 3 states that "[n]o employer shall discriminate against or for any worker by reason of nationality, creed or social status in wages, working hours and other working conditions."

In January 1997, Japan's Supreme Court awarded wage compensation to an undocumented migrant worker from Pakistan who was injured while working in Japan. The issue of contention was whether income losses should be estimated based on his income in Japan or on his expected income in Pakistan. Supporting the decision of the Tokyo High Court, the Supreme Court ruled that while estimated losses should not be calculated differently based upon the worker's nationality, "the estimated period of future work in Japan should take into consideration the foreigner's individual situation." The judge said in the ruling that undocumented workers could not work for long in Japan, and therefore decided that his losses should be estimated based on three years of work in Japan (at 170,000 yen per month) and thirty-nine years of work in Pakistan (at 30,000 yen per month). ("Illegal Foreign Worker Awarded Three Year's of Income Lost Because of On-the-Job Accident," *Japan Labor Bulletin,* vol. 36, no. 4, April 1, 1997. Available:http://www.jil.go.jp/bulletin/year/1997/vol36-04/05.htm. November 1999.)

[507] *Tsutatsu* are bureaucratic orders that are issued by upper level ministry officials and then strictly followed by the ministry's staff at all levels of the government. The Japan Export Information Center at the U.S. Department of Commerce defines "tsutatsu" as "written administrative guidance given by government officials to related parties/organizations/companies" (Japan Export Information Center, *Destination Japan: A Business Guide for the 90s (Second Edition),* May 1994.   Available: http://www.gwjapan.com/ftp/pub/business/destjpn/destjpn2.txt. September 1999.)

These orders are considered interpretations of the law, and are often given more weight than the law itself, though in many cases they are not clearly described or disseminated to the public. (See Human Rights Watch interviews with Toru Takahashi, Immigration Review Task Force member, Tokyo, Japan, April 8, 1999; and with Atty. Yoko Yoshida, Kyoto, Japan, April 13, 1999.)

discourage undocumented migrants from seeking their assistance.[508] In 1991, the Compensation Division of the Labor Standards Bureau issued a tsutatsu instructing its staff not to inform the immigration authorities when illegals ask for assistance before the worker receives compensation, although it did not say what should be done after any such compensation had been obtained.[509] Then in 1993, the Labor Minister announced that labor officials should give higher priority to reducing labor violations than to reporting immigration violations. This position was later confirmed by the Minister of Justice, who was asked by the Japanese Diet to comment on the potentially conflicting duties arising out of the immigration reporting requirement. The Minister issued a general statement providing that, if the reporting requirement might interfere with a government official's primary job, the official may prioritize his or her primary job. This was an important step forward with implications for a variety of government officials, including those in the Ministry of Labor and the Ministry of Health, apparently allowing them to ignore the immigration reporting requirement in certain circumstances without fear of recrimination.

Lack of labor rights protections in the sex industry
The labor rights of trafficked women in the sex industry are also unclear because of the nature of the work. Protections in the Labor Standards Law are limited to employees of specified industries, namely "hotels, restaurants, snack bars, allied trades and recreation hall enterprises."[510] Although this would appear to cover hostesses in snack bars, the law was written before such businesses were defined and categorized by the Entertainment Businesses Law, and the meaning of "snack bar" for the purposes of the law is not clear.[511] In addition, the LSL applies only when a worker "is employed in the abovementioned enterprises or offices . .

---

[508] The Forum on Asian Immigrant Workers, *Citizen's Report on the Human Rights of Foreign Workers in Japan,* April 17, 1993, p. 33.

[509] Compensation Division Statement no. 7, March 25, 1991. (Akira Hatade, "Labor Movement Regarding Foreign Workers," in Hiroshi Takana and Takashi Ebashi [eds.], *Rainichi Gaikokujin Jinken Hakusho [White paper on human rights for foreigners in Japan]* (1997), p. 106).

[510] Article 8(14). If the term "allied trades" in Article 8(14) is interpreted to include the business of procuring women for the snack bars, then brokers are within the purview of the law as well.

[511] Human Rights Watch interview with a local government labor official, Tokyo, Japan, April 14, 1999.

. and receives wages therefrom."[512] Snack bar owners and managers often describe hostesses as "freelance" workers, rather than "employees" of the snack bar, thus circumventing the responsibilities that go with being an "employer" under the law even though, in practice, they maintain high levels of control over the terms and conditions of the women's work on a consistent basis.

In addition, the very illegality of businesses of "prostitution" makes it unclear whether they fall within the scope of any labor laws. The law provides penalties for women engaged in public solicitation, and while there are no penalties provided for the act of exchanging sexual intercourse for compensation, it is also prohibited under the law. Moreover, the illegal status of "prostitution" stigmatizes all women in the industry as persons in need of "guidance" and "resocialization."[513] It has thus reinforced a climate in which women working in the sex entertainment industry — both legally and illegally — try to hide their occupation, thus reducing these women's access to employment-related government benefits, including the services of labor protection offices.[514] And the Prostitution Prevention Law does not provide any provisions for wage or other compensation when prostitutes' labor rights are violated. As noted above, even the punishments for coercive labor practices under the PPL are substantially less than those imposed for such practices under LSL.

Denial of access to critical public services, such as subsidized health care

The Japanese government not only fails to offer services specifically designed to provide redress to women victims of trafficking and debt bondage, it explicitly denies such women access to basic public services on the basis of their undocumented immigration status. One clear example is the blanket exclusion of undocumented women from public women's shelters.[515] Another example that has

---

[512] Article 10. Note that Article 11 defines "wage" as "the wage, salary, allowance, bonus and every other payment to the worker from the employer as remuneration of labor under whatever name they may be called."

[513] While no longer common in practice, women convicted of violating the PPL may be sentenced to "guidance disposition" in a women's guidance home. Like other correctional institutions, the woman's guidance home is administered by the Ministry of Justice's Correction Bureau, but it is designed to give women "protection and guidance as well as medical treatment necessary for their resocialization." Correction Bureau, Ministry of Justice, Japan, "The Women's Guidance Home." Available: http://www.moj.go.jp/ENGLISH/CB/cb-02.htm. September 1999.

[514] Human Rights Watch interview with Momocca Momocco, founder of SWEETLY (Sex Workers! Encourage, Empower, Trust and Love Yourselves!), Kyoto, Japan, April 12, 1999.

[515] Note that the effects of this rule may be mitigated in some shelters where staff practice a "don't ask, don't tell" policy regarding immigration status.

drawn enormous criticism from advocates in Japan is the discriminatory treatment of migrants in Japanese health care policies. These policies are described at some length below, as access to health care is repeatedly cited as a key concern by both women victims of trafficking and by representatives of local NGOs who work with these women.

Trafficked women, like many other foreigners in Japan, face a variety of problems in obtaining adequate access to health care. These obstacles include language barriers — very few medical facilities offer interpreters — and a lack of information about available services. Women held in debt bondage face additional problems stemming from their lack of wages and the strict control that employers exercise over their freedom of movement. They must rely on their mamas to bring them to the doctor, provide them with funds to pay for their visit and any necessary medication, and accurately share the doctor's assessment, while respecting their confidentiality.

Rather than assist women in overcoming these obstacles, the Japanese government has exacerbated these problems with health care policies that discriminate against trafficked women on the basis of their immigration status. Japan has taken significant steps over the last several decades to ensure the highest attainable standard of health for its citizens. However, as a member of the Japanese delegation to the United Nations Human Rights Committee made clear during the discussion of Japan's Fourth Periodic Report on compliance with the ICCPR, immigration control considerations have been given priority over health when it comes to migrant populations:

> With respect to medical assistance for illegal aliens: the national medical insurance and other medical insurances and medical aid within public assistance, these would not be applied to illegal foreigners residing in Japan. If these systems are applied to illegal aliens, there is the potential of encouraging illegal sojourn or illegal residence in Japan, and we do not think this is favorable.[516]

These policies contravene Japan's obligations as a party to the International Covenant on Economic, Social and Cultural Rights (ICESCR). Under the ICESCR, Japan is obligated to "recognize the right of everyone to the enjoyment of the highest attainable standard of physical and mental health" and to take the steps

---

[516] Suginaka, Ministry of Health and Welfare, 1716 meeting of HRC, October 29, 1998

necessary "for the creation of conditions which would assure to all medical service and medical attention in the event of sickness."[517] The covenant expressly forbids discrimination of any kind in the provision of these rights, including discrimination against non-nationals.

Discrimination in access to emergency health care

The most dramatic example of Japan's discriminatory policies is the 1990 decision by the Ministry of Health and Welfare to limit "livelihood protection" to Japanese citizens and permanent residents. The Japanese health care system is based on the principle of universal health insurance coverage,[518] but a final safety net is provided by the Livelihood Protection Law which, among other things, reimburses hospitals for the cost of emergency medical care when patients are unable to pay their bills. This funding is provided regardless of employment or residency status and is designed as a final measure to ensure the safeguarding of individuals' life and health.[519] Undocumented and short term migrants are excluded from Japan's national health insurance schemes on the rationale that admitting undocumented migrant workers into the system would encourage illegal stays in the country.[520] But for more than forty years, the livelihood protection system had been available to all persons, regardless of immigration status. In 1990, despite the pleas of advocates and various local authorities, such protection was removed by

---

[517] Article 12. Ratified by Japan on June 21, 1979.

[518] The majority of Japanese citizens, about seventy million, are covered under the Health Insurance Law, which provides health insurance to laborers in a position of regular employment at a fixed place of business. Another forty-two million people are insured under the National Health Insurance system, which applies by law to all residents of Japan who have a specific address in a town, city, or village. These policies include both physical and mental health care needs. (Japan Civil Liberties Union, "1998 Report Concerning the Present Status of Human Rights in Japan (Third Counter Report)", October 1998; "The Japanese National Health Insurance Scheme," *MF-MASH News,* no. 17, September 1998, p. 5.; Dr. Takashi Sawada, e-mail to Human Rights Watch, October 9, 1999.)

[519] Japan Civil Liberties Union, "1998 Report Concerning the Present Status of Human Rights in Japan (Third Counter Report)."

[520] While the laws governing these insurance schemes make no distinction based on immigration status, the Ministry of Health and Welfare has issued directives excluding undocumented workers from coverage under either scheme. ("State must supply health care for illegal aliens, panel says," *Japan Times,* May 27, 1995.)

administrative order.[521] This order removed resources previously available for the emergency health care of undocumented (and legal, non-permanent) foreigners, directly contravening Japan's obligation under ICESCR to work towards the progressive realization of the rights enshrined in the convention.[522]

Doctors and hospitals still have an obligation to accept all persons in need of emergency medical care, but by deciding that it would no longer reimburse unpaid bills for foreigners (with the exception of permanent residents), the government has deterred medical professionals from meeting this obligation when the patients are foreigners.[523] In a few prefectures, the effects of this policy have been mitigated by local government decisions to reimburse hospitals when foreigners fail to pay their medical bills.[524] But in other prefectures, local governments have refused to carry such expenses. Dr. Takashi Sawada, a doctor at the Minatomachi Medical Clinic, which serves foreign patients, told us that "in Tokyo and Kanagawa prefectures, where they have this [reimbursement] system, it is much better than in Chiba and Ibaraki, where they don't and acceptance of uninsured migrants is low."[525]

---

[521] Japan Civil Liberties Union, "1998 Report Concerning the Present Status of Human Rights in Japan (Third Counter Report)."

Note that emergency psychiatric care is still available to all persons regardless of immigration status under the Mental Health and Welfare Act, which provides free treatment for severe cases in which patients are in danger of harming themselves or others.

[522] ICESCR, Article 2(1). According to Article 14(e) of the Maastricht Guidelines on Violations of Economic, Social and Cultural Rights, (Maastricht, January 22-26, 1997): "Violations of economic, social and cultural rights can occur through the direct action of States or other entities insufficiently regulated by States. Examples of such violations include . . . The adoption of any deliberately retrogressive measure that reduces the extent to which any such right is guaranteed."

[523] See Human Rights Watch interview with Nigoon Jitthai, researcher at the Graduate School of Medicine, Tokyo University, Tokyo, Japan, April 17, 1999; Hiroshi Hayakawa, "Dr. Haruto takes charge in Yokosuka Chuo Clinic," MF-MASH News, no. 11, June 1995, p. 7; Human Rights Watch interview with Dr. Takashi Sawada of the Minatomachi Medical Clinic, Tokyo, Japan, April 7, 1999.

[524] In particular, there have been efforts to employ provisions of a law originally designed to protect domestic (Japanese) travelers and persons without money or a residence, under which hospitals are reimbursed for outstanding medical bills by local governments. Since the Ministry of Health and Welfare's 1990 decision to withhold livelihood protection from foreigners without permanent residency, this law has been used in some areas to cover undocumented migrants.

[525] Human Rights Watch interview, Tokyo, Japan, April 7, 1999.

Denial of subsidized treatment for HIV/AIDS

Trafficked women are also denied access to government subsidies for HIV/AIDS treatment — which are available to all Japanese citizens and long-term legal residents in Japan — on the basis of their immigration status.[526] This policy stands in contravention to the recommendations of the Committee on the Elimination of All Forms of Discrimination Against Women (CEDAW), which noted that trafficked women are particularly vulnerable to HIV/AIDS and should be guaranteed access to HIV/AIDS-related services without discrimination. In 1999, CEDAW stated that "issues of HIV/AIDS and other sexually transmitted disease are central to the rights of women and adolescent girls to sexual health" and, specifically, recommended that all states "should ensure, without prejudice and discrimination, the right to sexual health information, education and services for all women and girls, including those who have been trafficked, even if they are not legally resident in the country."[527] CEDAW went on to explain:

> While biological differences between women and men may lead to differences in health status, there are societal factors which are determinative of the health status of women and men which can vary among women themselves. For that reason, special attention should be given to the health needs and rights of women belonging to vulnerable and disadvantaged groups, such as migrant women, refugee and internally displaced women, the girl child and older women, women in prostitution, indigenous women and women with physical or mental disabilities.[528]

---

[526] Government-subsidized HIV/AIDS treatment is provided under the Welfare Act for Disabled People, and only citizens and foreigners with at least a one-year work visa are covered. (Human Rights Watch interview with Dr. Takashi Sawada, Tokyo, Japan, April 7, 1999.)

Rutsuko Shoji, Director of HELP Asian Women's Shelter, told Human Rights Watch how Japan's discriminatory policy regarding HIV/AIDS treatment was reducing one woman's chance of returning to Thailand before she dies. The woman was a third generation Vietnamese "refugee" who was born and raised in a refugee camp in Thailand and trafficked into Japan at age sixteen. HELP and others were trying to persuade the Thai government to allow her to return to Thailand, but in the meantime, she remained in Japan, where she was being denied access to medication that could prolong her life.(Human Rights Watch interview, Tokyo, Japan, April 8, 1999.).

[527] Committee on the Elimination of Discrimination Against Women, "General Recommendation No. 24," 20th session, 1999, paragraph 18.

[528] Ibid., paragraph 6.

The particular vulnerability of female trafficking victims and other foreign women to HIV/AIDS in Japan was confirmed by Japan's National AIDS Surveillance Committee. This found that from 1985 through 1997, non-Japanese females accounted for thirty-four percent of all HIV cases and eight percent of all AIDS cases and non-Japanese males accounted for fourteen percent of HIV cases and twenty percent of AIDS cases. While "non-Japanese" may include foreigners whose residency status qualifies them for coverage under the Welfare for Disabled People Act, the National AIDS Surveillance Committee notes that "the peak of HIV cases seen in 1992 was due to non-Japanese females, mainly young women from Southeast Asia."[529] Given Japanese immigration policies, it is unlikely that many, if any, of them qualified for state-funded HIV/AIDS treatment. And given the research conducted by Human Rights Watch and other organizations, it is very likely that many of these women were victims of trafficking from Thailand and other countries. The proportion of non-Japanese among the overall number of HIV/AIDS sufferers is much higher in areas that receive large numbers of migrant women from Thailand. One study found, for example, that more than ninety percent of all non-hemophiliac cases of HIV and AIDS in Nagano and Ibaraki prefectures involved foreign migrants, with most of those infected coming from Thailand and other Asian countries, and no less than ninety-nine percent of them illegally overstaying their visas.[530] In accordance with CEDAW's recommendations, the government should take urgent steps to ensure that trafficked women who are infected with HIV/AIDS are provided with all appropriate medical care and treatement on the same basis as others.

Discrimination in access to reproductive health care

Japanese health care policies regarding maternal and child health also discriminate against undocumented migrants in contravention of the reproductive health guarantees in the Women's Convention.[531] Under the 1965 Maternal and Child Health Law, the government provides pre-natal and post-natal medical care, including check-ups during pregnancy, check-ups for infants, and vaccinations for children free of charge to all women who register their pregnancies. Upon registration, women receive a maternal and child health care handbook and coupons

---

[529] National Institute of Infectious Diseases, "AIDS/HIV Surveillance in Japan, 1985-1997," *Infectious Agents Surveillance Report,* vol. 19, no. 4 (no. 218). Available: http://idsc.nih.go.jp/iasr/19/218/tpc218.html. September 1999.

[530] Kijo Deura and Takashi Yokota, "Medical Care and HIV Infection of Foreign Immigrant Workers in Japan," Regional Meeting on Traffic in Women in Asia and Pacific, February 19-22, 1997, Bangkok, Thailand.

[531] Article 12.

for the free services. But while the handbook is available to everyone, the free vaccinations and free check-ups for pregnant women, new mothers, and infants are available only to legal residents in Japan. Undocumented women — and their children — are not covered. According to Dr. Sawada, in a few prefectures, public health professionals may have bypassed this regulation by not asking about women's immigration status, but this is unusual.[532] Discriminatory maternal and child health policies inevitably increase the health risks facing undocumented migrant women and their children, despite their being a particularly vulnerable group. This was evidenced in a survey published in October 1999 by an associate professor of nursing at the Tokyo Women's Medical College, which found that the rate of stillborn births among Thai women in Tokyo in 1997 was more than double (2.1 times higher) that of Japanese women. Moreover, babies born to Thai mothers were 2.5 times more likely to die before their first birthday than those born to Japanese mothers.[533]

Immigration reporting requirement

In practice, undocumented migrants are deterred from seeking medical care because of the fear that any attempt to use government health services could lead directly to their deportation. According to Japan's Immigration Control Act, employees of government health clinics and public hospitals, like all other civil servants, are required to report those they suspect of being illegal immigrants to the immigration authorities. The Minister of Justice's statement authorizing civil servants to give higher priority to their primary functions than to the immigration reporting requirement may mean that doctors can ignore that requirement, but the Immigration Control Act has not been modified to reflect this statement, and actual government policy is ambiguous. Hospitals have also used the immigration reporting requirement to discourage foreigners from seeking their services. In 1998, for example, a hospital at the Tokyo Women's Medical University was criticized for displaying a sign in its outpatient ward stating, "This Medical Hospital is Obligated to Report to the Immigration Office." The statement, in English on the assumption that foreigners would be more likely to understand English than Japanese, was falsely attributed to the "Japanese Immigration Control Office" —

---

[532] Human Rights Watch interview, Tokyo, Japan, April 7, 1999.
[533] "More non-Japanese having babies," *Asahi Shimbun* (English version), October 8, 1999.

an office that does not, in fact, exist. The sign was removed, however, after vigorous complaints by activists.[534]

Even though medical professionals may, in practice, avoid reporting undocumented migrants, the fear that they might be reported deters some migrants from seeking necessary medical care. By retaining the requirement to report undocumented immigrants in the Immigration Control Act, even if it is not currently being enforced, the government inevitably exacerbates this concern among migrants. This was shown in a study of undocumented workers from the Philippines in the mid-1990's, which found that there were no recorded incidents of hospitals turning in patients to immigration authorities, yet "this fear [was] prevalent" among the migrants.[535] Dr. Irohira Tetsuro of the Saku General Hospital in Nagano Prefecture told Human Rights Watch that this fear is common among undocumented women from Thailand, who are reluctant to attend the hospital for treatment because they fear they might be deported.[536]

Assistance provided by local advocates and private service providers

A growing lobby of Japanese NGOs and advocates is pushing for recognition of the plight of women victims of trafficking in Japan and for assistance for such women through the establishment of shelters, the provision of medical care, and the provision of legal services. Their efforts, Human Rights Watch found, have contributed significantly to mitigating some of the negative effects of Japanese policies, but can be only of limited effect while those policies remain flawed. Private organizations are typically under-funded and can provide only limited services, in limited areas of Japan. While Human Rights Watch commends their efforts, it is still the Japanese government which has the responsibility under international law for protecting the human rights of trafficked persons and remedying the abuses they have faced.

Private organizations provide shelter, health care, and other services

Certain Japanese nongovernmental organizations have done a lot to help foreign women victims of trafficking, forced labor, and other abuses. Various privately-run women's shelters, for example, offer their services to all foreign women, regardless of their immigration status, and several of the victims

---

[534] Human Rights Watch interview with Dr. Takashi Sawada, Tokyo, Japan, April 7, 1999; Human Rights Watch interviews with Kimiko Ogasawara, Tokyo, Japan, April 19, 1999 and January 21, 2000.
[535] Sarah Y. Usuki, "Filipino Migrant Workers in Japan: Their Behavior on Health Problems," *Asian Migrant,* vol. 9, no. 3, July - September 1996, p. 70.
[536] "Holding out a helping hand," *The Nation* (Bangkok, Thailand), May 8, 1993.

interviewed by Human Rights Watch had benefited from this, often having been referred there by Japanese or Thai government officials. At such shelters, women are not only accommodated, but can receive counseling, legal assistance, easier access to medical care, and help in arranging safe travel back to their country of origin.

Some private organizations are also offering low cost or free health care to the foreign community, with guarantees that undocumented foreigners will not be reported to immigration authorities. For example, in 1991, the Minatomachi Foreign Migrant Workers' Mutual Aid Scheme for Health (MF-MASH) was created to offer undocumented migrants access to a health insurance policy providing premiums and benefits similar to that of the government's National Health Insurance Scheme. Members, who pay 2000 yen (in 1999, approximately US$17) per month, then qualify to receive medical care at the Minatomachi Medical Center in Yokohama city for thirty percent of the full cost of such treatment. This program has provided subsidized medical care for thousands of foreign patients.[537]

Volunteer advocates have provided some victims with a measure of redress

The committed efforts of Japanese advocates have also provided a few trafficked women with a small degree of redress, but the experiences these advocates describe indicate that police and immigration officials tend to impede their efforts, rather than facilitating them. In one case, three women trafficked from Thailand successfully sued their employers at a snack bar under Japanese labor laws. But the circumstances that made their success possible were extraordinary. These three plaintiffs were the women from the "Shimodate Incident," who were being detained in Japan on murder charges, so they had not been deported. The snack bar owners revealed incriminating evidence against themselves while testifying in the murder trial, and the women's team of volunteer defense lawyers seized upon the owners' testimony and initiated a civil case against them for labor violations. The snack bar owners had testified that they had paid 3000 yen (US$20) per hour in wages for the three women and that the money had been given to the mama-san to distribute.[538] As one of the owners explained in his statement to the police at the Shimodate Police Station, "[t]he bar is open around 7 p.m. to midnight. Hourly pay is 1,000 yen [approximately US$7 at 1991 exchange rates], and I paid

---

[537] Hiroshi Hayakawa, "Over 3 years in existence: Foreign workers still need *MF-MASH*," *MF-MASH News,* no. 10, January 1995, pp. 1-3, 6.

[538] Abigail Haworth and Kyoko Matsuda, "Flesh and Blood: part two," August 1994.

it everyday, but I paid the salaries for [the three defendants] to [their mama-san]."[539] So the defense lawyers filed a civil suit claiming compensation for unpaid wages; according to the Labor Standards Law, wages must be paid *directly* to the workers.[540] The case was successful. In 1995, the women were awarded back wages, at the rate of 1000 yen (approximately US$10) per hour each, in addition to compensation for emotional distress. In all, the owners were ordered to pay more than 12 million yen (US$127,000), 3,242,000 yen each to two of the women and 5,715,000 to the third.[541]

In another ground-breaking case, a Thai woman successfully pressed criminal charges against a snack bar owner for forcing her into sex work and against a client for sexually assaulting her by inserting a whiskey bottle into her vagina. She and the other women working at the snack bar had been forced to work twelve hours a day in addition to providing sexual services to at least three men every night, but they received only 5,000 yen (US$45) per client out of the 15,000 to 20,000 yen (US$135 to 180) clients paid their boss. During a police raid of the snack bar in November 1993, the owner was arrested by police for violating labor laws concerning wage remuneration, and a Thai woman worker was arrested for immigration violations. The Japanese NGO OASIS quickly came to her assistance and convinced her to press charges against the owner of the bar and against the client who had assaulted her. Human Rights Watch was unable to find out the nature of the charges for which the owner and client were prosecuted, but we did learn that both defendants were convicted. In December 1993, the snack bar owner was ordered to pay compensation of 850,000 yen (US$7,700), and the client was ordered to pay another 700,000 yen (US$6,300); neither defendant was imprisoned. Unfortunately, OASIS reported that the Thai woman did not collect any of the money that was awarded to her; she returned to Thailand before the case was completed and as of January 1994, OASIS was unable to find her.[542]

There have been a few other cases as well in which Japanese activists have realized limited success in pursuing legal claims for trafficked women. An OASIS staff member told Human Rights Watch about a case in which a snack bar owner

---

[539] "Record of Testimony," name: Toshihisa Sasaki, testified at Shimodate Police Station on September 30, 1991 to Police Officer Sugita.

[540] Human Rights Watch interview with Atty. Kazuko Kawaguchi, Japan, March 9, 1994. Attorney Kawaguchi was one of the six lawyers representing the women.

[541] Shima Kobayashi, "Summary of Due Process Violations found in the Key Court Cases — Trafficking of Thai Women to Japan," July 11, 1997. Though as noted in the discussion above, efforts to file criminal charges against their employers failed. See the previous chapter for more information about the murder trial.

[542] "What Price Freedom?," *The Nation* (Bangkok, Thailand), January 29, 1994.

was actually sentenced to jail time after a Thai woman who had been working in debt bondage for two years pressed charges under Japan's labor laws and the Prostitution Prevention Law: "In October 1992, the police raided a snack bar and arrested seven women as illegal aliens. OASIS encouraged each woman to press charges, but only one, Keak, agreed. So, Keak signed the papers and gave permission to the OASIS lawyer to press charges against the owner and broker. The lawyer fought for 150 bai [US$12,000] and won 95 bai [US$7500]. The broker had to pay 65 bai [US$5100] and the owner 30 bai [US$2400]. In addition, the owner was jailed for two years."[543] In another case that year, a support group was formed on behalf of five Thai women charged with murdering their Singaporean mama-san in Mobara city, Chiba prefecture in 1992. The women explained that they had been held against their will, watched twenty-four hours a day by video camera, and forced to perform sexual services for customers to repay debts of 3.8 million yen (US$30,000) each. So the support group filed charges against the mama-san's partner for illegal confinement under the Penal Code and for violations of the Prostitution Prevention Law. The man was convicted, but received only a 25,000 yen fine.[544]

These cases provide important precedents for future efforts to obtain justice for trafficking and related abuses. However, Human Rights Watch found that the limited success these women enjoyed was possible only with the vigorous assistance of Japanese advocates, who encouraged the women to press charges, helped them throughout their trials, and publicized their cases to gain public support. These advocates received no payment for their efforts, faced reluctant and biased civil servants at every stage of the process, had to pursue the cases over long periods of time, and in some cases, had to represent victims in absentia, as they were deported while the trial was still underway. In sum, the extraordinary circumstances of these cases — and the enormous amount of effort required on the part of advocates — provide only further evidence of the Japanese government's indifference to the human rights violations suffered by trafficked women.

---

[543] Human Rights Watch and FOWIA interview with OASIS staff member, Japan, 1995. Note that Human Rights Watch was unable to find out the exact nature of the charges for which the owner was imprisoned. U.S. dollar amounts are calculated using the average exchange rate from 1992.

[544] Yayori Matsui, "Trafficking in Asian Women and Prostitution in Japan," *Asia-Japan Women's Resource Center Newsletter*, No. 1, August 1995, p. 30.

X. RESPONSE OF THE THAI GOVERNMENT

The Thai government has identified the eradication of trafficking in women and children for sexual purposes as a priority. Its response to the problem has been articulated largely through the framework of its "National Policy and Plan of Action for the Prevention and Eradication of the Commercial Sexual Exploitation of Children" (hereinafter, National Plan of Action), adopted in 1996.[545] Although the policy's primary goal is the eradication of the sexual exploitation of children, many of its provisions apply equally to adult women, and there is a strong emphasis on the problem of trafficking in persons for sexual purposes, both into and out of Thailand. The government has also highlighted specifically the problems of Thai women trafficked to Japan for sex work. On September 28, 1999, the Thai Embassy in Tokyo organized a conference to identify the problems that Thai sex workers face in Japan and to discuss solutions. Officials from the Thai and Japanese governments as well as representatives from Japanese NGOs were invited to participate. The Thai government estimated that there were more than 30,000 Thai women working illegally in Japan as of March 1999, and the Thai ambassador to Japan, Sakthip Krairiksh, insisted, "These women are not criminals. Instead, we must find more effective ways to deal with gangsters who bring them in and exploit them inhumanely."[546]

Thai policy-makers' commitment to combating trafficking in women has yielded some positive results. Nonetheless, trafficking abuses have remained largely undeterred and unpunished. In part, this is due to flaws in the design and implementation of their anti-trafficking initiatives. The attention given to this issue by the Thai government has increased awareness among Thais of the risks of female migration to Japan, and useful services have been provided for trafficking victims who need assistance in returning home to Thailand. Government efforts have also been notable for their strong emphasis on cooperation with nongovernmental and intergovernmental organizations in Thailand. However, the effectiveness of these efforts has been limited. Government policies have been undermined by gender stereotypes and weak enforcement of anti-trafficking legislation. Ultimately, women do not have access either to sufficient employment opportunities in Thailand

---

[545] National Committee for the Eradication of Commercial Sex, National Commission on Women's Affairs, Office of the Prime Minister, Thailand, "National Policy and Plan of Action for the Prevention and Eradication of the Commercial Sexual Exploitation of Children," 1996.

[546] Sanitsuda Ekachai, "Conference seeks help for Thai victims: These women are not criminals-envoy," *Bangkok Post,* September 28, 1999; "Govt, NGO officials meet on Thai women's problems," *The Daily Yomiuri,* September 28, 1999.

to deter overseas migration nor to the information and/or to services they would need to protect their rights in the course of such migration. In some cases, government practices have even infringed on women's rights to equality and freedom of movement. In addition, women from the "hilltribes,"[547] who are among the most disadvantaged and vulnerable populations in Thailand, have been largely excluded from both prevention efforts and victim services.

Combating Trafficking in Women

Education and Awareness-Raising Programs
The Thai government's efforts to combat "trafficking" in women are premised on an understanding of the term that includes both consensual and non-consensual migration for sex work. The National Plan of Action identifies the provision of universal access to education and/or vocational training, along with efforts to raise public awareness about the dangers of child prostitution and of sending children abroad as commercial sex workers, as key strategies for preventing the commercial sexual exploitation of children. Thus, for example, the National Education Act adopted in 1999 promises that compulsory education will be extended from six years to nine years.[548] This could ameliorate the problem of child prostitution both by keeping girls in school longer — many girls enter the sex industry soon after graduating from sixth grade at ages as young as twelve or thirteen — and by preparing girls for a wider variety of jobs. The Thai government has also tried to increase education and employment opportunities for adults, and particularly for women, through vocational training programs. The Occupational Assistance Division of the Department of Public Welfare, for example, operates seven provincial vocational centers across the country, offering three to six month courses for women aged fourteen to thirty-five years old.[549] These programs are explicitly designed to provide poor women and girls with means for alternative employment, so that they do not become involved in prostitution.[550]

Efforts to raise public awareness regarding prostitution and trafficking have consisted of large-scale information campaigns in villages warning women about

---

[547] They are also referred to as "tribal people."

[548] "Educational-reform panel must stick to its guns to succeed," *The Nation* (Bangkok), January 12, 2000.

[549] Human Rights Watch interview with Suwaree Jaiharn, Occupational Assistance Division, Department of Public Welfare, Ministry of Labour and Social Welfare, at the Department of Public Welfare office, Bangkok, Thailand, April 28, 1999.

[550] Napat Sirisambhand, *Social Security for Women in the Informal Sector in Thailand,* January 1996, p. 9.

the dangers of entering the commercial sex industry, as well as the dangers of seeking employment abroad. The government's warnings against overseas migration have been reiterated as new incidences of trafficking into forced sex work are revealed.[551] Some government warnings have focused on Japan specifically, telling women how hard life would be in Japan, that they would be beaten and otherwise abused,[552] and posters have been distributed cautioning women that, if they try to go to Japan, they might be forced into prostitution.[553] These campaigns have not, however, included information that might assist women in migrating safely, such as information about their rights as overseas workers or about services available to them in Japan.

In addition to long-term education and development policies, the government has also tried to prevent trafficking in women—understood by the government to include any facilitated migration for sex work—by denying passports to "potential victims." While preventing trafficking is obviously an important goal, this policy constitutes an invasion of women's and girls' privacy and results in unacceptable restrictions on women's and girls' freedom of movement on the basis of their suspected status as victims, or potential victims, of a crime. An informational booklet published by the Ministry of Labour and Social Welfare's Department of Public Welfare (DPW) explains that one of DPW's "Services for Women" is "investigating the background of women between fourteen and thirty-six years old who have requested passports from the Ministry of Foreign Affairs (MFA), and have been suspected by MFA of being procured to sexual business in foreign countries."[554] An official at the Occupational Assistance Division of DPW, who participates in these reviews, described the process to Human Rights Watch:

> Women apply for passports with the following reasons: most to travel as a tourist, some to marry, and some to work. If they are suspicious of a woman's reasons, the Ministry of Foreign Affairs sends the names of the women here. To see if the woman should be approved for a passport, we ask the provincial official to visit her home, look at the status of her family, and talk to her mother,

---

[551] For example, see "IN BRIEF: Thais warned against lure of foreign land," *The Nation* (Bangkok), March 10, 1999.

[552] Human Rights Watch interview, with Chitraporn Vanaspong, Information Officer, ECPAT International, Bangkok, Thailand, April 22, 1999.

[553] "Thai Government Warning to Thai Women Going to Japan," *Yomiuri Shimbun,* May 10, 1994 (translated from Japanese).

[554] The Department of Public Welfare, Ministry of Labour and Social Welfare, "Welcome to The Department of Public Welfare, Ministry of Labour and Social Welfare," Thailand, 1998, p. 9.

father, and other family members. If the woman has said that she wants to go abroad to marry someone, we ask her about the occupation of her proposed husband, how high a salary he makes, how long they've known each other, and whether he visits her here. We recommend approval for about half of the cases and rejection for the other half, but the final decision is up to the Ministry of Foreign Affairs. Reasons for rejection include: she doesn't have work in Thailand; her family doesn't have enough money to give her to travel; her documents, such as her marriage license, aren't valid; the address she gave for her boyfriend — if she says she is going abroad to marry — isn't correct.[555]

Officials from the Ministry of Labour and Social Welfare also examine Thai passengers departing for Japan at Don Muang airport in an effort to weed out persons going to Japan to work illegally on tourist visas.[556] And in 1995, Thai Labour and Social Welfare Minister Sompong Amornwiwat met with officials from the Japanese government and explained that many Thai workers had been lured into Japan and cheated by illegal businesses there. He urged senior officials from Thai Ministry of Labor and the Japanese Embassy to strictly inspect Thai nationals traveling to Japan and to tighten screening procedures for visa applications in Thailand.[557]

---

[555] Human Rights Watch interview with Suwaree Jaiharn, Occupational Assistance Division, Department of Public Welfare, Ministry of Labour and Social Welfare, Bangkok, Thailand, April 28, 1999.

[556] "Japan-bound Thais 'need more scrutiny,'" *The Nation* (Bangkok, Thailand), January 7, 1995.

In October 1999, fifteen Thai nationals submitted a petition to the Don Muang airport immigration chief, complaining that they were subjected to abusive and insulting questioning from immigration officials who suspected them of seeking jobs overseas. They were part of a group of thirty-five nongovernmental organization representatives flying to Malaysia to take part in an international AIDS meeting. The fifteen were first-time air travelers, and they were detained by officers asking them questions such as: "Where are you going? People with your looks don't seem to be the ones who will be attending a meeting." Police Lieutenant-General Chidchai Wanasathit, the immigration police commissioner, explained that it was the policy for immigration officers to be strict with first-time travelers, though not abusive or insulting. ("AIDS activists protest over airport abuse: Officials accused of insulting behavior," *Bangkok Post,* October 28, 1999.)

[557] See "Japan-bound Thais 'need more scrutiny,'" *The Nation* (Bangkok, Thailand), January 7, 1995; and "Minister seeks to curb illegal labour," *Bangkok Post,* January 8, 1995.

Legislative Reform

Thailand has also engaged in substantial legislative reform in an effort to suppress child prostitution and trafficking in both children and women. In 1996, the Prevention and Suppression of Prostitution Act was revised to reduce the penalties on women engaged in prostitution[558] and to increase the penalties on all other persons involved in the prostitution business, especially in cases involving children (persons under eighteen). Though this law is targeted primarily at the domestic sex industry in Thailand, it also applies to cross-border recruitment for sex work. Section 9 prescribes penalties of one to ten years of imprisonment and a fine of 20,000 to 200,000 baht for "[a]ny person who procures, seduces or takes away[559] any person for the prostitution of such person, even with her or his consent and irrespective of whether the various acts which constitute an offence are committed within or outside of the Kingdom."[560] Section 12 could also be applied to international trafficking agents in cases in which women are detained while their travel arrangements are being made:

> Any person who detains or confines another person, or by any other means, deprives such person of the liberty of person or causes bodily harm to or threatens in any manner whatsoever to commit violence against another person in order to compel such other person to engage in prostitution shall be liable to imprisonment for a term of ten to twenty years and to a fine of two hundred thousand to four hundred thousand baht.

---

[558] Section 4 of the Act defines "prostitution" as "the acceptance of sexual intercourse, or the acceptance of any other act, or the commission of any other act in order to gratify the sexual desire of another person in a promiscuous manner in return for earning or any other benefit, irrespective of whether the person who accepts the act and the person who commits the act are of the same sex or not."

[559] Note that other government publications translate "takes away" as "traffics."

[560] If this offense is committed against a child, penalties can be as high as twenty years.

Here and below, excerpts from the Prevention and Suppression of Prostitution Act were taken from the English translation of the law provided in Save the Children Fund (U.K.)'s "Thailand's National Policy, Plan of Action and Legal Measures in the Elimination of Sexual Abuse and Exploitation of Children." The translation was completed by Wanchai Roujanavong, Deputy Executive Director, International Affairs Department, Office of the Attorney General, Chairperson of FACE.

In 1997, several amendments to the Penal Code were adopted with provisions similar to those in the Prevention and Suppression of Prostitution Act. Section 282 now provides penalties of one to ten years of imprisonment and a fine of 2,000 to 20,000 baht for anyone who, "for the sexual gratification of another person, procures, lures,[561] or traffics a man or woman for an indecent sexual act, even with his or her consent."[562] And section 283 raises the penalties to five to twenty years of imprisonment and a 10,000 to 40,000 baht fine for offenders employing "deceitful means, threats, physical assault, immoral influence, or mental coercion by any means."[563] The revisions also established penalties for the trafficking of children under the age of eighteen for non-sexual purposes.[564] The extraterritorial scope of sections 282 and 283 was established by adding them to the list of laws in section 7 of the Penal Code for which an offender may be tried in the Kingdom, even if the offenses were committed outside of the Kingdom. These changes were confirmed in the substantially revised Measures in Prevention and Suppression of Trafficking in Women and Children Act (hereinafter, Trafficking Act) that was adopted on the same day in 1997.

The Trafficking Act does not create additional criminal offences, except in establishing penalties for attempting to commit acts related to trafficking and for conspiring to commit such offenses.[565] Rather, it grants additional powers to law enforcement officials to facilitate their efforts to suppress crimes already prohibited

---

[561] "Lures" is also translated as "deceives."

[562] Here and below, excerpts from the Penal Code were taken from the English translation of the amendments provided in Save the Children Fund (U.K.)'s "Thailand's National Policy, Plan of Action and Legal Measures in the Elimination of Sexual Abuse and Exploitation of Children." The translation was completed by Wanchai Roujanavong, Deputy Executive Director, International Affairs Department, Office of the Attorney General, Chairperson of FACE.

[563] In both provisions, there are higher penalties for committing these offenses against persons under eighteen years of age.

[564] Section 312: "Whoever, for gaining illegal benefit, receives, sells, procures, lures, or traffics a person over fifteen years but not yet over eighteen years of age, even with the consent of that person, shall be punished with imprisonment not exceeding five years, or a fine not exceeding ten thousand baht, or both. If the commission of the offence in the first paragraph is committed against a person not yet over fifteen years of age, the offender shall be punished with imprisonment not exceeding seven years, or a fine not exceeding fourteen thousand baht, or both."

[565] Section 6 provides that attempting to commit any of the offenses specified in Section 5 is subject to the same penalties as committing the offense. Section 7 prescribes a maximum sentence of five years of imprisonment and a 10,000 baht fine for conspiring to commit any of the offenses specified in Section 5.

by other legislation.[566] Section 5 of the Act describes the types of offences covered by this law:

> In committing an offence concerning the trafficking in women and children, buying, selling, vending, bringing from or sending to, receiving, detaining or confining any woman or child, or arranging any woman or child to receive any act, for sexual gratification of the third person, for an indecent sexual purpose, or for gaining any illegal benefit for him/herself or another person, with or without the consent of the woman or girl, which is an offence under the Penal Code, the law on prostitution prevention and suppression, the law on child and youth welfare, or this Act, the official is authorized to enforce power under this Act.[567]

The actions officials are authorized to take in order to facilitate the prevention, investigation, and prosecution of such crimes include the following:

- Section 8 instructs superior administrative or police officials "to inspect, examine, and monitor at airports, seaport, railway stations, bus stations, entertainment establishments, factories and public places to prevent the offense [of trafficking] from being committed."

---

[566] The Trafficking Act is designed to: "provide measures to authorized officials to undertake proceedings . . . whenever offences have been committed relating to the traffic of women and children constituting offences according to the Criminal [or Penal] Code, the law on the prevention and suppression of prostitution, or the law on child and youth welfare, to more widely facilitate the prevention, suppression and assistance to women and children victimized by such offences." National Committee for the Eradication of Commercial Sex, National Commission on Women's Affairs, Office of the Prime Minister, Thailand, "National Policy and Plan of Action for the Prevention and Eradication of the Commercial Sexual Exploitation of Children," 1996, p. 33.

[567] Here and below, excerpts from the Trafficking Act were taken from the English translation of the law provided in Save the Children Fund (U.K.)'s "Thailand's National Policy, Plan of Action and Legal Measures in the Elimination of Sexual Abuse and Exploitation of Children." The translation was completed by Wanchai Roujanavong, Deputy Executive Director, International Affairs Department, Office of the Attorney General, Chairperson of FACE, and Pen Suwannarat, Program Coordinator, Mekong Region Law Center.

- Section 9 provides that in the course of this inspection, the official has the right to search the body of a woman or child if the official "has reason to believe that she/he is the victim" of a trafficking offense. Only female officers may conduct body searches of women and girls.

- Section 10 authorizes a superior administrative or police official to detain suspected victims "for factual clarification, or checking documents or evidence," in order to prevent or suppress an offense specified under Section 5 or to rescue a woman or child who may be the victim of such an offense. The period of detention should not exceed half an hour, but it may be extended to twenty-four hours if the Director General of the Police Department in Bangkok, or the provincial governor elsewhere, is notified without delay. Moreover, with the Director General or provincial governor's permission, this period of detention may be extended to up to ten days.

- Section 12 allows a public prosecutor to bring a victim of an offense specified under Section 5 to testify in court immediately, even if the offender has not yet been arrested. The court shall instantly examine the witness, and may also grant an interested party in the case, or his/her counsel, the right to cross-examine the witness. If the offender is later indicted, "the deposited testimony of the witness shall be used as evidence in the trial."

In addition to measures specifically targeted at trafficking offenses, new legislation was proposed in 1999 to overcome the obstacles involved in suppressing a variety of organized crime activities, including trafficking in persons. This legislation could make an important contribution to Thailand's efforts to investigate and prosecute traffickers. These laws include a money laundering bill, which was enacted in April 1999, and a witness protection law, proposed by the Justice Ministry in mid-1999.[568] The Anti-Money Laundering Bill allows officials to seize the proceeds from the following types of illegal activities: narcotics trafficking, prostitution, fraud against the public, fraud against banks and finance companies and violations of stock trading laws, abuses of authority by government officials, extortion, and contraband smuggling.[569] It can be used to target recruiters and traffickers who are involved in fraudulent job recruitment and recruitment

---

[568] "Cream of bureaucrats eyed for anti-laundering office," *The Nation* (Bangkok, Thailand), May 17, 1999; "Witnesses need protection, say academics," *The Nation* (Bangkok, Thailand,), August 9, 1999; "Witness protection law being drafted," *The Nation* (Bangkok, Thailand), July 8, 1999.

[569] "Bill receives Senate's nod," *The Nation* (Bangkok, Thailand), March 20, 1999.

(fraudulent or otherwise) for prostitution, as well as corrupt government officials who profit from these activities.[570] The proposed witness protection law was still in the drafting process a year later, in mid-2000, when this report was being prepared, so it could not be evaluated. However, effective measures to protect witnesses could address a crucial obstacle to the successful prosecution of trafficking agents and escorts, who are often connected to dangerous criminal networks. As a police colonel in northern Thailand explained, "Witnesses are afraid to testify and the best we can do is tell the local precinct to watch them for a limited period of time — and even then not twenty-four hours a day — and after that time period they're on their own."[571]

Weak enforcement efforts
    The usefulness in practice of the revised trafficking legislation could not be assessed at the time this report was prepared, because there had been little effort to enforce it. Human Rights Watch found that many law enforcement officials, in fact, were unaware that the new law existed. In April 1999, two years after the revised Trafficking Act had been enacted, a high-ranking police officer in one of the provinces in northern Thailand — where trafficking in women and girls from neighboring countries into Thailand is a significant problem — insisted to Human Rights Watch that no such law existed.[572] Activists involved in encouraging the investigation and prosecution of trafficking abuses in Thailand explained that they often found themselves instructing police about the content of the revised legislation.[573]
    At the time this report was being prepared, government efforts were underway to address this problem. On June 30, 1999, the Thai government produced a document with detailed instructions regarding the implementation of trafficking

---

    [570] The bill could have negative effects as well. While it was under consideration in early 1999, many people, including a senior politician and several human rights activists, expressed concern that several of its provisions, such as those allowing the appointed enforcement panel to tap telephone wires and seize assets of crime suspects, constitute infringements of individual rights. ("Crime assets bill 'close to approval,'" *The Nation,* January 21, 1999).
    [571] Human Rights Watch interview with a Police Colonel, northern Thailand, April 26, 1999.
    [572] Human Rights Watch interview with a Police Colonel, northern Thailand, April 26, 1999.
    [573] Human Rights Watch interview with Sudarat Sereewat, Secretary General of FACE, Bangkok, Thailand, April 22, 1999; Human Rights Watch interview with Wanchai Roujanavong, Chairman of FACE: coalition to Fight Against Child Exploitation and Senior Expert State Attorney, Bangkok, Thailand, April 22, 1999.

legislation. The "Memorandum of Understanding on Common Guidelines of Practices for Agencies Concerned with Cases Where Women and Children are Victims of Human Trafficking" (hereinafter, Memorandum of Understanding) was drafted in cooperation with a number of nongovernmental and intergovernmental organizations and contains useful information for police officers that is sensitive to the needs and rights of trafficked persons. While much of the document is devoted to the problem of trafficking in women and children into Thailand, it also contains a number of provisions regarding the trafficking of Thai women and children out of the country. In these cases, the memorandum instructs officers to file criminal charges against persons suspected of committing trafficking offenses and to "immediately coordinate with a public prosecutor in order to file a petition for the court to take an early deposition of the testimony of the witness," as is allowed under the revised trafficking law. It explains that all victims under the age of eighteen should be referred to shelters — not detention centers — operated by the Department of Public Welfare and that vocational training programs should be arranged for victims over the age of eighteen "if the woman wants" to receive such assistance. The memorandum also directs police officers to inform the Department of Public Welfare or a nongovernmental organization of all trafficking cases so that a social worker, psychologist, psychiatrist, or other person "with experience in working with women or children" may be involved in the initial inquiry, investigation, and trial of the case.[574]

Policies that incorporate gender discrimination and stereotypes violate women's rights and are ineffective in combating trafficking

In its efforts to combat trafficking, some of the policies that Thailand has adopted are overly-broad and infringe on women's rights to freedom from discrimination and freedom of movement. The most striking example is the extra scrutiny to which the passport applications of women and girls (only) are subjected. This constitutes discriminatory treatment as well as a violation of the right to freely

---

[574] Office of the National Commission on Women's Affairs, Office of the Permanent Secretary, Office of the Prime Minister, Thailand, "Memorandum of Understanding on Common Guidelines of Practices for Agencies Concerned with Cases where Women and Children are Victims of Human Trafficking, B.E. 2542 (1999)." The memorandum was translated into English by Wanchai Roujanawong, Senior Expert State Attorney, International Affairs Department, Office of the Attorney General, Chairman of FACE (the Coalition to Fight Against Child Exploitation), with the support of IOM through Senator Saisuree Chutikul.

leave and enter one's country, rights firmly established under international law.[575] In 1997, DPW recommended that more than one thousand women be denied passports out of the 2,300 names referred by MFA. The number of cases referred to DPW dropped dramatically to 575 in 1998, but still, hundreds of women were denied passports on the ground that they might enter the sex industry if they traveled abroad.[576] Thus, women were penalized for their vulnerability to abuse; they were denied the necessary documents to travel abroad based on the suspicion that they would become victims of sexual exploitation. Moreover, even those whose applications were eventually approved suffered intrusions into their privacy, as applicants and their family members were interrogated about financial and other personal details of their lives.

Similarly, the Trafficking Act appears aimed at suppressing all migration of women suspected to be seeking work in the sex industry, failing to differentiate between consensual and non-consensual migration. As noted above, it is too early to assess the impact of the revised law. However, Human Rights Watch is concerned that the protective approach toward both children and (adult) women travelers adopted in certain provisions of the Trafficking Act has the potential to infringe on these persons' right to privacy, to freedom of movement, and to freedom from arbitrary detention. In determining the appropriate treatment of suspected victims of trafficking, it is important to emphasize that such persons have not been charged with any criminal activity and that their treatment must be consistent with the intent of protection. Body searches should never be carried out without a person's consent on the basis of her/his status as a suspected *victim* of a crime. In addition, while briefly restricting a woman or child's freedom of movement for the purpose of factual clarification and document verification may be appropriate, any further deprivation of liberty must be consistent with the right to be free from arbitrary detention.

---

[575] ICCPR, Article 12:

1. Everyone lawfully within the territory of a State shall, within that territory, have the right to liberty of movement and freedom to choose his residence.

2. Everyone shall be free to leave any country, including his own.

3. The above-mentioned rights shall not be subject to any restrictions except those which are provided by law, are necessary to protect national security, public order (ordre public), public health or morals or the rights and freedoms of others, and are consistent with the other rights recognized in the present Covenant.

4. No one shall be arbitrarily deprived of the right to enter his own country.

[576] Human Rights Watch interview with Suwaree Jaiharn, Occupational Assistance Division, Department of Public Welfare, Ministry of Labour and Social Welfare, Bangkok, Thailand, April 28, 1999.

Placing a person in protective detention on the basis of her/his suspected status as a victim of trafficking is an extreme measure that must be subject to a high level of judicial oversight. Notifying — or obtaining permission from — the Director General of the Police Department or a provincial governor (as provided in Section 10 of the Trafficking Act) is not a sufficient protection against arbitrary detention, and the process provided for pursuing claims of "wrongful" detention under Section 13 of the Trafficking Act does not provide adequate assurance of a fair and prompt hearing.[577] Sections 10 and 13 should be revised to ensure that all persons detained as suspected trafficking victims have immediate access to a court that may decide the lawfulness of their detention and that all due process protections, including the right to legal counsel, are afforded. In addition, the Thai government should take concrete steps to ensure that persons who are placed in protective detention are not treated punitively. The Trafficking Act goes a long way to address this issue by providing that persons detained under Section 10 should be held in an "appropriate place, which shall not be a detention cell or prison." The Memorandum of Understanding (discussed above) goes further by defining "appropriate" places as a primary shelter, a DPW shelter, or a private shelter approved of by that department; by providing that all detained children be afforded medical examinations; and by instructing police to notify the DPW or an NGO about all trafficking cases. These protections should be strengthened to ensure that all persons detained as suspected trafficking victims have access to the medical, social, and other services they need, without delay. In addition, if a child is detained, all efforts should be made to locate the child's family members and facilitate the child's prompt reunification with his/her parents or guardians, unless the best interests of the child dictates otherwise.

The overly-broad scope of Thailand's anti-trafficking policies also undermines their effectiveness in combating trafficking in women. Women who voluntarily decide to migrate may later find themselves victims of trafficking, having been sold into servitude abroad. However, efforts to forcibly prevent women's travel are counterproductive. They alienate women migrants — by encouraging women to take steps to evade or overcome the government's restrictions on their travel — rather than empowering women to protect their rights during the course of their

---

[577] Section 13 allows "the victimized woman or child, spouse, relative, or person with related interests to the woman or child" to challenge instances of "wrongful" detention under section 10, but there is no indication of what would be considered "wrongful" or what the remedy would be in those instances. Furthermore, such challenges are not heard by a judge — they are decided by the Director General of the Police Department in Bangkok or by the provincial governor in other provinces, and if that authority finds the detention lawful, the case is referred to the Minister of Interior for final judgement

migration. And, while they may make traffickers' tasks more complicated, they simultaneously make the services of traffickers even more essential to women who want to migrate but cannot negotiate the legal obstacles themselves. At the Department of Public Welfare, an official acknowledged to Human Rights Watch that rejecting passport applications only leads women to employ deceptive tactics. "If a woman's application is rejected," the officer explained, "then she will change her surname and try again."[578]

The Thai government's awareness-raising campaigns have been criticized on similar grounds. They have provided valuable information about the dangers of migration, but they would be more effective in protecting women from abuse if they combined such warnings with information that helped women migrate safely. This could include information about laws and policies in countries of destination, as well as information about services and resources available to Thai women abroad. As one NGO representative put it, the effectiveness of warnings alone is limited as "women still want to go because they are so poor."[579]

The government's skill development programs for women could also be improved. Efforts should be made to overcome traditional preconceptions regarding women and women's roles and to change the focus on traditional "female" skills that prepare women only for very low-paying occupations.[580] As Naiyana Supapung, former director of Friends of Women in Asia (FOWIA),[581] explained:

> The government says it provides vocational training, but this training prepares women for jobs with little income. Women don't want this. The government officials don't understand; they have a bad attitude and look down on the women who are prostitutes. They don't believe these women have the potential

---

[578] Human Rights Watch interview with Suwaree Jaiharn, Occupational Assistance Division, Department of Public Welfare, Ministry of Labour and Social Welfare, Bangkok, Thailand, April 28, 1999.

[579] Human Rights Watch interview with Chitraporn Vanaspong, Information Officer, ECPAT International, Bangkok, Thailand, April 22, 1999. See also Human Rights Watch interview with Naiyana Supapung, Bangkok, Thailand, April 28, 1999.

[580] In *Social Security for Women in the Informal Sector in Thailand* (January 1996, p. 14), Napat Sirisambhand notes that while a woman might be able to support herself on the income from such skills, women often have families (particularly parents) to support and thus need higher income occupations.

[581] This was a Bangkok-based NGO that assisted women both in preparing for migration overseas and in returning to Thai society.

to study. We tried to contact the Ministry of Labor to get them to change their programs, and not just offer cooking and hair dressing, but also electronics and computers, subjects that can lead to good jobs. When I visited the vocational programs, only men were in those courses. Officials say it's the women's fault, that they don't choose electronics, but I think it's the officers' attitude about what is appropriate for women. It is not a written rule, but an orientation on the part of the advisor at these programs. And teachers are not supportive of having women in technical courses.[582]

Senator Saisuree Chutikul, one of the primary participants in drafting the government's National Plan of Action and the Memorandum of Understanding on trafficking, agreed that proactive efforts are needed to ensure that skill training programs are more responsive to markets. Currently, she said, "Girls will say, 'I want sewing,' because they don't know about anything else, and the Department of Public Welfare has sewing teachers, so arranging these classes is convenient for them."[583]

Hilltribe women's vulnerability to trafficking is exacerbated by discriminatory nationality policies that violate their right to a nationality, to education, and to freedom of residence and movement
Another critical problem is the discrimination faced by hilltribe populations in Thailand. There are approximately 800,000 to 900,000 hilltribe people living in the border region of northern Thailand. They suffer from disproportionate levels of poverty in relation to the general population of Thailand, and, while estimates vary, as many as seventy percent lack citizenship cards. As non-citizens, these hilltribe people face a variety of discriminatory policies. They do not have access to government-subsidized health care. Although they may attend primary school at local officials' discretion, they are not allowed to receive primary school diplomas, thereby preventing them from attending higher education and limiting their employment opportunities. And their freedom of movement is sharply limited. In an effort to regularize the status of hilltribe populations, local authorities in some provinces have issued identity cards and short term visas. But these papers are

---

[582] Human Rights Watch interview with Naiyana Supapung, former Director of FOWIA, Bangkok, Thailand, April 28, 1999.
    [583] Human Rights Watch interview with Saisuree Chutikul, Senator, Chairperson, Senate Committee on Women, Youth and the Elderly, and Advisor, Office of the Permanent Secretary, Office of the Prime Minister, Bangkok, Thailand, April 30, 1999.

issued on an ad hoc basis, and, while they accord limited rights of residency and employment, they typically prohibit travel outside of one's home province without permission.[584]   There have also been central government programs to register hilltribe people, but they have been overwhelmed by the volume of applications and little progress has been made.   In January 2000, Thailand's Registration Administration Bureau announced that a new plan was underway. A mobile unit was going to be launched in cooperation with the United Nations International Children's Emergency Fund (UNICEF) to issue identification cards to members of hilltribe groups and displaced people along Thailand's border. At the time this report was prepared, it was too early to assess the effectiveness of this effort.[585]

The discrimination that hilltribe women and girls face in access to educational and employment opportunities in Thailand exacerbates their vulnerability to trafficking by increasing their incentive to seek work abroad. Moreover, those without citizenship papers cannot travel overseas through legal channels. These factors combine to make the offers of recruiters and trafficking agents — who promise to arrange lucrative employment as well as safe passage — more appealing.

The policies that make these women and girls more vulnerable to the human rights violations of trafficking and forced labor also violate a number of other human rights, including the right to freedom of movement and residence[586] and the right to education.[587]   In addition, by perpetuating the problem of statelessness, Thailand's hilltribe policies stand in blatant disregard of the persistent appeals by the international community — through conferences, conventions, declarations, and

---

[584] See "Citizenship is gift sought on Children's Day," *The Nation* (Bangkok, Thailand), January 9, 2000. Malee Traisawasdichai, "Hilltribe take woes to Denmark," *The Nation* (Bangkok, Thailand), July 12, 1999; "Battling Pride & Prejudice," *The Nation* (Bangkok, Thailand), July 14, 1999; pamphlets and newsletters published by the Daughters' Education Program of the Development and Education Programme for Daughters and Communities Centre. There are also a large number of Burmese who reside in Thailand after fleeing from Burma, but have not been granted any refugee or residency status. They are in a particularly precarious position, and face the same vulnerabilities described with regard to hilltribe populations below.

[585] "ID Cards for hilltribes," *The Nation* (Bangkok, Thailand), January 4, 2000.

[586] ICCPR, Article 12(1).

[587] The right to free, compulsory education, as well as access to higher education on the basis of capacity, is guaranteed under the Convention on the Rights of the Child (Article 28(1)). According to Article 2(1), "States Parties shall respect and ensure the rights set forth in the present Convention to each child within their jurisdiction without discrimination of any kind, irrespective of the child's or his or her parent's or legal guardian's race, color, sex, language, religion, political or other opinion, national, ethnic or social origin, property, disability, birth or other status."

resolutions — that states work to reduce statelessness and devote efforts to guarantee individuals' fundamental right to citizenship.[588] These goals have been echoed by the Executive Committee of UNHCR (EXCOM),[589] of which Thailand is a member. In 1995, EXCOM issued the "Conclusion on the Prevention and Reduction of Statelessness and the Protection of Stateless Persons," in which it "calls upon States to adopt nationality legislation with a view to reducing statelessness, consistent with fundamental principles of international law."[590]

Nongovernmental organizations in Thailand have provided some assistance to hilltribe communities. The Thai government has called on such organizations to participate in its educational programs; in launching the "Education and training programme for teachers, parents and young girls at risk"[591] in 1995, for example, Pimpa Chanprasong, Minister to the Prime Minister's Office, noted, "The government alone cannot solve these problems."[592] The nongovernmental partner in that program was DEP, the Daughters' Education Program of the Development and Education Programme for Daughters and Communities Centre, which runs schools and vocational programs in Chiang Rai province. DEP's primary objective

---

[588] The 1961 Convention on the Reduction of Statelessness, for example, aims "to provide for the acquisition and retention of nationality by those who would otherwise be stateless and who have an established link with the State concerned through factors of birth or descent." (UNHCR Training Program 1996, "Training Package: Statelessness and Related Nationality Issues," p. 25.) See also the 1948 Universal Declaration of Human Rights, Article 15; the Declaration on the Right to Leave and the Right to Return adopted by the Uppsala Colloquium in 1972; General Assembly Resolution 50/152, 9 February 1996, paragraph 16; the 1961 International Covenant on Civil and Political Rights, Article 24; and the 1965 International Convention on the Elimination of All Forms of Racial Discrimination, Article 5(d)iii. In addition, the Convention on the Rights of the Child (Article 7) guarantees children the right to acquire a nationality. It does not specify which state has the obligation to grant a child nationality, but it instructs states to ensure the implementation of this right "in particular where the child would otherwise be stateless." Thailand acceded to this treaty on March 27, 1992, but it submitted a reservation regarding Article 7, stating that its application "shall be subject to the national laws, regulations and prevailing practices in Thailand."

[589] EXCOM was created under General Assembly Resolution 1166 (XII) of November 1957. Its first session was held early in 1959. EXCOM tasks include advising the High Commission for Refugees in his/her work and approving the High Commissioner's assistance programs.

[590] Conclusion No. 78 (XLVI).

[591] "At risk," refers specifically to girls "at risk of entering the commercial sex trade."

[592] "Government and NGOs cooperate to help young women," *DEP Newsletter*, March 1995, p. 1.

since its initiation in 1989 has been to prevent girls from being forced into the sex industry. Its programs target "girls likely to enter the commercial sex industry," and DEP has paid particular attention to providing educational and employment opportunities to hilltribe girls. The Director, Sompop Jantraka, has noted that hilltribe persons without identification papers are particularly vulnerable to "unscrupulous employers" in the sex industry because of the difficulties they face in obtaining legal employment.[593]

Services for Victims

In addition to its efforts to prevent and suppress trafficking, the Thai government provides assistance for trafficking victims. Thai officials facilitate women's safe repatriation to Thailand, and temporary shelter and skills training are provided to those who want it. But while these services are important, they are not designed to adequately address the economic burdens that motivated the women to go to Japan in the first place. Training programs typically prepare women only for low-paying jobs, and no steps are taken to assist trafficking victims in seeking compensation or redress for violations suffered in Japan. Moreover, hilltribe and refugee women who have been trafficked from Thailand are denied permission to reenter Thailand on the grounds that they are non-nationals, leaving them stranded in Japan, separated from their homes and families.

Assistance in repatriation

In Japan, officials at the Royal Thai Embassy bear the primary responsibility for responding to the needs of Thai nationals, in cooperation with the Division of Consular Affairs of the Thai Ministry of Foreign Affairs in Bangkok. Embassy services are not provided specifically for victims of trafficking, but embassy records indicate that most of the women who seek its help migrated to Japan through what it terms "the trafficking process": their travel and employment was facilitated by networks of agents, escorts, and brokers, and they worked as indebted sex workers for at least one year after they arrived in Japan.[594] With the help of Thai officials — who issue CI papers and help women raise funds to cover their travel[595] — Thai

---

[593] "Project covers province," *DEP Newsletter,* March 1995, p. 2.

[594] Consular Section, Royal Thai Embassy, Tokyo, "Information Concerning Thai Commercial Sex Workers Including Statistics on Thai Women Arrested for Prostitution in Japan," October 21, 1998.

[595] See "Deportation as 'illegal aliens'" chapter for a discussion of how these policies are implemented. It is worth repeating that government loans for travel expenses are only granted once all other avenues for raising money from friends and relatives have been exhausted, and women may not leave Thailand again until the money has been repaid.

women are often able to return home within a few weeks. In some cases, Embassy officials have even gone to considerable lengths to help women escape from debt bondage in snack bars or brothels, and they often work closely with Japanese NGOs, referring women to private women's shelters when they need a place to stay while they await repatriation.[596] In recognition of the work such groups do to assist Thai women, the Thai government donated US$400,000 to Japanese NGOs in 1994,[597] and in 1998, the Thai Labor Office in Tokyo, along with the Tokyo Metropolitan Government, the Japanese Ministry of Labor, and the Social Welfare Office, assisted the HELP Asian Women's Shelter in publishing a Thai language handbook on Japanese laws.[598]

Shelter and vocational training in Thailand

Women returning from Japan also have access to shelters and vocational training programs in Thailand, either through the services established under the Prevention and Suppression of Prostitution Law or through the Department of Public Welfare's more general services for women. Under the prostitution law, four reception homes and four welfare protection and vocational development centers have been established to provide institutional care to women found guilty of prostitution-related offenses. Until 1996, all women convicted under this law could be remanded to such institutions for up to one year. Under the revised law, these services are optional for women over the age of eighteen, but girls under eighteen may be forcibly placed in a protection and vocational development center for up to two years.[599] There are also women's shelters operated by Thai NGOs, such as the Women's Desk of the Catholic Commission on Migration, that have been used by women returning from trafficking and forced labor abuses in Japan, and there are a variety of skill development programs provided by the Department of Public Welfare and other government agencies, which can serve both preventative and rehabilitative functions.

---

[596] Human Rights interview with First Secretary Nopporn Ratchewej, Royal Thai Embassy, Tokyo, Japan, April 15, 1999. The Thai Embassy will also register children born in Japan as Thai citizens, so that women do not have to go through an arduous process of establishing their children's nationality after returning to Thailand.

[597] "Support for Japanese NGOs from the Thai Government," *Asahi Shimbun,* May 12, 1994 (translated from Japanese).

[598] Human Rights Watch interview with Rutsuko Shoji, Director, HELP Asian Women's Shelter, Tokyo, Japan, April 8, 1999.

[599] Sections 33-37. Section 38 allows shelters and protection and vocational development centers to request police assistance in pursuing persons who have escaped from such facilities.

Violations of the right to return to one's own country

The services that the Thai government provides to trafficking victims suffer from some of the same prejudices as the efforts to prevent and punish trafficking described above. A devastating result of the government's discriminatory nationality policies, for example, is its refusal to permit the repatriation of women who had not obtained official Thai citizenship at the time they left the country. This policy constitutes a violation of the women's right to return to their "own country,"[600] and typically results in indefinite separation from their family members as well, in contravention of Thailand's international legal obligation to protect the family unit.[601] When persons with refugee status in Thailand are trafficked to Japan they face similar problems. Thailand is not a signatory to the Convention relating to the Status of Refugees or the Protocol Relating to the Status of Refugees, but it has granted more than 100,000 refugees a limited right to reside in Thailand, as long as they remain within the confines of designated refugee camps. Refugees also pass their status on to their children, so there are now thousands of second and third generation refugees who were born and raised in Thai territory, but have no right to return to the country once they have left.[602]

---

[600] One's "own country" under Article 12 of ICCPR is not equivalent to one's country of citizenship. As the Human Rights Committee explained in its General Comment on Article 12, "The scope of 'his own country' is broader than the concept 'country of his nationality.' It is not limited to nationality in a formal sense, that is, nationality acquired at birth or by conferral; it embraces, at the very least, an individual who, because of his or her special ties to or claims in relation to a given country, cannot be considered a mere alien." (Human Rights Committee, "General Comment No. 27," General Comments under Article 12 of the International Covenant on Civil and Political Rights (Freedom of Movement), sixty-seventh session, 1999.)

[601] ICCPR, Article 23(1).

[602] EXCOM has issued a number of other conclusions related to long-term refugee situations, exhorting states to find durable solutions to refugee situations, to facilitate refugee's ability to travel internationally, and to promote family reunification. See conclusions no. 69 (1992), no. 49 (1987), and no. 24 (1981), among others. In conclusion no. 69, EXCOM specifically addresses the situation of long-term refugees, and recommends that States not only consider an appropriate status for persons who refuse to repatriate due to fear of persecution, but also that "appropriate arrangements, which would not put into jeopardy their established situation, be similarly considered by relevant authorities for those persons who cannot be expected to leave the country of asylum, due to a long stay in that country resulting in strong family, social and economic links there" (Conclusion No. 69 (XLIII), "Cessation of Status," 1992, paragraph (e)). This statement applies directly to those persons classified as "refugees" in Thailand, but who were born in the country, inheriting their "refugee" status from their parents, or even their parents' parents.

While denying persons the right to return to their own country is always unacceptable, it is particularly egregious in the case of trafficking victims, whose initial decision to leave Thailand was made under deceptive or otherwise coercive conditions. In April 1999, Human Rights Watch spoke to the First Secretary at the Thai Embassy about this continuing issue, and, while he expressed sympathy for the women's situation, he explained insisted that there was nothing his office could do: "We have to follow the Ministry of the Interior's immigration law," he explained.[603]

Biases undermine usefulness of skills training programs

For women who are able to return to Thailand, the programs designed to facilitate their rehabilitation and reintegration into Thai society are undermined by the same gender stereotypes that affect other government training programs for women. At the centers established under the Prevention and Suppression of Prostitution Act, these stereotypes are compounded by biases against the "former prostitutes" participating in the programs. Not only do women learn skills that prepare them only for low-income work, "the status of these schools is low because people know that these schools are for 'bad women.'"[604] Naiyana Supapong suggested that "[t]he government shouldn't have separate schools for former prostitutes — they should mix them in with the other vocational schools."[605]

No effort to assist women in seeking compensation for violations

Finally, the policies and practices of the Thai government consistently reveal the perception that while women who have engaged in sex work abroad are in need of certain types of assistance, protection, and rehabilitation, they are not in need of assistance as migrant workers. Thus, the services that the Thai Embassy and other Thai government officials provide for women victims of trafficking and other abuses abroad do not include legal assistance in fighting for unpaid wages or financial compensation or in understanding or challenging deportation proceedings. Thai Embassy First Secretary Nopporn Ratchawej said that this is largely because women do not ask for such assistance, adding that because most of the women have been in Japan for several years they can communicate with immigration officials themselves and do not need help with interpretation or translation. Typically, he said, the Embassy is not contacted by immigration officials or detainees until after deportation orders have been issued, and then the Embassy will try to facilitate the detainees' return. Nopporn found that women's priority is quick repatriation; "the

---

[603] Human Rights Watch interview, Tokyo, Japan, April 15, 1999.

[604] Human Rights Watch interview with Naiyana Supapung, former Director of FOWIA, Bangkok, Thailand, April 28, 1999.

[605] Ibid.

women want to return home quickly, so they don't want to press charges. . . . Men sometimes ask for unpaid wages, but women do not."[606]   Our interviews with advocates and women confirm that many women are reluctant to testify about their experiences for fear that this will delay their return home and, for those who have been arrested, prolong their period of detention. However, we also found that Thai officials, like Japanese government officials, show little interest in pushing for justice or financial compensation for the labor abuses and other violations women have suffered in Japan.

This disinterest stems from the fact that the great majority of migrant Thai women in Japan are employed in the sex industry. While most of the labor the women perform as hostesses is legal — and thus in theory subject to minimum wage protections and other labor law guarantees — Thai officials do not consider the women's activities "work." The government's bias against these women is perhaps best illustrated by the absolute disinterest evinced by the Thai Labor Attache in Japan. When Human Rights Watch spoke to the Minister-Counsellor of the Thai Office of Labor Affairs in Tokyo, Pranee Sukkar, and requested a meeting to discuss services provided for migrant Thai women working in Japan, her response was, "If you are interested in women, you should speak to the First Secretary at the Thai Embassy. We don't work with women."[607] We followed up on this statement in a telephone interview with an official in the Division of Foreign Affairs Coordination at the Thai Ministry of Labor and Social Welfare in Bangkok. She gave the following description of the Labor Attache's responsibilities in Japan:

> The Labor Attache at the Labor Office in Japan is responsible to protect the Thai people. But her responsibilities are different from those of the Thai Embassy — she is only responsible for labor issues. The Labor Office helps both legal and illegal laborers, asking for the rights they should have in Japan. For example, if an employer doesn't pay the correct wage, the employee can go to the Labor Attache, who will help him collect the proper wages.[608]

She went on to explain that "[the Labor Attache] has a separate responsibility from the Embassy Officer who cares for the illegal Thai women, whether they are

---

[606] Human Rights Watch interview, Tokyo, Japan, April 15, 1999.

[607] Human Rights Watch telephone conversation with Pranee Sukkar, Minister-Counsellor, Office of Labor Affairs, Tokyo, Japan, April 7, 1999.

[608] Human Rights Watch telephone interview, Jintana, Division of Foreign Affairs Coordination, Ministry of Labor and Social Welfare, Bangkok, Thailand, April 29, 1999.

workers or not. So that is why she says 'we don't help women.' Usually, women go to Japan through agents with deception. The woman thinks she's going for work, but then it's really not the case." As the conversation continued, the official admitted that Thai women in Japan might, in fact, be working, but insisted that Thai government "classifies this work differently. . . . It's unusual work so it's not covered by the Labor Attache. Many other Thai government offices care for these women, such as the Department of Public Welfare."[609] But while the Department of Public Welfare does provide certain services to Thai women returning from abusive conditions in Japan, it does not provide any assistance to women in collecting unpaid wages or other compensation for the labor violations and other abuses suffered in Japan.

---

[609] Ibid.

XI. INTERNATIONAL RESPONSE

Trafficking in persons is a global phenomenon of large-scale proportions. Incidents of trafficking have been reported in all regions of the world, and, while the number of persons trafficked each year is impossible to determine, estimates range from hundreds of thousands to millions of victims worldwide. The international community has taken note of this egregious human rights violation, and efforts are underway in domestic, regional, and international fora to address the problem and define appropriate state responses. Mary Robinson, the United Nations High Commissioner for Human Rights, has been particularly vocal on this issue, calling on states to take concrete measures to prevent, punish, and provide redress for trafficking abuses. Several inter-governmental organizations have also renewed their commitment to protecting the rights of undocumented migrants. While this is a different issue, their efforts could have important implications for victims of trafficking, whose immigration status is typically undocumented.

This chapter provides a brief overview of some of the initiatives that Human Rights Watch believes have the most potential to affect the experiences of women trafficked from Thailand to Japan and influence the Japanese and Thai governments' response to this problem.

Government Efforts: Multilateral and Bilateral

One important multilateral government initiative is the United Nations' effort to establish international standards for states' response to trafficking in persons as part of its larger effort to combat the activities of cross-border crime syndicates. In December 1998, the U.N. General Assembly adopted a resolution calling for the elaboration of a convention against transnational organized crime, supplemented by a protocol on trafficking in women and children. The Ad Hoc Committee on the Elaboration of a Convention against Transnational Organized Crime (Ad Hoc Committee) was created by this resolution, with the responsibility of drafting the convention and the trafficking protocol by the end of 2000. In 1999, the committee agreed to expand the trafficking protocol to cover all trafficking in persons, with special attention to women and children. Delegations from both the Japanese and Thai governments are participating in these Ad Hoc Committee negotiations. At the time this report was being prepared, the convention and the trafficking protocol were still under negotiation. Human Rights Watch believes that if appropriate human rights protections are included in the protocol, it could significantly facilitate the prosecution of traffickers and increase the protections, services, and access to redress available to victims.

The Group of Eight (G8) meetings have provided another high-profile and potentially effective forum where member governments — Japan, the United States,

Canada, Australia, Germany, the United Kingdom, France, and Russia — have discussed the problem of trafficking in persons. In October 1999, the G8's Senior Experts' Group on Transnational Organized Crime (the "Lyon Group") released the "Guiding Principles and Plan of Action to Combat the Smuggling of and Trafficking in Human Beings," in which it agreed to "intensify its efforts to develop, enact and facilitate national, multilateral and international principles, agreements, strategies and actions to prevent and counter the smuggling of and trafficking in human beings." This statement recognized the potential importance of the trafficking protocol discussed above and called for the enactment of domestic legislation to facilitate the prosecution of traffickers. Unfortunately, however, while the action plan details numerous steps that must be taken to improve law enforcement efforts, there is little reference to the measures states must take to uphold the rights of trafficking victims. The action plan states only that for those persons who provide information for the investigation and prosecution of their smugglers or traffickers, states should, "where appropriate," ensure the availability of protection, assistance, and support.[610] Human Rights Watch hopes that the G8 will continue to devote attention to this issue, with an increased emphasis on the rights and needs of trafficking victims.

Japan and Thailand have participated in a number of regional discussions regarding trafficking in persons as well. In January 2000, Japan's Ministry of Foreign Affairs hosted the Asia-Pacific Symposium on Trafficking in Persons in Tokyo, with participants from Japan, Thailand, and other countries in the region. In his key-note speech, Japan's Senior State Secretary for Foreign Affairs, Shozo Azuma, described trafficking as a serious crime of increasing proportions and expressed his government's hope that the symposium would serve to deepen participants' understanding of the problem. In March 2000, Japan and Thailand sent delegations to the Asian Regional Initiative to Combat the Trafficking of Women and Children (ARIAT), co-hosted by the United States and the Philippines in Manila. The objective of the meeting was to discuss national action plans and regional strategies to prevent trafficking, protect victims, reintegrate trafficking victims into society, and prosecute traffickers. The participants adopted an action plan that included, among other provisions, commitments to:

• improve information sharing within and between states;

---

[610] Ministerial Conference of the G-8 Countries on Combating Transnational Organized Crime (Moscow, October 19-20,1999), "Communiqué, Annex 2: Guiding Principles and Plan of Action to Combat the Smuggling of and Trafficking in Human Beings." Available: http://www.library.utoronto.ca/g7/adhoc/crime99.htm#annex2. March 2000.

- develop anti-trafficking information materials for dissemination to diplomatic and consular missions that include information on where to seek assistance;
- promote cooperation among governments and nongovernmental organizations in the prevention, protection, prosecution, repatriation and reintegration aspects of trafficking in persons;
- provide comprehensive and immediate assistance for trafficked persons;
- promote education, vocational training, scholarship programs, and employment opportunities for children and women to reduce their susceptibility to being trafficked;
- improve states' ability to prevent and prosecute trafficking through legal reform and training, as necessary; and
- facilitate trafficked persons' repatriation and safe reintegration in their countries of origin.

Participants also agreed to periodically assess their progress in implementing the action plan and to promote the participation of both state and non-state actors in that implementation.[611]

In addition, there are bilateral and domestic initiatives in some countries with potentially important implications for the Japanese and Thai governments' responses to the trafficking of women from Thailand to Japan. The United States government and the European Union, for example, have strong ties with both of these governments and regularly interact with them in a variety of bilateral and multilateral fora. These fora could provide important opportunities to raise the issue of trafficking in persons and promote appropriate government responses. In addition, the United States and the European Union are engaged in international anti-trafficking activities that could — and in some cases already do — involve collaboration with Japanese and/or Thai officials.

In the United States, training programs on combating trafficking in persons form a significant component of these activities. Foreign law enforcement officials receive such training through a number of U.S. agencies, including the Immigration and Naturalization Service (INS), which opened a training office in Tokyo in 1997; the Bureau for International Narcotics and Law Enforcement Affairs (INL) of the Department of State, which established the International Law Enforcement Academy in Bangkok in 1999; the Federal Bureau of Investigation, whose international training activities include the Pacific Rim Training Initiative (PTI); the Child Exploitation and Obscenity Section of the Department of Justice, which is

---

[611] "ARIAT Regional Action Plan Against Trafficking in Persons, Especially Women and Children," March 29-31, 2000, Manila, Philippines. Available: http://secretary.state.gov/www/picw/trafficking/riarap.htm. June 2000.

involved in international training activities regarding child exploitation and the trafficking of women and children for sexual purposes; and the Bureau of Educational and Cultural Affairs of the Department of State (formally of the U.S. Information Agency), whose International Visitor Program has included bringing foreign law enforcement officials to the United States to discuss anti-trafficking tactics.[612] These training activities typically address trafficking in persons within the context of efforts to combat transnational organized crime and/or illegal migration, and frequently focus on enforcing laws against undocumented immigration. Greater attention is needed to the steps states must take to protect the human rights — and physical safety — of trafficked persons.

The United States' response to trafficking in women and children in Asia has also included foreign assistance programs funded by the U.S. Agency for International Development and the Department of State. These programs are designed to prevent trafficking — through disseminating information warning women of the dangers of trafficking and/or creating additional economic opportunities for women and girls at home — and facilitate the repatriation and reintegration of trafficking victims.[613] So far these activities have been carried out primarily in South Asia, but there are plans to increase prevention and reintegration efforts in Southeast Asian countries, including Thailand. Finally, when this report was being prepared in mid-2000, the United States Congress was considering legislation that would establish a mechanism for monitoring governments' responses to trafficking in persons worldwide, and draft versions of the bill included a set of

---

[612] IOM, *Trafficking in Migrants*, Quarterly Bulletin, September 1997; Weekly Special Report, January 28, 2000, "International Issues: Clinton on Administration Action on Human Trafficking." http://www.telecom.net.et/~usis-eth/wwwh6708.htm. Available March 2000.; Bureau for International Narcotics and Law Enforcement Affairs, Department of State, "Crime Programs." Available: http://www.state.gov/www/global/narcotics_law/crime.html. March 2000; The FBI Academy, "International Training Program." Available: http://www.fbi.gov/programs/academy/itp/itp.htm. March 2000; Child Exploitation and Obscenity Section, Criminal Division, Department of Justice,"International Aspects of Child Exploitation." Available: http://www.usdoj.gov/criminal/ceos/internatl.htm. March 2000; Department of State, "International Visitor Program." Available: http://e.usia.gov/education/ivp. March 2000.

[613] Weekly Special Report, January 28, 2000, "International Issues: Clinton on Administration Action on Human Trafficking." Available: http://www.telecom.net.et/~usis-eth/wwwh6708.htm. March 2000; USAID, "Democracy Programs: Asia Regional." Available: http://www.info.usaid.gov/democracy/ane/traffic.html. March 2000.

"minimum standards for the elimination of trafficking," providing for assistance to countries who met those standards and sanctions on those who did not.

The European Union (EU) has also demonstrated a strong interest in combating trafficking in persons. The DAPHNE Initiative, for example, has provided funding to several nongovernmental organizations in Europe who work to prevent trafficking and assist its victims. This initiative was proposed by the Commission of the European Communities (European Commission) in 1997 and was designed to support NGOs involved in combating violence against women and children. In implementing the program, the Commission has recognized the importance of addressing trafficking in women and in children as a part of this effort.[614] In 1998, the European Commission issued a communication on trafficking in women reaffirming that the practice represented "an unacceptable violation of women's rights," and that the issue remained "high on the political agenda of the EU." The communication further provided that any policy in this field should prioritize "help and support to the victims of this serious and degrading violation of human rights."[615]

To date, the focus of the EU's anti-trafficking activities has been trafficking into and/or out of European states.[616] However, as a significant donor of humanitarian aid in Asia, and a regular participant in high-level meetings with the governments of Japan and Thailand, the EU is in a good position to raise the problem of trafficking in women from Thailand to Japan and to engage in collaborative efforts to improve prevention and response mechanisms. As noted in the European Commission's 1998 communication on trafficking, existing EU aid programs already address some of the root causes of trafficking, such as poverty and unemployment, but more could be done. In particular, the European Commission suggested supporting collaborative projects in developing countries

---

[614] European Commission Press Release, "The DAPHNE Initiative: Commission supports new projects to combat violence against women and children," IP/99/40, Brussels, January 21, 1999. Available: http://europa.eu.int/rapid/start/cgi/guesten.ksh (search using document number and/or date). May 2000.

[615] Commission of the European Communities, "Communication from the Commission to the Council and the European Parliament: For Further Actions in the Fight Against Trafficking in Women," Brussels, December 9, 1998, COM(1998) 726 (see "General Introduction" and "Main Policy Principles").

[616] It has also focused almost exclusively on the trafficking of women for sexual exploitation. Human Rights Watch would encourage the European Union to adopt a broader understanding of the problem that includes the trafficking of women, men, or children into servitude in any occupation or labor sector.

to improve legislation, judicial and police training against trafficking in women, and prevention and awareness-raising actions.[617]

Intergovernmental Organizations Address Trafficking in Persons

Intergovernmental organizations that address labor and migration issues have increasingly recognized the importance of incorporating efforts to address trafficking abuses into their work. The International Labor Organization (ILO) has noted that there is a close connection between protecting the rights of undocumented workers and addressing the problem of trafficking. As ILO Asia Pacific Regional Director, Mitsuko Horiuchi, has explained, "The one foolproof way to curtail clandestine migration and exploitation of migrants by traffickers, intermediaries and unscrupulous employers is simply to respect the rights of migrant workers."[618] To support such efforts, ILO experts are working with governments to assist them in drafting relevant legislation and policies to prevent trafficking and to protect the rights of migrant workers and their families. The ILO has also urged states to ratify the "Convention concerning Migrations in Abusive Conditions and the Promotion of Equality of Opportunity and Treatment of Migrant Workers," which it adopted in 1975.[619]

The International Organization for Migration (IOM) also recognizes that trafficking in persons often occurs within the context of larger migratory flows. IOM's policy on trafficking in migrants attributes the rise in this practice to the "market for irregular migration services" that has resulted from reduced opportunities for legal migration coupled with a large pool of potential labor migrants in some countries and a persistent demand for foreign labor in others. IOM's efforts to combat trafficking in migrants have included organizing regional and global seminars, conducting research, publishing reports, engaging in technical

---

[617] Commission of the European Communities, "Communication from the Commission to the Council and the European Parliament: For Further Actions in the Fight Against Trafficking in Women," Brussels, December 9, 1998, COM(1998) 726 (see Part III.2: Cooperation with Developing Countries).

[618] Statement by Mitsuko Horiuchi, ILO Asia Pacific Regional Director, to the International Symposium on Migration: Towards Regional Cooperation on Irregular/Undocumented Migration, Bangkok, 22 April 1999. Available: http://www.ilo.org/public/english/region/asro/bangkok/speeches/1999/iommigr.htm. March 2000.

[619] As of May 15, 2000, there were twelve States Parties to this Convention and an additional three signatories (Office of the United Nations High Commissioner for Human Rights, "Status of Ratifications of the Principal International Human Rights Treaties, as of 15-May-00"). The Convention will enter into force when at least twenty States have accepted it.

cooperation activities with governments, participating in information dissemination programs in countries of origin, and promoting the safe return and reintegration of trafficking victims.[620] In addition, IOM has highlighted the need for counseling, legal aid, and medical support for trafficking victims and other migrants. In October 1999, IOM signed a memorandum of understanding with the World Health Organization (WHO), agreeing to pursue concrete measures and detailed recommendations to "better meet the health needs of migrants and other displaced persons."[621]

Several of these programs have the potential to improve the Thai and Japanese government responses to trafficking in women. In Thailand, ILO and IOM have already been instrumental in the government's efforts to formulate a response to the trafficking in persons into and out of the country. Representatives of both organizations were members of Thailand's National Committee on Combating Trafficking in Women and Children, which drafted the "Memorandum of Understanding on Common Guidelines of Practices for Agencies Concerned with Cases where Women and Children are Victims of Human Trafficking" in 1999. IOM's technical cooperation activities in East and Southeast Asia include developing guidelines for police and immigration officials to distinguish between trafficked migrants and other migrants in an irregular situation, in order to adjust their practices and procedures accordingly. IOM also published a report in April 1999 describing trafficking abuses suffered by women who migrate from Thailand to Japan, entitled *To Japan and Back: Thai Women Recount their Experiences.* Two years earlier, IOM released a study on trafficking in women into Japan from the Philippines.[622]

---

[620] IOM, "Trafficking in Migrants: IOM Policy and Responses." Available: http://www.iom.ch/iom/policies/trafficking. March 2000.

[621] WHO, "WHO, IOM to Strengthen Collaboration on Migration and Health Issues," Note for the Press, no. 22, October 4, 1999. Available: http://www.who.int/inf-pr-1999/en/note99-22.html. March 2000.

[622] IOM, *Trafficking in women to Japan for sexual exploitation: a survey of Filipino women,* April 1997.

XII. RECOMMENDATIONS

To the Japanese Government

1. Actively investigate, prosecute, and punish perpetrators of trafficking in persons and/or servitude, imposing penalties appropriate for punishing the grave nature of the slavery-like abuses involved and for deterring further such abuses. Take measures to ensure that the undocumented immigration status of trafficking victims does not impede investigation or prosecution of labor law violations and other offenses.

(1) Adopt legislative changes necessary to provide appropriate penalties for all acts and attempted acts related to the recruitment, transport, transfer, sale, or purchase of human beings by force, fraud, deceit, or other coercive tactic, for the purpose of placing them into conditions of servitude, in which labor is extracted through physical and/or non-physical means of coercion, including debt bondage, blackmail, fraud, deceit, isolation, threat or use of physical force, and psychological pressure. Such changes could include:

> (a) Amending Article 226 of the Penal Code — which forbids kidnapping, buying, or selling a person for the purpose of transporting the same out of Japan, as well as transporting a person who has been kidnapped or sold out of Japan — so that it applies to cases in which persons are transported *into* Japan. In addition, add language prohibiting all transport, sale, or purchase of persons for the purpose of placing them into servitude in a country not their own (whether or not "kidnapping" in the country of origin can be proven).

> (b) Amending Article 73-2 of the Immigration Control Act and Article 7 the Prostitution Prevention Law to provide penalties against the use of coercive tactics in job placement and employment that are equal to those provided under the Labor Standards Law and the Employment Security Law for similar practices.

> (c) Amending the Labor Standards Law and the Employment Security Law to prohibit — and penalize — the confiscation of a person's passport, travel documents, or other identification papers by employers or job brokers. Add penalties to the recently enacted provision of the Entertainment Businesses Law

216

that prohibits the use of high debts to extract labor (Article 18(2)).

(2) Any evidence of trafficking and/or the commission of compulsory labor offenses against migrants that is collected by immigration officials — including any information provided by detainees during questioning — should be referred to police and/or labor officers, as appropriate, in order that they can investigate and, where there is adequate evidence, prosecute those responsible. Such information should also be made available to the migrants themselves and their advocates.

(3) Evidence and allegations of official complicity in trafficking or servitude abuses should be thoroughly investigated, and any officials against whom there is adequate evidence prosecuted.

(4) Develop and provide specific training and awareness programs for police, labor officials, immigration officials, prosecutors, and judges regarding the situation of foreign laborers and the abuses they commonly face during their travel to Japan, their job placement, and their employment, particularly when they are undocumented. Train officials to effectively recognize trafficking abuses — including coercive job placement and debt bondage — as well as other violations suffered by undocumented migrant workers, to collect evidence of such violations, to file appropriate charges, and to prosecute the perpetrators. This should include aggressive investigation and prosecution of evidence of coercion in the entertainment industry and businesses of prostitution. Such training should be carried out with the active involvement of relevant NGOs.

2. **Amend laws, including the immigration law, to exempt victims of trafficking and/or servitude from being prosecuted or otherwise penalized for any crimes or illegal status that have resulted directly from these practices. While repatriation may be appropriate, punitive measures, including detention pending deportation, should be waived.**

3. **Guarantee victims of trafficking and/or servitude access to redress for abuses they have suffered, facilitating their ability to seek compensation for damages, withheld wages, and restitution.**

(1) Facilitate foreigners' access to interpretation services and legal counsel in immigration proceedings as well as civil court proceedings, ensuring that

assistance from the Legal Aid Association is available without discrimination based on immigration status. This is particularly important in cases in which there is evidence of trafficking or forced labor.

(2) Instruct labor officials to increase their efforts to protect the labor rights of both Japanese and non-Japanese women working in the entertainment industry. Train officers on the labor rights of women in this industry and launch a public information campaign informing women of these rights. Such a campaign should pay particular attention to reaching foreign women. Labor office investigators should set up special late shifts to facilitate investigation of labor rights violations that occur outside of normal business hours.

(3) Issue temporary residence visas to foreign nationals pending the resolution of any criminal, civil or other legal actions relating to offenses they have suffered. During this time, victims of trafficking should be provided with the right to work and/or other means of support.

4. **Protect the safety of victims of trafficking and/or servitude, with measures that include strong witness protection provisions and the opportunity to seek asylum.**

(1) In the investigation and prosecution of traffickers, take steps to protect victims or witnesses who cooperate in these proceedings, with measures to ensure their safety, physical and psychological well-being, dignity, privacy, and right to timely repatriation to their country of origin. Measures should be available not to disclose information, or to delay disclosure, where victims' or witnesses' security would be adversely affected, and victims and witnesses should be notified in advance of decisions relating to such disclosure. Witness protection measures should be made available, and methods of taking testimony in advance and/or via communications technology should also be considered. None of these measures should be prejudicial to, or inconsistent with, the rights of the accused to a fair and impartial trial.

(2) In coordination with UNHCR officers, ensure that victims of trafficking and/or servitude have the opportunity to seek asylum.

5. **Ensure that victims of trafficking and/or servitude have access to essential government services, including appropriate shelter and medical care.**

(1) Amend Article 62 of the Immigration Control Act to explicitly exempt medical professional and labor officials from civil servants' obligation to report suspected illegal immigrants to the immigration office.

(2) Open government women's shelters to undocumented migrant women and provide government funding to privately-run shelters that currently provide assistance to such women.

(3) Ensure that victims of trafficking and/or servitude have access to adequate medical care, including access to government-subsidized HIV/AIDS treatment when appropriate. Measures to facilitate their access to such care could include: amending the Livelihood Protection Law, the Health Insurance Law, the National Health Insurance Law, the Welfare Act for Disabled People, and the Maternal and Child Health Law to explicitly provide that they apply to all persons in Japan, on a non-discriminatory basis; and providing training for medical personnel that encourages them to be sensitive to the physical and mental health needs of foreigners and assists them in effectively communicating with foreigners.

(4) Encourage the establishment of health clinics in all major cities in collaboration with NGOs and provide free, anonymous testing for HIV/AIDS and other STDs. These clinics should be accessible to undocumented migrants without the threat of their being reported for immigration violations.

6. **Amend detention and trial procedures in both the criminal justice system and the immigration control system to ensure that the rights of detainees, as established by international human rights guidelines, are upheld. Facilitate independent monitoring of procedures and conditions, and thoroughly and promptly investigate all allegations of misconduct.**

(1) Establish an independent body to monitor legal proceedings and detention conditions, and to investigate and address allegations of due process violations and mistreatment of detainees and/or suspects by immigration officials, police, and prison staff.[623]

---

[623] Concluding observations by the Human Rights Committee, November 5, 1998, paragraph 10: "More particularly, the Committee is concerned that there is no independent authority to which complaints of ill-treatment by the police and immigration officials can be addressed for investigation and redress. The Committee recommends that such an independent body or authority be set up by the State Party without delay."

(2) Fully protect the civil rights of all detainees. This includes ensuring that detainees fully understand the nature of the charges against them, are informed of their right not to incriminate themselves and of their right to an attorney; have access to immediate consular assistance and legal counsel (all persons charged with criminal offenses must have access to legal counsel free of charge if they cannot afford to pay); may meet in private with their attorneys; are tried before a fair and impartial tribunal within a reasonable time; and have a right of appeal to a higher court. They should also have access to adequate translation and interpretation services during all legal proceedings.

(3) Eliminate the "detention in principle" policy for foreigners who are awaiting deportation after being taken into custody by immigration officials; all efforts should be made to release detainees, either to their own residences or to appropriate shelters. In addition, a system of periodic review should be established to assess the need for continued detention when detention is prolonged due to difficulties in securing the funding and/or documentation for a person's deportation.

(4) Ensure that conditions in all detention facilities are in full compliance with the Standard Minimum Rules for the Treatment of Prisoners. Compose and make public detailed standards of treatment, including provisions that: protect detainees' right to communicate through visits and written correspondence with lawyers, family members, and friends; require that women officers are present during all interactions with women detainees; and strictly limit the use of restraint mechanisms and solitary confinement. Thoroughly investigate all allegations of mistreatment of detainees; vigorously prosecute and punish those guilty of such abuse.

7. **Ratify relevant international conventions, including the Slavery Convention; the Supplementary Convention on the Abolition of Slavery, the Slave Trade, and Institutions and Practices Similar to Slavery; ILO Convention concerning the Abolition of Forced Labour, no. 105; and the International Convention on the Protection of the Rights of All Migrant Workers and Members of Their Families.**

To the Thai Government
1. **Expand and improve the services available to women trafficked from Thailand to Japan, so as to facilitate their access to compensation and redress in Japan, guarantee their safe repatriation, and ensure that they have access to appropriate social services upon their return to Thailand.**

(1) Train labor attaches and embassy officials in Japan regarding the rights of Thai nationals in Japan and strategies for promoting these rights. Explicitly instruct the Thai Labor Attache in Japan to assist all women from Thailand who have suffered from violations of Japanese labor laws, regardless of their immigration status or occupation.

(2) Ensure that Thai women have access to information about their rights and to legal assistance in Japan, so that they may pursue civil and/or criminal claims related to trafficking, debt bondage, and any other abuses they have suffered.

(3) Protect trafficked women from further victimization by taking all necessary precautions to protect their confidentiality. In addition, when issuing Certificates of Identity,[624] inform women verbally and in writing that they are not liable for any fine or other penalty upon their arrival in Thailand.

(4) Work with appropriate NGOs to expand the services available to trafficked women after they return to Thailand. Such services should include counseling, safe shelter, medical care, vocational training, and information about job opportunities, women's groups, and other support networks throughout the country. Ensure that all services offered to women over the age of eighteen are strictly voluntary and non-punitive; in providing services to children, the best interests of the child should in all cases be given primary consideration, taking into account the expressed wishes of the child and her family members.

2. **Improve law enforcement efforts to prevent and punish the trafficking of persons out of Thailand, including efforts to crack down on official complicity in such crimes.**

(1) Prohibit the trafficking of women into conditions of servitude in any labor sector in the penal code; these changes also should be reflected in the application of the Trafficking Act.

(2) Enact legislation establishing a witness protection program that could be used by women who testify against traffickers in Thailand or abroad.

---

[624] Certificates of Identity are temporary travel documents issued by the Thai Embassy to Thai nationals who lack valid passports.

(3) Evidence and allegations of official complicity in trafficking or servitude abuses should be thoroughly investigated, and any officials against whom there is adequate evidence prosecuted.

(4) Provide training to judges, prosecutors, immigration officials and police regarding special considerations in trafficking cases, including victims' fear of retaliation and need for confidentiality. Using the "Memorandum of Understanding on Common Guidelines of Practices for Agencies Concerned with Cases where Women and Children are Victims of Human Trafficking,"[625] train officials to use the provisions in the Trafficking Act that are aimed at overcoming obstacles to prosecution, such as section 12, which authorizes police to bring women to court immediately to give their testimony, even if the suspect has not yet been apprehended.

3. **Take steps to reduce women and girls' vulnerability to trafficking by expanding their education and employment opportunities in Thailand and empowering them to protect their rights as workers overseas.**

(1) Implement the National Education Act's promise to extend free and compulsory education nationwide, with a particular emphasis on ensuring girls' access to education.

(2) Promote skills training for women in accordance with market demand, rather than with traditional conceptions of appropriate women's work. Provide training to staff of vocational training programs, teaching them to avoid gender stereotyping both in advising women on course selection and in instructing (men and) women in the classroom.

(3) Establish labor information centers with up-to-date, practical information regarding labor migration and the rights of migrant workers abroad. This should include information about relevant laws and regulations in destination countries as well as about governmental and nongovernmental services (such as medical care, shelters, legal counsel, etc.) available to foreign migrants, both documented and undocumented. In the case of Japan, where so many Thai women are employed in the entertainment industry, particular attention should be given to conditions in this industry, and Japanese laws and regulations

---

[625] This documented was drafted and adopted by a coalition of Thai government and nongovernmental representatives in 1999)

regarding entertainment businesses and prostitution. Also include information about the services and duties of Thai Embassy and Consulate officials and Thai Labor Attaches abroad.

4. **Protect women's right to freedom of movement, including international travel.**

(1) Amend the Trafficking Act to protect the rights of women and children travelers. While briefly restricting a woman or child's freedom of movement for the purpose of factual clarification and document verification may be appropriate, compulsory body searches are unacceptable and the right to be free from arbitrary detention must be protected. Remove the language in Section 9 that permits officials to search the bodies of women and children based on their status as "suspected victims." Amend Sections 10 and 13 to ensure (a) that all persons detained as suspected trafficking victims have immediate access to a court that may decide the lawfulness of their detention; (b) that all due process protections, including the right to legal counsel, are afforded to such persons; and (c) that detainees have access to the medical, social, and other services they need.

(2) Eliminate the discriminatory practice of referring passport applications of (only) women ages fourteen to thirty-six to the Department of Public Welfare for review when the women "have been suspected by MFA of being procured to sexual business in foreign countries." Do not in any way discriminate against women who wish to travel overseas, regardless of the purpose of their travel.

5. **Take steps to address the particular vulnerability of hilltribe and refugee women to trafficking and to facilitate their safe repatriation when trafficking abuses occur.**

(1) Strengthen efforts to regularize the status of hilltribe persons in Thailand by providing them with provisional legal residency status — including the right to work — as well as the opportunity to apply for citizenship.

(2) Allow all children residing in Thailand to attend school and receive diplomas, regardless of their citizenship status.

(3) Allow all persons trafficked out of Thailand who can provide evidence of a genuine effective link with the country, such as long-term residence

(including residence in refugee camps within Thai borders), to reenter the country, regardless of their citizenship status.

6. **Ratify relevant international conventions, including the Slavery Convention and the Supplementary Convention on the Abolition of Slavery, the Slave Trade, and Institutions and Practices Similar to Slavery; the Convention relating to the Status of Refugees; the Protocol relating to the Status of Refugees; the Convention on the Reduction of Statelessness; and the International Convention on the Protection of the Rights of All Migrant Workers and Members of Their Families. Remove reservations from Article 7 of the Convention on the Rights of the Child, thereby recognizing the right of *all* children to be registered immediately after birth and to acquire a nationality.**

To the Japanese and Thai Governments

1. Discuss and implement concrete measures to reduce migrant Thai women's vulnerability to labor exploitation in Japan. Such measures could include expanding the opportunities for legal labor migration by women from Thailand to Japan, and conducting awareness-raising activities for migrant Thai women in both Thailand and Japan.

    (1) Reevaluate immigration policies, taking into account the labor market demands in Japan and the labor supply in Thailand.

    (2) Continue awareness-raising activities in both Thailand and Japan that include information on services available to assist migrant women in escaping traffickers and abusive employers, and in seeking compensation and redress for violations.

2. **Work cooperatively — and in coordination with relevant Japanese and Thai NGOs — to ensure the safe and humane repatriation of victims of trafficking, servitude, and other abuses.**
    Ensure that all women from Thailand have access to the identification and funds needed for travel expenses. Cooperate with NGOs, including women's shelters, to ensure that women have access to temporary housing and other necessary services before and after repatriation, as needed. At all times, strong precautions should be taken to protect the women's confidentiality.

3. **Establish a monitoring body, with the financial support of both governments, to assess the cross-border trafficking situation; identify**

loopholes in existing laws; make recommendations for coordinating government policies to enhance access to services for victims of trafficking and improve the effectiveness of law enforcement efforts; and monitor and publicly report on the implementation of such policies. This body should include representatives from nongovernmental organizations (NGOs) and the Japanese and Thai governments, and should seek input from relevant intergovernmental organizations, such as the International Organization for Migration and the International Labour Organization. The monitoring body should prepare a joint operational plan that both governments are committed to implementing within a reasonable, designated period of time.

To All Governments

- Ensure that the "Protocol to Prevent, Suppress and Punish Trafficking in Persons, especially Women and Children," currently being drafted as a supplemental protocol to the United Nations Convention against Transnational Organized Crime, incorporates strong provisions for the protection of the human rights and physical safety of trafficking victims.
- Ratify the International Convention on the Protection of the Rights of All Migrant Workers and Members of Their Families. This convention emphasizes that all migrant workers, whether documented or undocumented, are to be accorded fundamental human rights. These rights include the right to life, the right to be free from cruel, inhuman or degrading treatment or punishment, the right to be free from slavery, servitude, and forced or compulsory labor, and the right to due process. While it does not propose new human rights for migrant workers, this convention draws attention to a vulnerable population whose human rights are often exempted from state protection.
- Raise the problem of trafficking in persons, and particularly the trafficking of women from Thailand into compulsory labor in Japan, in high-level discussions with the Japanese and Thai governments.
- Ensure that any anti-trafficking training programs that involve Japanese and/or Thai law enforcement officials emphasize the importance of protecting the rights of victims, ensuring their physical safety, and providing them with access to necessary services. Allow for outside monitoring of training programs — including curricula and instructors — by NGOs with expertise regarding the rights and needs of trafficked persons.
- Allow for outside monitoring of trafficking prevention and reintegration programs carried out in Thailand. These activities should be designed and implemented in a way that empowers women and girls to protect themselves from trafficking abuses and to seek redress for violations. Efforts to prevent

trafficking of women from Thailand should include the promotion of viable economic opportunities for women and girls and information dissemination regarding legal overseas migration opportunities for women and their rights overseas.   Particular attention should be given to reaching vulnerable populations, such as hilltribe and refugee women and girls.[626]

To Intergovernmental Organizations

United Nations High Commissioner for Refugees (UNHCR)
•   In accordance with UNHCR's mandate to address the problem of statelessness,[627] UNHCR protection officers in Japan and Thailand should work with Japanese and Thai officials to arrange durable solutions for women whose citizenship is disputed or unclear, including repatriation to Thailand.
•   UNHCR protection officers in Japan should work to ensure that those victims of trafficking and servitude who fear retaliation in Thailand have sufficient opportunity to apply for refugee status.

International Organization For Migration (IOM)
•   Include Japan in technical cooperation activities, urging the Japanese government to adopt policies and legislation that will not create unnecessary obstacles for legal migration, impose heightened criminal penalties for trafficking, provide trafficking victims with incentives to testify against traffickers, and treat trafficked migrants as victims rather than offenders.
•   Work with the Thai government in implementing and evaluating the "Memorandum of Understanding on Common Guidelines of Practices for

---

[626] According to USAID's description of "Preventing the Trafficking in Women and Children in South and South East Asia," "The primary beneficiaries of this assistance will be those populations in each country considered most vulnerable to being trafficked, as well as the community-based organizations engaged in assisting these populations." USAID, "Democracy   Programs: Asia   Regional," http://www.info.usaid.gov/democracy/ane/traffic.html. Available March 2000.

[627] Excom Conclusion No. 78 (1995), the Conclusion on the Prevention and Reduction of Statelessness and the Protection of Stateless Persons, instructs UNHCR to "undertake the functions foreseen under Article 11 of the 1961 Convention on the Reduction of Statelessness;" namely, to serve as "a body to which a person claiming the benefit of this Convention may apply for the examination of his claim and for assistance in presenting it to the appropriate authority."   In addition, Excom Conclusion No. 78 "[f]urther requests UNHCR actively to promote the prevention and reduction of statelessness through the dissemination of information, and the training of staff and government officials; and to enhance cooperation with other interested organizations."

Agencies Concerned with Cases where Women and Children are Victims of Human Trafficking."

- Adopt concrete measures and detailed recommendations for the promotion of the health of migrant workers, as called for in the Memorandum of Understanding signed by WHO and IOM in October 1999 to "better meet the health needs of migrants and other displaced persons."

International Labor Organization (ILO)[628]

- Assess the situation of migrant workers in Japan, with particular attention to the labor rights abuses suffered by foreign women working in the entertainment or sex industry.
- Make concrete recommendations to the Japanese government regarding legislative measures, training activities, and other steps that could be implemented to improve the protection of the rights of all migrant workers, both documented and undocumented.

World Health Organization (WHO)

- Adopt concrete measures and detailed recommendations for the promotion of the health of migrant workers, as called for in the Memorandum of Understanding signed by WHO and IOM in October 1999 to "better meet the health needs of migrants and other displaced persons."
- Urge Japan to apply health policies without discrimination based on migration status; in particular, urge Japan to provide undocumented migrant women (and especially victims of trafficking and servitude in the sex industry) with access to confidential HIV/AIDS testing, counseling, and treatment on an basis equal to Japanese citizens.
- At the WHO research center in Kobe, Japan, study the health needs of migrant workers (including those in the sex industry), looking at their access to medical care.

---

[628] The ILO has a constitutional mandate to address migrant workers issues and has initiated a special program to combat discrimination against migrant workers and ethnic minorities.